The Inflammation Cure Cookbook

Kimberly B. Myers, PhD, MHS, RDN, LDN
William Joel Meggs, MD, PhD, FACMT, FACEP

abbott press®

A DIVISION OF WRITER'S DIGEST

Abbott Press books may be ordered through booksellers or by contacting:

Abbott Press
1663 Liberty Drive
Bloomington, IN 47403
www.abbottpress.com
Phone: 1-866-697-5310

ISBN: 978-1-4582-0951-1 (sc)
ISBN: 978-1-4582-0952-8 (e)

Library of Congress Control Number: 2013910999

Printed in the United States of America.

Abbott Press rev. date: 11/5/2013

Table of Contents

Pasta Dishes

Salad Creations

Sandwiches

Soups

Baked Goods

Foreword

Inflammation is the culprit in chronic and degenerative diseases and in aging. The body produces pro-inflammatory cytokines for many reasons, but excesses contribute to debilitating conditions over time. By choosing a wise diet, people can reduce their risk of developing the diseases related to inflammation, such as stroke, heart disease, asthma, and several forms of arthritis and cancer.

Most people eat three times a day, and the resulting internal environment can either be rich or poor in nutrients and phytochemicals. The Western diet encourages high intakes of red meat and refined grains. Thus, to counteract this trend, individuals must be fully conscious of the foods they choose on a daily basis. Adding key foods to the daily intake, such as salmon, other fatty fish, nuts, green tea, olive and canola oils, can counteract the negative effects of the Western diet.

Using herbs and spices can also be protective. Turmeric (curcumin, cumin) has been shown to have significant anti-inflammatory properties. Garlic and onions, apples, oranges, broccoli and other cruciferous vegetables are now considered to be "functional foods" because they have such strong health-promoting properties. Functional foods may be conventional foods, fortified or enriched foods, additives, or enhanced foods that have been carefully developed.

Diet affects how the body expresses genes, so an anti-inflammatory diet can, over time, turn off some of the systemic processes that debilitate and age a person. This book provides not only the evidence-based science about inflammation but also provides important choices for living in a healthy manner. Thus, I highly recommend this book. I encourage the reader to focus on the tips and the positive steps that can be taken to live a rich, full and healthful life.

Sylvia Escott-Stump, MA, RDN, LDN
President, The Academy of Nutrition and Dietetics, 2011-2012

Introduction

A one year old boy's mother who fancied herself an expert in healthy cooking made his birthday cake of wholesome, healthy ingredients. One hundred percent rice flour was used. Instead of sugar, the cake was sweetened with dried apricots that were as hard as shoe leather. There was neither fat nor yeast. The boy's uncle took one bite of the dense dry concoction and remarked, "When this boy gets his first bite of chocolate cake, he's going to run away from home."

Healthy eating when properly done can be fine cuisine, as the recipes gathered here prove. Combining wholesome ingredients to create a delectable dish is no harder than cooking unhealthy foods. *The Inflammation Cure*, published in 2003 by the Contemporary Books Division of McGraw-Hill, discusses the role of inflammation in chronic and degenerative diseases including the aging process. It outlines five lifestyle components that have been scientifically proven to reduce one's risk of developing diseases related to inflammation.

These are:
What we eat
What we do
Where we live
What medications can do
Mind/body solutions

What we eat was discussed first and foremost because of the immense importance of diet in overall health. *The Inflammation Cure Cookbook* presents recipes for healthy eating that will reduce one's risk of diseases related to inflammation, ranging from heart disease and stroke to obesity, asthma, and diabetes. In addition, it updates the explosive growth of knowledge of the role of inflammation in disease that has occurred since *The Inflammation Cure* was published.

In Part I, the rationale for the inflammation cure diet is presented, including the burgeoning evidence that there are healthy fats and unhealthy fats, essential fatty acids that must be balanced in the diet, protein requirements that are essential to manufacturing proteins that perform essential body functions, and the different types of carbohydrates which should be eaten in moderation. We must be compulsive label readers who know what we are getting in every prepared food that we buy and have the knowledge to avoid prepared foods that attempt to rope us in with unhealthy ingredients, such as too much sugar, too much salt, and the wrong types of fat.

Part II presents the inflammation cure recipes. The bulk of these recipes stem from the culinary genius of Dr. Kimberly Myers, who in addition to being a creative cook, has a PhD degree in human nutrition and is a Registered Dietitian Nutritionist. Dr. William Meggs, a physician with a strong interest in diet and health, contributed some of his favorite recipes.

Eating healthy foods is not sufficient for good health. The whole grains wheat, barley, and rye contain health promoting fibers, proteins, and energy sources of carbohydrates along with vitamins and minerals. These grains, however, can be devastating for individuals with an intolerance to gluten. Lactose, the sugar in cow's milk, is split into glucose and galactose by the enzyme lactase in our small intestine. People who lack the ability to produce lactase can have a devastating intolerance to milk and other dairy products. All foods contain a host of organic chemicals which have biological activity in the human body, ranging from caffeine to naturally occurring insecticides that plants use to ward off destructive insects. Just as a person can have adverse reactions to drugs, food chemicals can cause highly individualized adverse reactions. Part III of this book is a manual for those with health problems to determine if specific foods can be the source of these problems. Many cases of chronic illness have gone into remission with dietary modifications. The problems addressed in Part III are very different from the problems addressed in Part I, for which the recipes given in Part II are helpful. The recipes in Part II address the problem of eating a diet that reduces one's risk of chronic diseases related to inflammation and aging such as heart attacks and strokes. The dietary recommendations in Part III are for a different problem; that is, specific food intolerances which do not affect everyone.

Eating a healthy diet is not enough. For example, a chain smoker could eat the healthiest of diets and still have accelerated aging and suffer heart attacks and strokes at a young age. The air we breathe can modify our health, so tips on avoiding unhealthy air are presented. Mind states can be deleterious to health, as can a stressful job or lifestyle. Tips to handle stress will be discussed. When all else fails, there are medications that those of us cursed with certain genes have to consider. As we age, genes are switched on and off as part of the aging process, so we have to be cognizant of that and intervene appropriately with medications.

The authors wish to thank Sylvia Escott-Stump for contacting Dr. Meggs about Dr. Myers' interest in anti-inflammation cuisine and as a collaborator on future editions of *The Inflammation Cure,* and for her help in the planning stages of this project. We are also grateful for her interest, encouragement, and providing the Foreword. The authors wish to thank Susan Martin Meggs for providing the illustrations. We are grateful to Thomas Clute Meggs for photographing the front cover. The excellent proof reading skills of Libby Phillips Meggs have been invaluable. We owe a special debt to Michael Bourret of Dystel and Goderich Literary Management for his encouragement and tireless efforts to promote the book to a publishing industry in turmoil. The invaluable help from the staff at Abbott Press is also appreciated.

Part I

The Inflammation Cure Food Choices

Inflammation is an altered state of a body part that suggests a flame. Inflamed tissue is on fire. It is hot and red and painful. It can take many forms and have many causes. Sometimes inflammation is appropriate as part of the body's response to infection or injury. In these cases, inflammation takes hold of a body part, fights off the infection, repairs the damage, and subsides, returning the tissue to its normal state of health.

Inflammation can become a permanent fixture and cause diseases like rheumatoid arthritis and multiple sclerosis. Rheumatoid arthritis is a pattern of inflammation that usually begins in the joints but can spill over into other parts of the body. Multiple sclerosis is an inflammatory disease that results when one's immune system starts attacking the sheaths that surround nerve fibers. A host of other diseases can result from abnormal patterns of inflammation and will be discussed briefly.

Inflammation occurs when the body mistakes some harmless substance in the environment as a threat to life. Such inflammation is behind allergies, asthma, and skin rashes like that of poison ivy. When ragweed throws its microscopic pollen grains into the air, the noses and sinuses of millions of people act as if they are breathing in dangerous germs and become inflamed in an effort to battle the invasion. This leads not only to sneezing and wheezing, but can impair sleep, concentration, ability to think, and in some cases cause overwhelming generalized fatigue.

The body uses inflammation as part of the mechanism to beat us down as we age. The planned obsolescence built into bodies is to a great extent the result of inflammation. In a magnificent example of biological economy, the same system that protects us from germs when we are young does us in when we get old. Though there is nothing we can do to prevent aging, we can do things to slow the process of aging. The flip side is that we can also make dangerous choices—from smoking to using cocaine—that accelerate the aging process. Degenerative diseases of aging, such as hardening of the arteries leading to heart attacks and strokes, can be forestalled by a healthy lifestyle, anti-inflammation food choices, and other modalities discussed in Part IV of this book.

The *Inflammation Connection* refers to the fact that inflammation in one part of the body influences inflammation elsewhere. Evidence of this comes from research that shows correlations between diseases related to inflammation. We now know that inflammation of the lining of the blood vessels is behind heart attacks and strokes. People with heart attacks and strokes are at increased risk to have inflamed gums. People with inflamed gums are more like to have heart attacks and strokes. Inflammation is related to obesity, insomnia, depression, and diabetes. Allergies and asthma are related to insomnia and depression. Obese people are more likely to develop asthma than people with normal weight. People with rheumatoid arthritis are more likely to develop heart disease. Inflammation connections are everywhere we look.

All sorts of things in our environment increase the risk of diseases associated with heart attacks. The small particulates in the air from burning fossil fuels can inflame the linings of our arteries and lead to heart attacks. So can cigarette smoke, whether from smoking or breathing someone else's smoke. Leaky furnaces can also play a role when we seal up our houses in winter and have roaring fires inside our homes.

The importance of food choices in reducing one's risk of inflammation, avoiding diseases associated with inflammation, and even slowing down the process of aging, is overwhelming. There are several ways that diet plays a role in the inflammatory process. Foods are complex mixtures of a host of chemicals with diverse sizes and shapes. These can have profound positive and negative effects on the body. In addition to chemicals that occur naturally in foods, wild assortments of chemicals are added to foods from farms to processing and distribution networks. Some of these food chemicals—both naturally occurring and added—are pro-inflammatory and increase our risk of diseases associated with inflammation. Other food chemicals reduce the risk of inflammation by providing essential nutrients or by providing potent antioxidants to counteract the dangerous effects of oxidants that damage inflamed tissues.

Sometimes a single food or collection of foods drives inflammation in an individual's body. Identifying these highly individualized problem foods and eliminating them from the diet can result in remission of chronic diseases. Techniques for identifying personal problem foods are presented in Part III.

The Inflammation Cure recipes presented here are designed to be appealing, nutritious, and healthful.

Nutrition Primer

Knowledge of the basics of nutrition is essential to eating properly and maintaining good health. Most have studied nutrition in school health and science courses. The nutrition primer given here is presented as a refresher course for those who want to review the basics. Others may want to skip this section. The basic chemistry classes of nutrients are proteins, fats, carbohydrates, minerals, a group of bioactive organic chemicals that include vitamins and antioxidants, and water. The energy yielding nutrients, carbohydrates, fats and proteins, plus water are the major proportion of most foods. Vitamins and minerals, while they do not provide direct energy, aid in the process of energy production within our cells. Without the proper mix of the energy yielding and non-energy yielding nutrients our bodies cannot function properly. All are necessary for ideal nutrition but must be consumed in an appropriate balance. Too much of a good thing, most importantly for the metals, can cause serious diseases. Further, there are preferable fats and carbohydrates and others that should be eaten in moderation or avoided.

Proteins

This class of compounds consists of chemicals called amino acids hooked together like the boxcars on a train to make a long chain. Just as train cars have couplers that hook together to join two cars, the amino end (consisting of a nitrogen atom and three hydrogen atoms) of one amino acid hooks to the acid end (consisting of a carbon atom, two oxygen atoms, and a hydrogen atom) of another to couple them. Once the protein chain is complete, the long line folds to form a three dimensional structure. Different proteins have different functions in the body. Hemoglobin is a protein that carries oxygen in the blood stream, greatly increasing the amount of oxygen that can be carried to our tissues. Others are enzymes that effectively speed up chemical reactions. Many proteins, including insulin, are hormones. Still others form receptors on the surface of our cells that when stimulated cause things to happen. Clearly, proteins are necessary for life. If even one amino acid in a protein is wrong, disease and even fatalities can result. Sickle cell anemia results from just one mistake in the amino acids that form hemoglobin.

There are 20 amino acids that the human body needs to form proteins. A deficiency of even one amino acid can be fatal because proteins necessary for life cannot be manufactured. Non-essential amino acids are those that most people can manufacture internally and do not need to obtain from the diet, though some people with genetic mutations may need to obtain these from their diets. Essential amino acids have to be obtained from the diet because humans do not have the enzymes required to manufacture them internally. The essential and non-essential amino acids are given in Table I-1. The non-essential amino acids marked with an asterisk are those that some individuals need from the diet.

Some amino acids are essential building blocks for neurotransmitters, and some even function as neurotransmitters. Serotonin is a neurotransmitter that is essential for proper functioning of the brain. Depression is treated by drugs that increase the amount of serotonin in the synapses that connect our brain cells and allow our nerve cells to talk to each other. Too much serotonin or drugs that mimic serotonin such as LSD can cause hallucinations. Schizophrenia is treated by giving drugs that block the action of the neurotransmitters serotonin and/or dopamine. Our bodies manufacture serotonin by modifying the amino acid L-tryptophan.

The amino acid L-tyrosine is the starting molecule to manufacture the neurotransmitters dopamine, nor-epinephrine, and epinephrine that are found in systems of nerve cells that play vital roles in our brains. Dopamine is involved in a wide range of activities, from memory, mood, thinking, learning, sleep, and regulation of movement. Toxins that damage the system of nerve cells that use dopamine to communicate disrupt regulation of movements, leading to a Parkinsonian syndrome. Nor-epinephrine and epinephrine are the major neurotransmitters and hormones involved in the sympathetic branch of the autonomic nervous system which are essential to what are termed *flight and fight* responses. When we exercise vigorously or sense danger, nor-epinephrine is released from the adrenal glands to speed up body functions, with increased heart rate and metabolism of energy, to shunting blood away from the gut and to skeletal muscles.

Another amino acid essential to making neurotransmitters is glutamic acid, the starting point for manufacturing the neurotransmitter GABA (short for gamma-aminobutyric acid). GABA is the major inhibitory amino acid in the brain. The system of neurons that use GABA to talk to each other calm down the firing activity of other systems of neurons. It is no surprise that drugs that increase the action of GABA are used to treat seizures, depression, anxiety, and muscle spasms. Glutamic acid is itself an important excitatory neurotransmitter.

It is important to remember that just as with the carbohydrates and fats, it is possible to consume too much protein. Extra calories consumed from protein that are not utilized at that time by the body for maintenance will be converted to triglycerides and stored for future energy use in our adipose tissues. So while it is important to consume enough protein, you do not want to consume too much. A simple formula for most people to calculate their protein needs is to take their healthy body weight in kilograms (kg) and to multiply it by 0.8. The example listed below is for a 150 pound person.

150 pounds divided by 2.2 = 68 kg

68 kg x 0.8 g of protein per kg of body weight = 54.4 g of protein

The person in this example has a healthy body weight of 150 pounds. When the 150 pounds is converted to kg, the person's body weight is then measured as 68 kg. The 68 kg of healthy body weight multiplied by 0.8g indicates that this person needs about 54 grams of protein each day. Keep in mind that individuals with certain conditions such as cancer, endurance athletes, those recovering from surgery, burn victims, or pregnant women will need more daily protein and more overall nutrition. But as a general guide this formula works well for the general population. Consuming extra protein will only result in an extra burden on the kidneys and other organs, increase the inflammatory process and lead to excess weight stored in the adipose tissue.

Table 1-1.

Essential amino acids that must be obtained from food	Non-essential amino acids that humans can manufacture
Histidine	Alanine
Isoleucine	Arginine*
Leucine	Asparagine
Lysine	Aspartic acid
Methionine	Cysteine*
Phenylalanine	Glutamic acid
Threonine	Glutamine*
Tryptophan	Glycine
Valine	Proline*
	Serine*
	Tyrosine*

* amino acids that some individuals need from their diets

Fats

Dietary lipids and fats are high energy compounds consisting of carbon atom chains that also contain hydrogen atoms. The human body can extract more energy from fat than any other class of nutrient. While a gram of fat provides 9 calories of energy, a gram of protein or carbohydrate can only provide 4 calories of energy. The American Heart Association recommends that your total fat intake should be 30% or less of your total calories for a day. Of that 30%, only 7% should come from saturated fats and none should come from trans fats. We must recognize there are healthy fats, unhealthy fats, and essential fats that must be obtained from the diet. Let's explore the structure and types of fats a little more.

Each carbon atom in a fat can be thought of as having four arms to grab onto other atoms. To produce a fat, two arms have to be used to join other carbon atoms to form the chain. The other two can join two hydrogen atoms to produce a saturated fat. If one or both of the remaining arms produce a double bond to a neighboring carbon atom, the fat is unsaturated. A fat with all single bonds between the carbon atoms is said to be saturated because it has grabbed as many hydrogen atoms as possible. A fat with double bonds between carbon atoms is called unsaturated. Animal fats tend to be saturated while vegetable oils are unsaturated. This difference is why animal fats are generally solids (such as lard and butter) and vegetable oils tend to be liquid.

There is an abundance of scientific evidence that suggests unsaturated fats are healthier than saturated fats. Vegetarians have a lower risk of heart attacks than meat eaters, and the types of fat in meat is one of the main reasons, though the anti-oxidants, fiber, and other beneficial effects of fruits, vegetables and whole grains also play a role. A study comparing groups in southern and northern Europe found that both groups consumed 40% of their calories as fat. The northern Europeans ate saturated fats from meat and butter while the southern Europeans got their fat from olive oil. The southern Europeans had half the risk of heart attacks of the northern Europeans. The USDA and the American Heart Association recommend that one should limit the consumption of animal fats and use vegetable oil, such as canola oil or olive oil, instead. Meat eaters should stick to lean cuts that are mostly protein and limit their portions to 4 ounce servings.

One of the great travesties of the last century was the industrial process of hydrogenating vegetable oils to produce margarine. This process increases the shelf life of baked goods while producing a spreadable solid similar to butter. These so-called trans fats turned out to be at least two times worse than saturated fats.

Another pitfall with fats is what happens to them during cooking. Whether in frying, baking, or grilling, high heat changes the composition of cooking oils by oxidizing them. The oxidation of fatty acids leads to the production of free radicals and makes the dietary fat less healthy. This effect is most pronounced in frying. Though fried foods acquire a tasty character and pleasing appearance, we recommend limited fried foods because healthy vegetable oils decrease their advantage through the oxidation that takes place with frying. Fried food vendors that advertise, *Fried with Canola Oil*, may be misleading the public into believing that frying with these oils is healthy. While frying foods in healthier fats such as canola and olive oil is believed to be healthier than frying foods in saturated fats such as lard, we recommend limiting or even avoiding the consumption of fried foods.

Essential Dietary Fatty Acids

There are dietary fatty acids necessary for proper functioning of the human body that we cannot manufacture internally. They must be obtained from the diet or from supplements. Pills or capsules containing essential fatty acids are truly nutritional supplements. Linoleic acid (an omega-6 fatty acid) and alpha-linolenic acid (an omega-3 fatty acid) are essential polyunsaturated fatty acids that humans need for their well-being. These fatty acids are modified in our bodies to make a host of important molecules that control inflammation while also affecting mood and behavior. These are omega-6 (n-6) and omega-3 (n-3) fatty acids, which refers to the fact that the chain of carbon atoms has a double bond in the sixth and third bonds from the omega end of the chain, respectively. Good health requires a balance of omega-3 and omega-6 fatty acids. Essential fatty acids can be obtained from fish, vegetable oils, linseed (flax seed) and canola oil, walnuts, leafy vegetables, pumpkin seed, and sunflower seeds. A typical Western Diet is high in n-6 fatty acids due to the high consumption of processed foods prepared with inexpensive vegetable oils and is low in n-3 fatty acids due to low consumption of fish. It is important to consume enough n-3 fatty acids from the longer chain n-3s, which are found in fish, blue-green algae, and functional foods such as omega-3 enriched eggs and omega-3 fortified soymilk, since our bodies are not capable to elongate the shorter alpha-linolenic acid into the longer chain fatty acids, eicosapentaenoic acid (EPA) and docosahexaenoic acid (DHA), in sufficient amounts.

Omega-3 fatty acids decrease inflammation, while omega-6 fatty acids increase inflammation. For those at risk of diseases related to inflammation, supplementation with omega-3 fatty acids is recommended. The pros and cons of taking fish oil tablets and other omega-3 supplements are discussed in section IV, under supplements.

Carbohydrates

Carbohydrates are compounds composed of carbon, hydrogen, and oxygen. Sugars are small carbohydrate molecules that hook together to form larger starch molecules. Carbohydrates are combined with oxygen inside the cells of our bodies to form high energy phosphate bonds that are used to power cell functions. Carbohydrates are the body and mind's preferred source of energy. Complex starches are preferred to simple sugars to avoid the glycemic rush, or rapid rise in blood sugar, that can have adverse health effects.

Minerals

Salt (table salt) is a simple compound consisting of a sodium atom hooked to a chloride atom. Virtually all foods contain salt, but additional salt is added to many prepared foods as a flavor enhancer or stabilizer. As the amount of salt in the diet increases, one's risk for high blood pressure, heart attacks, and strokes goes up. The American Heart Association recommends limiting salt intake to 1.5 grams per day or 1500 mg per day, which is only achievable if no additional salt is added to foods. Most processed foods and food from fast food restaurants are spiked with unhealthy amounts of salt. Many cheeses contain high amounts of salt. Chips, nuts, and nachos are coated with salt. Excessive salt in the diet should be avoided. It is important to learn how to read food labels so that you can identify processed foods you purchase that contain unhealthy amounts of salt and to make appropriate substitutions for these foods. Most canned vegetables and soups have low sodium or no sodium added options. You can also drain canned vegetables containing high amounts of salt in a strainer and rinse with or soak in cold water; this helps to remove the excess salt in which the product was packaged.

Cholesterol

Cholesterol is an important sterol within the body. It is synthesized in the liver daily and used to make bile acids, sex hormones such as estrogen, progesterone, and testosterone, adrenal hormones such as cortisol, and vitamin D. Cholesterol is also incorporated into every cell membrane within our body. More than 90% of the cholesterol within our bodies resides within the cell. Cholesterol, while essential within the body, is NOT an essential nutrient because the body is able to manufacture all of the cholesterol it needs, every day. Dietary cholesterol is only from animal products. Consuming animal products contributes to serum cholesterol levels (the amount of cholesterol floating around in our blood). Plaque is formed when too much cholesterol accumulates within the walls of our arteries. Over time, plaque can build up and cause atherosclerosis (hardening of the arteries). The risk of heart attacks and strokes increases as the level of cholesterol in the blood rises. It is therefore important to limit the amount of dietary cholesterol to the recommendations set by the American Heart Association, which is no more than 300 milligrams per day. Dr. Myers has an easy way for you to remember which foods contain cholesterol. "If it had a face or comes from something that had a face, it contains cholesterol". Remember to limit your animal protein foods and to balance them with healthy plant-based proteins such as soybean products, nuts and beans.

Dietary Fiber

Dietary fiber consists of materials in fruits and vegetables that add bulk to the diet and plays an important role in digestion. Many fibers have a long thin thread-like structure, which gives the class its name. Fiber is sometimes referred to as roughage. It is not digested in the stomach or small intestines and passes into the colon where it plays an important role in the formation of feces. Fiber can be soluble in water or insoluble—plants contain a mixture of the two types. Insoluble fiber absorbs water and produces a softer bulky stool that is more readily and rapidly passed. A diet low in fiber can lead to constipation and increase the risk of hemorrhoids and colon cancer. Soluble fiber undergoes fermentation by bacteria in the colon producing substances of benefit. In the United States, authoritative sources recommend eating 20 to 35 grams of dietary fiber a day, though the average intake is only 16 grams per day. A diet with adequate dietary fiber is known to lower cholesterol and reduce the risk of diseases related to inflammation including heart disease, stroke, and cancer. A person eating five to ten servings of fruits and vegetables a day and whole grains will consume adequate fiber.

Toxins in Foods

Foods contain a host of toxins, including natural toxins as well as synthetic chemicals found in preservatives, artificial coloring agents, and flavoring agents. Residues of highly toxic fungicides, insecticides, and herbicides occur in doses that, except in unusual cases, do not cause *acute* toxicity in the majority of people. Due to the high burden of natural toxins in foods, our bodies have evolved a highly efficient system to eliminate toxins. Toxins in food are absorbed from the gastrointestinal tract into the portal vein and transported directly to the liver. The liver acts like a big sponge to remove toxins before nutrients are released to the rest of the body. If our detoxification mechanisms are overwhelmed, diseases can result. Hence it is prudent to avoid toxins to the extent that is possible—no small chore in today's polluted world—and to take steps to enhance our ability to detoxify the poisons that we inhale and ingest daily. Eating a variety of foods and avoiding food jags—eating a large amount of a single food as might occur with food addictions (chocoholics beware) – is crucial.

A startling example of how eating a large amount of even a food considered healthy was presented at the Bellevue Toxicology Conference at the New York City Poison Center. A woman was diagnosed with new onset diabetes mellitus and declined medication in favor of a natural treatment popular in Chinese culture. Two weeks later she sought medical attention for being sluggish, swelling of her body, and lack of energy. Her thyroid gland had stopped producing the thyroid hormone, T4. Bok choy is reported to help with diabetes in Chinese medicine, so the woman ate a pound of bok choy for breakfast and another pound for dinner every day for two weeks. Unfortunately for her, bok choy and other members of the cruciferous family contain a toxin that poisons the thyroid gland (http://www.nejm.org/doi/full/10.1056/NEJMc0911005). When these vegetables are eaten in moderation, our livers are able to remove it before it gets to our thyroid gland. Most of us can eat bok choy, broccoli, cabbage, and brussels sprouts in moderation without danger.

A number of cases of inadvertent poisonings have occurred from misuse of pesticides. A graduate of our Emergency Medicine residency program called Dr. Meggs one afternoon from a rural hospital where he was on duty in the Emergency Department. Seven farm workers had shared a watermelon and become sick with nausea, vomiting, confusion, and other symptoms. The farmer denied using any pesticides in the field, other than rat poison. The farm workers recovered immediately after receiving the antidotes for insecticides that poison the enzymes cholinesterase. Samples of the watermelon were obtained and sent to an analytical chemistry laboratory. The laboratory found toxic amounts of the insecticide aldicarb. The use of aldicarb on watermelon plants is illegal because it is incorporated into watermelons. When aldicarb was used on a watermelon crop in California, a few hundred people became ill and several died.

Contamination of foods by heavy metals is an area of concern. Of particular concern is the contamination of fish by mercury. Methyl mercury is a neurotoxin with a long half life in the brain. At high levels it is devastating to the developing fetus, as was dramatically learned in Japan. Children born to women who ate fish from Miamata Bay in Japan during pregnancy were severely disabled. There are known benefits associated with eating fish, but these must be balanced against the toxicity of organic mercury compounds. The amount of mercury in fish varies greatly, depending on the species, the extent of contamination of their habitat, and where they are located on the food chain. Some large predator fish that are high on the food chain and live longer store more mercury in their bodies than other fish. Examples include swordfish, tile fish, king mackerel, and shark. Fish with lower mercury content include salmon, catfish, pollock and shrimp. Canned light tuna has less mercury than albacore tuna and tuna steaks. The Environmental Protection Agency and state health departments monitor mercury levels in fish and issue advisories on the safety of locally caught fish. These studies are generally available at state government web sites and in government reports that are available online. EPA data on the ranges of mercury found in various fish species is available at http://www.fda.gov/Food/FoodSafety/Product-SpecificInformation/Seafood/FoodbornePathogensContaminants/Methylmercury/ucm115644.htm. Developing fetuses and small children are most susceptible to the neurotoxic effects of mercury and organic mercurial compounds. Hence, pregnant women and small children should be especially careful of their fish consumptions. The US Environmental Protection Agency recommendation is that these special populations eat no more than 12 ounces (two average servings) of fish that are low in mercury each week, while avoiding those species with high mercury content.

Antioxidants

Antioxidants have been shown in scientific studies to reduce the effects of free radical damage. Free radicals are natural by-products of the metabolism of lipids – this occurs every day, all day long, in our bodies. Some individuals increase their exposure to free radicals by engaging in activities such as smoking cigarettes or cigars, using other tobacco products, increased exposure to sunlight and working with or handling pesticides. High levels of free radicals can increase a person's risk for certain types of cancer, including skin, lung and gastrointestinal cancers. Free radicals also increase your risk for cardiovascular disease, Alzheimer's disease, and macular degeneration.

Antioxidants come in many forms and have different functions depending on where they originated; therefore, it is important to eat a wide variety of foods that contain the different antioxidants to ensure a good mixture of all of the identified antioxidants. Antioxidants can compete for absorption along the gastrointestinal tract. If a large volume of one antioxidant is consumed, for example through high doses of a dietary supplement, it can decrease the absorption of other antioxidants. Instead of taking megadoses of a specific antioxidant, you should try to consume a wide variety of the whole foods listed in Table I-2. Antioxidants include Vitamins A, E, and C and the mineral Selenium. Other antioxidants, to name a few, include Beta-carotene, lycopene, lutein, luteolin, resveratrol and glutathione. Antioxidants are abundant in fruits, vegetables, whole grains, green tea, herbs and spices. This is a great example of why you should *eat your colors!*

Table I-2: Whole Foods Containing Antioxidants

Blueberries	Hazelnuts	Gala Apples	Kiwi
Blackberries	Prunes	Black Beans	Pineapple
Cranberries	Raspberries	Pinto Beans	Pistachios
Red Kidney Beans	Strawberries	Avocados	Almonds
Artichokes	Red Delicious Apples	Spinach	Green Tea
Russet potatoes	Granny Smith Apples	Sweet Potatoes	Oats grains
Pecans	Sweet Cherries	Broccoli	Cloves
Walnuts	Black Plums	Green and Red Pears	Cinnamon
Ginger	Oregano	Turmeric	Dark Chocolate
Pomegranate	Mango	Red Wine	Grape Juice
Zucchini	Yellow Squash	Cumin	Garlic

Organic Foods

Organically grown foods constitute a fast growing segment of the food market. While difficult to find ten to twenty years ago, most grocery store chains now stock a host of fresh, frozen, canned, and packaged organic foods. All produce in some grocery store chains is now labeled as either *organic* or *commercial*. Many people have voted with their pocket books: they are willing to pay a premium to purchase organic foods. Advocates of organic foods believe that large scale commercial agriculture is toxic to the environment, with chemical fertilizers and pesticides polluting ground water, lakes, and rivers. Over time wild life can be damaged. Humans can be sensitive to chemicals added to foods such as sulfites. There are fears that pesticide and other chemical residues on foods can cause neurodegenerative diseases such as Parkinson's disease. An increased risk of cancer from chemicals on foods is also of concern to many. Scientific studies of health benefits of eating organic foods to humans are limited. There are theoretical reasons that support avoiding foods with pesticide residues for those who believe in the precautionary principle, particularly with regards to residues that are known or suspected to cause cancer.

Read Food Labels

Only a very small percentage of the American population knows how to read and interpret the information presented on food labels. The current food label is designed to provide the consumer with the basic information regarding a specific product to help them to decide if the product fits into their overall diet. Let's review a few basics of the food label. Food labels are based on a 2000 calorie diet, meaning it assumes that you are consuming 2000 calories most days. This generality does not fit all people. For some individuals 2000 calories is way too high and for others it is way too low. It is important to keep this in mind along with your specific nutritional needs so that you can adjust appropriately the amounts required to maintain your optimal health.

On the far right side of the food label are the Percent Daily Values (%DV). These numbers are based on 100% of the daily value for each individual nutrient. Keep in mind that these numbers are different than the Recommended Dietary Allowances. The %DV's are based on a 2000 calorie diet and were developed by the U.S. Food and Drug Administration (FDA). DVs have been established for 4 population groups: infants, toddlers, pregnant or lactating women, and people over four years of age. Keep in mind that these numbers are general guidelines. Your individual requirements for these nutrients will depend on your height, weight, general health, age, activity level and other health conditions.

The food label, as shown below, provides the amount of carbohydrate, fats and protein expressed in grams that is present in 1 serving of the food product. Using basic math, the consumer can then convert the number of grams for these different nutrients into calories.

Recall the calories for the different nutrients:

Fats: 9 calories per gram
Carbohydrates: 4 calories per gram
Proteins: 4 calories per gram

Nutrition Facts		
Serving Size 10 (18g)		
Servings Per Container About 14		

Amount Per Serving		
Calories 70	Calories from Fat 30	
	% Daily Value*	

Total Fat	3.5 g	**5%**
Saturated Fat	0.5g	**3%**
Trans Fat	0g	
Polyunsaturated Fat	1.5g	
Monounsaturated Fat	0.5g	
Cholesterol	0mg	**0%**
Sodium	140mg	**6%**
Potassium	20mg	**1%**
Total Carbohydrate	9g	**3%**
Dietary Fiber	0g	**0%**
Sugars	Less than 1g	
Protein	1g	

Vitamin A 0%	*	Vitamin C 10%	
Calcium 5%	*	Iron 2%	

* Percent Daily Values are based on a 2,000 calorie diet. Your daily values may be higher or lower depending on your calorie needs:

	Calories:	2,000	2,500
Total Fat	Less than	65g	80g
Sat Fat	Less than	20g	25g
Cholesterol	Less than	300mg	300mg
Sodium	Less than	2,300mg	2,300mg
Potassium		3,500mg	3,500mg
Total Carbohydrate		300g	375g
Dietary Fiber		25g	30g

To determine the amount of calories consumed from a specific calorie yielding nutrient, you simply need to perform some very basic math. For example if another food product contains 7 grams of fat, 22 grams of carbohydrate and 5 grams of protein, the calories consumed from a single serving of this food product would be:

7 grams of fat x 9 calories per gram = 63 calories from fat
22 grams of carbohydrate x 4 calories per gram = 88 calories from carbohydrate
5 grams of protein x 4 calories per gram = 20 calories from protein

The total caloric intake from consuming <u>one serving</u> of this food product is equal to the sum of these three nutrients.

63 calories from fat + 88 calories from carbohydrate + 20 calories from protein = 171 total calories

With this in mind, if you were to consume more than 1 serving of this food product at a sitting, you would need to adjust the nutrition information accordingly. This includes ALL of the nutrients that provide calories PLUS the non-caloric nutrients such as the dietary fiber, cholesterol, vitamins and minerals.

So let's assume you were really hungry and you ate 4 servings of this food product in one sitting. Below is a summary of your new caloric intake from this food product.

7 grams of fat x 4 servings x 9 calories per gram = 252 calories from fat
22 grams of carbohydrate x 4 servings x 4 calories per gram =
352 calories from carbohydrate
5 grams of protein x 4 servings x 4 calories per gram = 80 calories from protein

The total caloric intake from consuming <u>4 servings</u> of this food product is equal to the sum of these three nutrients.

252 calories from fat + 352 calories from carbohydrate + 80 calories from protein = 684 total calories

Using this example it is easy to see how calories can become a problem. It is important to consume a wide variety of whole foods and to pay close attention to serving sizes. When focusing on serving sizes, you will be able to monitor your overall nutrition status and to make adjustments based on your specific caloric and nutritional needs. Food labels are designed to provide consumers with the basic nutrition information contained within that product. It is important for you as a consumer to know how to read a food label and to determine which nutrients are the most important for your overall health. For example, if you have high blood pressure, it would be important for you to monitor the sodium you consume from foods. If you are trying to increase your dietary fiber to help lower your serum cholesterol level, it would be important for you to keep track of how much dietary fiber you are consuming. You should compare like products and purchase foods that are higher in dietary fiber. As you can see from the mathematical example above, the effects of nutrition are cumulative and your dietary selections should reflect the best possible options for your optimal health with consideration to any health condition that you may have.

When reading food labels, it is important to pay attention to the ingredient list which is located beneath the Nutrition Facts label. The ingredients are listed by weight, meaning the first ingredient listed is, by weight, the largest component of that food product. In the example below, the first ingredient is unbleached enriched flour; therefore, this product by weight contains more unbleached white flour than any other ingredient.

> INGREDIENTS: UNBLEACHED ENRICHED FLOUR, SOYBEAN OIL, WHOLE GRAIN WHEAT FLOUR, PARTIALLY HYDROGENATED COTTONSEED OIL, SUNFLOWER SEEDS, FLAXSEEDS, SUGAR, SALT, POPPY SEEDS, SALT, MILK CONCENTRATE

If you compare the ingredient list of a regular version of a food product to a low fat or low sugar version of the same food product, you can see what was removed from the original/regular version of the food and what has been added to a low fat or sugar free version. If fat or sugar has been removed from a food product, something must be added for the product to have an acceptable taste, feel and appearance.

Also notice that this ingredient list contains partially hydrogenated cottonseed oil, a trans fat, while falsely stating that it contains zero (0) grams of trans fat. Currently food labels can list that the product contains _no trans fats_ if the amount of **hydrogenated** or **partially hydrogenated** oil in each serving is less than 0.5 grams. If the listed serving size of a product is made small enough for the amount of trans fat to be below 0.5 grams per serving, the manufacturer is allowed to list on the Nutrition Facts label that the product contains zero (0) grams of trans fat. It is important to make note of this, since often times these fats are in snack foods. For some people it is easy to consume more than one serving in a sitting, which means they would be consuming unhealthy amounts of trans fats from that food product. Recall that trans fats have been shown to be more harmful to humans than saturated fats. Trans fats should be avoided, even if the label states zero grams of trans fat but contains hydrogenated vegetable oil. By reading food labels you can easily make substitutions to avoid foods that contain trans fats.

Summary: The Do's of the Inflammation Cure Food Choices
Do eat lots of fruits and vegetables.

Do eat a balance of protein (15%), complex carbohydrates (55%), and fats (30%).

Do eat a variety of foods—avoid a monotonous diet and food jags.

Do limit consumption of red meats and saturated fats, including animal fats and trans-fat.

Do limit consumption of cholesterol.

Do limit consumption of fried foods.

Do limit intake of table salt—ideally add no salt to food.

Do limit consumption of refined sugars, including cane sugar and corn syrup.

Do choose high fiber foods (whole grain and brown rice) over refined products (white bread and white rice).

Do choose organic products whenever possible and affordable.

Do not eat fish with high levels of mercury. Pregnant women and children should eat no more than two servings of fish low in mercury a week, while others can eat four servings a week.

Do read food labels. Know what you are eating and feeding your family.

Do shop locally, when possible. Support your local farmer!

Part II

Inflammation Cure Recipes

Whole foods, referring to foods that have not been processed by manufacturing companies or food production corporations, provide us with the healthy nutrients that our bodies need to grow, maintain and function properly. These nutrients include vitamins, minerals and a group of compounds called "phytochemicals". Whole foods, such as fruits, vegetables, nuts, dairy products, fish, herbs and spices are excellent sources of phytochemicals and provide numerous health benefits. Together these food properties aid in reducing inflammation; therefore, it is important not to focus on one specific food or food group but to eat a wide variety of foods each day. Listed here are ingredients used throughout the recipes we have created that provide a wide variety of vitamins, minerals, antioxidants and phytochemicals. This section was developed to help you identify the ingredients in these recipes and to aid you in focusing on healthy ingredients in recipes and foods that you prepare from other cookbooks or purchase at your local grocery store.

Herbs and Spices

Allspice, also referred to as Jamaican pepper, is widely used in Mexican dishes. This spice is found to have anti-inflammatory, warming, soothing and anti-flatulent properties. The spice includes the healthy oil eugenol, potassium, iron, copper and selenium, niacin and vitamin C. Selenium and vitamin C are antioxidants and aid in the prevention of free radicals.

Basil contains several polyphenolic flavonoids including orientin and vicenin which have been shown to have anti-oxidant protection for cells and assist in the reduction of inflammation and bacterial growth. Basil contains beta-carotene, cryptoxanthin, lutein, zeaxanthian and omega-3 fatty acids in the form of alpha-linolenic acid.

Bay leaf has a pleasant aromatic flavor and contains alpha-pinene, beta-pinene, myrcene, neral, and chavicol components which are highly volatile and are best known for possessing antiseptic, anti-oxidant, digestive and anti-cancer properties. Fresh leaves are a source of vitamin A, vitamin C, folic acid, niacin pantothenic acid and riboflavin. The B vitamins listed here play a role in metabolism. Vitamin C is one of the major antioxidants. Bay leaves contain insect repellent properties and have been used as a diuretic and appetite stimulant.

Black Pepper is known as the "king of spices" and is actually a berry obtained from the peppercorn plant. There are multiple colored peppercorns available in the market and are all derived from the same plant but simply harvested at different times of maturity. These peppers have been used since ancient times as anti-inflammatory, carminative and anti-flatulence. The oils present in peppercorns include piperine. They increase the absorption of selenium, beta-carotene and some B vitamins.

The presence of black pepper in the GI tract increases gastric enzyme secretions and aids in the movement of ingested food along the GI tract.

Caraway seeds are traditionally found in European cuisines. These seeds contain healthy oils with volatile compounds such as carvone, limonene, pinen, furfurol and thujone. These compounds are known to have antioxidant, digestive, and carminative properties. Caraway seeds are a source of dietary fiber, which has been shown to decrease the incidence of some types of GI cancers.

Cardamom is a seed pod and is used in traditional Indian dishes. These pods contain volatile oils such as pinene, sabinene, myrcene, phellandrene, terpinolene, citronellol, nerol, and geraniol, to name a few. These therapeutic properties have been used in many traditional medicines as antiseptics, diuretics, expectorants, stimulants and tonics. Cardamom is a source of potassium, calcium, magnesium, niacin, and vitamin C.

Celery is an herb and is very low in calories. This herb contains flavonoids such as zeaxanthin, beta-carotene and zeaxanthin which are known to protect against cancer. The antioxidant luteolin found in celery has been shown to increase the life expectancy of laboratory animals. Celery is a source of vitamin A, vitamin C, vitamin K, folate, potassium, calcium, and phosphorus.

Chives are small perennial herbs that provide a sweet, mild-onion flavor and possess thio-sulfinite anti-oxidants which have been shown to decrease cholesterol production. Due to the high amount of thio-sulfinites in chives, they have a role in decreasing blood pressure and reducing platelet clot formation in blood vessels which over time can decrease a person's risk for developing heart disease. This herb is a source of dietary fiber, folate, vitamin K, vitamin A, potassium, beta-carotene and lutein.

Cilantro is a native herb to the Mediterranean and Asia Minor. Due to this herb's antioxidants and dietary fiber content, consumption of cilantro can help reduce low density lipoproteins (LDL) cholesterol and increase high density lipoproteins (HDL) cholesterol. The leaves and stems contain several anti-oxidant polyphenolic flavonoids including asquercetin, kaempferol, rhamnetin and epigenin. This herb also contains folate, riboflavin, niacin, beta-carotene, vitamin C, vitamin K, iron and manganese.

Cinnamon has been used since biblical times and is grown in Bangladesh, China, Indonesia and India. This spice contains several oils including ethyl cinnamate, beta-caryophyllene, eugenol, linalool, cinnamaldehyde and methyl chavicol. Eugenol provides the sweet aromatic scent and is used as an antiseptic and cinnamaldehyde has been shown to provide an anti-clotting factor which aids in the prevention of plaque buildup in arteries and therefore decreases a person's risk for heart disease and strokes. Cinnamon contains niacin, folate, vitamin A, vitamin E, vitamin K, potassium, calcium, magnesium, manganese, phosphorus and zinc.

Cloves are known to contain antioxidants, anti-septics, rubefacient (warm and soothing properties), carminative and anti-flatulent properties. This spice contains the healthy oils eugenol, beta-caryophyllene and vanillin. Flavonoids are also present in this spice and include eugenin, kaempferol, rhamnetin and eugenitin. These ingredients my increase GI motility and enhance gastric enzyme secretions which aids in the prevention of indigestion and constipation. This spice is a source of vitamin K, B6, thiamin, vitamin C, potassium, beta-carotene and lutein.

Coriander is the tender hollow stems of the plant. It provides a pleasant aromatic and slightly spicy flavor to dishes. This herb contains several fatty acids including petroselinic acid, linoleic acid, oleic acid and palmitic acid. The seeds contain oils such as linalool, alpha-pinene, geraniol and camphene, just to name a few. Coriander contains dietary insoluble fiber, iron, copper, calcium, potassium, manganese, zinc, vitamin C and niacin. This herb has been used as carminative, to aid in digestion and as a remedy to rid unpleasant breath.

Cumin has a distinctive aroma and is commonly used in Middle Eastern, Western Chinese, Indian, Cuban and Northern Mexican cuisines. The main constituent in cumin is cuminaldehyde increases GI motility and enhances gastric enzyme secretions. This spice is a source of iron, copper, calcium, potassium, manganese, selenium, zinc, magnesium, thiamin, B6, niacin, riboflavin, Vitamin E, beta-carotene, zeaxanthin and lutein. Vitamin E and selenium are antioxidants and work together to prevent heart disease and strokes.

Dill is a perennial herb used in Mediterranean and European cuisines. Both dill leaves and seeds are used as seasonings. The volatile oils dillapiol, eugenol, DHC, limonene, terpinene and myristicin are present in both the leaves and seeds. Eugenol decreases serum glucose levels in diabetics. The oil extracted from dill seeds works as a sedative, aids in digestion, and helps to increase breast milk secretion. Fresh dill is a source of vitamin C, vitamin A, folic acid, riboflavin, niacin, copper, potassium, calcium, manganese, iron, and magnesium.

Fennel and fennel seeds are used in popular Mediterranean cuisines. This herb contains multiple flavonoid antioxidants such as kaempferol and quercetin which function to decrease the number of free radicals from the body and thereby protects against cancer, infections and aging. Fennel seeds increase the production of breast milk. Fennel is a source of dietary fiber, copper, iron, calcium, potassium, manganese, selenium, magnesium, zinc, vitamin A, vitamin C, vitamin E, niacin and riboflavin.

Garlic provides a strong flavor and contains numerous health properties. It contains thio-sulfinites that form allicin through enzymatic reactions. Allicin reduces the production of cholesterol within the body which can decrease total serum cholesterol, depending on the other components of the diet. Garlic consumption is associated with a decrease risk of stomach cancer. Garlic is a source of potassium, iron, calcium, manganese, zinc, magnesium, selenium, beta-carotene, zeaxanthin, vitamin C and folate.

Ginger is used in many cultural dishes, especially Indian and Chinese cuisine. The spicy and aromatic scent of ginger is from the oils and phenolic compounds present in the herb, including ginerols, farnesene, shogaols and zingerone. Gingerols improve GI motility, function as an anti-inflammatory, a painkiller, calms nerves, and contains anti-bacterial components. Zingerone has been shown to combat diarrhea caused by high levels of E. coli, primarily in children and the elderly. This herb is a source of Vitamin B6, pantothenic acid, magnesium, copper, potassium and manganese. Boiled slices of ginger root concocted with honey, sugar, lemon or other citrus fruits have been used to sooth the common cold and sore throats.

Mint contains menthol oil that produces a refreshingly cool sensation that radiates on the taste buds, palate and the throat. Menthol oil also functions as a pain killer, anesthetic and anti-irritant. Studies have shown that mint relaxes the GI wall and the sphincters that control the passage of food stuff along the GI tract. Hence, mint is used in the treatment of irritable bowel syndrome and other GI disorders. Mint is a source of folic acid, niacin, vitamin A, potassium, calcium, copper, iron magnesium, manganese and zinc.

Mustard and mustard seeds come in a variety of colors (white, black and brown) and are grown worldwide. The seeds are rich in phytonutrients and antioxidants. The oils and plant sterols, such as brassicasterol, stigmasterol, avenasterol, campesterol, sitosterol, oleic acid, palmitic acid, sinigrin, myrosin, and eicosenoic, provide multiple health benefits including relief from muscle and joint pain and inflammation. It is believed to aid in hair growth, but no scientific research could be found to support this claim. Mustard and mustard seeds are a source of dietary fiber, lutein, beta-carotene, selenium, manganese, magnesium, iron, calcium, potassium, vitamin E, folic acid and niacin.

Nutmeg is known as an aphrodisiac. The oils contained in the nutmeg seeds include myristicin, elemicin, safrole, eugenol, and trimyristin which contribute to the spice's therapeutic effects as an anti-depressant, anti-fungal, increasing GI motility and increased nutrient absorption, and carminative effects. This spice is a source of manganese, magnesium, copper, zinc, iron, potassium, calcium, folate, niacin, thiamin, cryptoxanthin (an antioxidant flavonoid) and beta-carotene.

Oregano is traditionally used in Greek and Italian cuisines. This herb contains thymol, carvacrol, limonene, pinene, ocimene, and caryophyllene. It is known as an anti-septic, diaphoretic, carminative, anti-spasmodic, stimulant and expectorant. It is believed to aid in gall bladder secretions. Some individuals find relief by taking oregano by mouth for colds, upset stomach, indigestion, mild fevers and menstrual cramps. This herb is a source of dietary fiber, poly-phenolic flavonoids, vitamin K, vitamin E, Vitamin A, niacin and folic acid.

Parsley is widely used in Mediterranean, American and European cuisines. This herb contains eugenol, an oil used by dentists as a local anesthetic and anti-septic agent. It is one of the best plant sources of antioxidant activity, as it contains the polyphenolic flavonoids apiin, apigenin, crisoeriol and luteolin. The fresh herb leaves contain vitamin A, vitamin C, lutein, phosphorus, zinc, iron, magnesium and vitamin K.

Paprika is native to America and was planted in Spain after the voyage of Columbus in 1492. The varieties of this spice include Hungarian paprika and Spanish paprika. This spice contains anti-inflammatory properties and has been shown to increase immune function and aid digestion. It helps regulate blood pressure. Paprika contains vitamin A, vitamin C, vitamin E, iron and phytosterols.

Poppy seeds have a light nutty flavor and are grown in Turkey, France, India and Eastern Europe. This spice contains many fatty acids and oils including oleic acid and linoleic acid (one of the two essential dietary fatty acids). Poppy seeds are a source of dietary fiber, which can lower serum LDL cholesterol. They also contain zinc, selenium, phosphorus, manganese, magnesium, iron, calcium, potassium and folate. The opiates codeine and morphine are contained in poppy seeds but have no known nutrient value.

Rosemary can easily be grown indoors in a small kitchen herb garden. This herb contains rosmarinin acid, a phenolic antioxidant, and the oils cineol, borneol and camphene which are known to have soothing, anti-inflammatory, anti-allergy and anti-septic components. Rosemary contains dietary fiber, magnesium, iron, calcium, potassium, vitamin A and folic acid. Consumption of dietary ingredients high in vitamin A has been shown to decrease a person's risk of lung and mouth cancers.

Sage is used in Mediterranean and European cuisines. There are four main types: Three –lobed sage, Pineapple sage, Clary sage and Azure sage. This herb contains cineol, borneol, tannic acid, fumaric, chloroganic, nicotinic acid, flavones and estrogenic substances which have been shown to have anti-irritant, ruberfacient, anti-inflammatory, anti-allergic, and anti-septic components. The oil constituents include thujone, an antagonist of the neurotransmitters gamma-aminobutyric acid and serotonin. Consumption is believed to increase attention span and aid in grief and depression. Three phytochemicals in sage are lutein, cryptoxanthin and beta-carotene. All three aid in the reduction of free radicals. This herb also contains folic acid, niacin, vitamin B6, vitamin A, vitamin C, vitamin E, vitamin K, potassium, calcium, iron, magnesium, manganese and zinc.

Tarragon, also known as dragon wort, is used in Mediterranean cuisines. Rich with phytochemicals and oils, this herb contains estrogole, cineol, phellandrene and ocimene. It has been used as an appetite stimulant and to lower serum glucose levels. Tarragon extracts have been shown in scientific studies to block platelet aggregation that occurs in heart attacks and strokes. This herb contains zinc, manganese, magnesium, iron, calcium, potassium, vitamin A, vitamin C, vitamin B6, niacin and folic acid.

Thyme contains multiple flavonoids (including zeaxanthin, lutein, pigenin, naringenin and tymonin) and has a high antioxidant level. Thymol, an oil present in thyme, has been shown to have anti-septic and anti-fungal properties. The nutritional components of thyme include dietary fiber, beta-carotene, zinc, manganese, magnesium, iron, calcium, potassium, vitamin C, vitamin A, niacin and folate.

Turmeric root is a traditional Indian and Chinese medicine with anti-inflammatory, antioxidant and cancer prevention properties. The oils contained in this herb include termerone, curumene, cineole, curione, and p-cymene. Curcumin, the primary pigment that gives tumeric its dark orange color, it thought to prevent tumors and treat arthritis, inflammation and heart ischemia. This herb contains zinc, phosphorus, manganese, magnesium, iron, copper, calcium, potassium, vitamin K, vitamin B6, niacin and folic acid.

Vanilla beans have been used since the time of the Mayans and are grown commercially in Madagascar, Indonesia, India and Puerto Rica. Vanilla, one of the more expensive spices on the market, is used worldwide. The main chemical compound is vanillin, which is known as an aphrodisiac. There is no current research to support these claims. This spice contains phosphorus and magnesium.

Whole Foods: Fruits, Vegetables, Nuts and Seeds

Almonds are rich with many vitamins, minerals and dietary fatty acids including zinc, selenium, phosphorus, magnesium, calcium, potassium, vitamin E, niacin, folate and monounsaturated fatty acids. Monounsaturated fatty acids have been shown to decrease low density lipoprotein (LDL) cholesterol and to increase high density lipoprotein (HDL) cholesterol, which aids in the prevention of heart disease. Almonds are gluten free and are used in numerous gluten free foods marketed to individuals with wheat allergies and celiac disease.

Apples are one of the most popular fruits and are low in calories. This fruit contains dietary fiber which increases GI motility and gut transit time while blocking the absorption of cancer causing agents in the large intestine. Apples contain antioxidants flavonoids and polyphenols including quercetin, epicatechin and procyanidin. The vitamins and minerals found in an apple include potassium, folate, vitamin A, vitamin C and small amounts of beta-carotene.

Apricots are commercially grown in Turkey, Italy, France, Iran, Syria, Spain, United States and China. This fruit is a source of vitamin C, vitamin A, folate, potassium, phytochemicals (lutein, zeaxanthin, beta-cryptoxanthins), beta-carotene and dietary fiber. Vitamin A and beta-carotene are both beneficial for vision. Vitamin C is a well established antioxidant that is helpful in the reduction of free radicals.

Asparagus is grown in China, Europe, Peru, United States and Australia. Like most vegetables, asparagus is low in calories with only 20 calories per half cup. This vegetable is a source of dietary fiber which aids in the reduction of serum cholesterol. A diet high in dietary fiber can decrease a person's risk of colon cancer. Asparagus has been used to aid in the relief of irritable bowel syndrome. Asparagus contains the phytochemicals lutein, zeaxanthin, beta-carotenes and cryptoxanthins which are known to decrease the effects of free radicals and to protect against cancers, neurodegenerative diseases and viral infections. Vitamins and minerals found in this vegetable include phosphorus, magnesium, potassium, vitamin K and niacin.

Avocados are high in monounsaturated fatty acids and are calorically dense. Scientific studies have shown that moderate amounts of monounsaturated fats in the diet can reduce blood levels of low density lipoprotein (LDL) cholesterol while increasing high density lipoprotein (HDL) cholesterol, hence reducing the risk of heart disease and strokes. This fruit is a source of dietary fiber which aids constipation, and tannins which have anti-inflammatory and anti-ulcer properties.

Bananas are available year round and are fairly inexpensive. This fruit contains dietary fiber, flavonoids, vitamin B6, vitamin C, potassium, vitamin A and folic aid.

Beans come in a wide variety of types including shell, pinto, white, red, black, pink and yellow. They are grown across the globe and available year round. Beans are a source of dietary fiber, protein, vitamin A, beta-carotene, lutein, zeaxanthin, folate, phosphate, vitamin K and potassium.

Bell peppers (red, yellow, orange and green) are native to Mexico and Central America and are available year round. Red peppers contain higher levels of nutrients than green peppers and contain the antioxidants lycopene and beta carotene. A red pepper on average contains three times the amount of vitamin C in an orange.

Broccoli is part of the cruciferous vegetable family and is a source of phytochemicals that have been shown to decrease the risk of prostate cancer and strokes. Low in calories, broccoli is packed with phytochemicals such as thiocyanates, indoles, sulforaphane, flavonoids and isothiocyanates which have been shown to protect against certain types of cancer including prostate, colon, pancreatic, breast and bladder. This vegetable is also a source of folate, vitamin A, vitamin C, vitamin K, potassium, calcium, iron, magnesium and selenium.

Brussels sprouts are said to have originated in Brussels but are consumed worldwide. Like broccoli, they contain sulforaphane and other cancer fighting chemicals. They are related to and similar to broccoli in nutritional value, being richly endowed with many vitamins and minerals.

Butternut squash is a winter squash grown in the Americas. This vegetable contains multiple phytochemicals that function as antioxidants. It is a source of dietary fiber, cryptoxanthin, beta-carotene, phosphorus, magnesium, calcium, potassium, vitamin C, vitamin A, niacin and folate.

Cabbage belongs to the cruciferous vegetable family and is loaded with healthful nutrients. Phytochemcials include thocyanates, lutein, zeaxanthin, isothiocyanates and sulforaphane which are antioxidants and protect against cancers such as breast, prostate and colon. Vitamins and minerals found in cabbage include vitamin K, pantothenic acid, vitamin B6, thiamin, folate, vitamin K, potassium, calcium and phosphorus.

Cauliflower is a member of the cruciferous family and is a source of multiple phytochemicals including sulforaphane and asindole-3-carbinol which have been shown to decrease the risk of prostate, cervical and ovarian cancers. Di-indolyl-methane is a lipid soluble compound in cruciferous vegetables and have been shown to be effective for immune modulation, anti-bacterial and anti-viral protection. Cauliflower is a source of vitamin C, vitamin K, niacin, potassium, magnesium and calcium.

Carrots are a root vegetable that are grown year round and are a well established source of vitamin A and beta-carotenes which have been shown to aid in vision and to protect the skin, lungs, and mouth from cancers. This vegetable is a source of vitamin C, vitamin K, folate, potassium, magnesium and phosphorus.

Cherries are native to Eastern Europe and Asia Minor. The pigments of cherries contain flavonoid compounds, the anthocyanin glycosides, that are strong antioxidants. Tart cherries have been shown to help prevent cancers, neurological diseases and diabetes. Cherries also contain the antioxidant melatonin which has soothing effects on brain neurons and has been shown to aid in insomnia and headaches. This fruit contains potassium, magnesium, phosphorus, folate and vitamin A.

Chili peppers are grown around the world and are a popular ingredient in Mexican cuisine. The chemical compounds in chili peppers include capsaicin which can reduce the risk of cancer and diabetes. The nutrients found in these peppers include folate, niacin, vitamin A, vitamin C, vitamin K, potassium, magnesium, phosphorus, beta-carotene. Chili peppers contain lutein which is important to central vision. Lutein reduced the risk of age-related macula degeneration in one study.

Coconut is high in fatty acids including lauric acid which increases high density lipoprotein (HDL) cholesterol. Coconut milk is full of carbohydrates, electrolytes, minerals and enzymes which aid in the process of digestion. The cytokinins found in coconut milk have been shown to prevent aging, cancer and high blood pressure. This fruit is a source of folate, potassium, magnesium manganese, phosphorus and selenium.

Corn is native to Central America and is naturally gluten free. The dietary fiber and carbohydrates work together to prevent rapid elevations of blood sugar. The yellow variety of corn contains phenolic flavonoid pigments rich with the antioxidants lutein, xanthins, cryptoxanthin and beta-carotene. Corn is also a source of ferulic acid which is recognized as an antioxidant that reduces the risk of cancer. It reduces inflammation and retards aging processes. Potassium, magnesium, vitamin C, niacin and folate are contained in corn.

Cranberries are rich with the antioxidant phytochemicals proanthocyanidin, cyanidin, quercetin and peonidin which have been shown to prevent the formation of atherosclerotic plaque in arterial walls. The phytochemical pro-anthocyanidin is known for decreasing the risk of cancer, inflammation, diabetes, bacterial infections, and neurological diseases associated with aging. Cranberries reduce the risk of urinary tract infections and alkaline kidney stones by making urine acidic. Cranberries are a source of vitamin A, vitamin C, vitamin E, vitamin K, potassium, magnesium and phosphorus.

Cucumbers are available year round and come in a variety of sizes, shapes and colors. This vegetable is a source of dietary fiber, potassium, vitamin C, vitamin A, vitamin K and lutein.

Eggplant is very low in calories and is a source of dietary fiber, magnesium, potassium, vitamin K, vitamin A and folate. This vegetable has been shown to reduce serum cholesterol. The dark pigmented skin of eggplant contains anthocyanins which may protect against inflammation, cancer, aging and neurological conditions.

Flaxseed has a light nutty flavor and is either brown or golden-yellow. Either type is a source of the omega-3 fatty acid, alpha-linolenic acid. Flaxseed consumed on a regular basis can help reduce low density lipoproteins (cholesterol) and increase high density lipoproteins (HDL) cholesterol. Omega-3 fatty acids have anti-inflammation properties that have been shown to lower blood pressure, protect against breast, colon and prostate cancers, and reduce the risk of heart disease and strokes. Flaxseeds also contain lutein, magnesium, zinc, iron, vitamin E, niacin and folate.

Leeks are in the allium family and are commonly used in European, Asian and American cuisines. This vegetable is a source of soluble and insoluble fibers and thiosulfinites which are antioxidants. Leeks are a source of beta-carotene, lutein, zinc, phosphorus, magnesium, calcium, potassium, vitamin K, vitamin C, vitamin A and folate.

Lemons are the most consumed fruit worldwide and are an excellent source of vitamin C (ascorbic acid). Low in calories and high in dietary fiber, this citric fruit is boasted as a natural preservative. Some studies have shown that citric acid, found in lemon juice, aids in the elimination of kidney stones. Lemons and oranges contain the phytochemcials hesperetin and naringenin which are antioxidants with anti-inflammatory action. This fruit is a source of potassium, copper, lutein, cryptoxanthin, vitamin A and folate.

Mango is one of the most popular fruits on the commercial market. This fruit reduces the risk of leukemia and cancers of the prostate, breast, and colon due to antioxidant properties. Mango contains potassium magnesium, cryptoxanthin, beta-carotene, vitamin B6, vitamin K, vitamin A, vitamin C and folate.

Mushrooms come in a wide variety of species of varying colors and shapes. Many are edible while some contain lethal poisons. White button mushrooms are the most popular form. The vitamin and mineral content of mushrooms vary depending on the type and where they are grown. As a group, edible mushrooms are a source of vitamin D, selenium, pantothenic acid, magnesium, folate, potassium, copper, fiber and energy primarily in the form of carbohydrate and a trace of protein.

Olives and olive oil contain a healthy ratio of monounsaturated fatty acids to saturated fats. They also contains the much desired polyunsaturated fatty acids, including alpha-linolenic acid (an omega-3 fatty acid) which makes them perhaps the healthiest choice for culinary uses. Extra virgin olive oil has a relatively high smoke point (450 degrees). The fruit and oil are sources of the fat soluble vitamins vitamin E and vitamin K.

Omega-3 Eggs are functional eggs that have been modified by changing the diet fed to the hen. Flaxseed or blue-green algae are feed constituents that increase the amount of omega-3 fatty acids incorporated into the egg. The amount of omega-3 fatty acid will vary by the brand of egg. Check at your local grocery store to see which brands of omega-3 eggs are sold in your area and select the one with the largest amount of omega-3 fatty acids.

Onions, a bulb vegetable and a staple in most kitchens, are a source of soluble fiber and the phytochemicals allium and allyldisulphide. Research suggests these properties protect against cancers and diabetes. Chromium, phosphorus, magnesium, potassium, vitamin C and folate are contained in onions.

Oranges are one of many tropical citrus fruits. They contain pectin, a dietary fiber, which functions as a laxative and may help decrease a person's risk of developing colon cancer by binding harmful agents and decreasing exposure time. Oranges contain the flavonoids narigenin and hesperetin which have antioxidant effects and aid in the reduction of inflammation throughout the body. Oranges are a source of lutein, cryptoxanthin, beta-carotene, magnesium, copper, potassium, vitamin A, vitamin C and folate.

Peanuts are a good source of energy and monounsaturated fatty acids that have been shown to help reduce the risk of heart disease and strokes. This nut contains the antioxidant resveratrol which is known to decrease the risk of stomach cancers, heart disease and Alzheimer's disease. Peanuts contain zinc, selenium, phosphorus, manganese, potassium, copper, vitamin E, niacin and folate.

Pecans have a buttery flavor and belong to the hickory family. Packed full of energy, this nut contains many health benefiting nutrients including monounsaturated fatty acids and antioxidants. Regular consumption of pecans have been shown to lower low density lipoprotein (LDL) cholesterol and raise high density lipoprotein (HDL) cholesterol. This nut is a source of phytochemicals that contribute to antioxidant activity including ellagic acid, beta-carotene, lutein, zeaxanthin and vitamin E. These have been shown to decrease the damage from free radicals and therefore protect the human body from diseases such as cancer, arthritis and infections. Pecans are also a source of zinc, selenium, magnesium, iron, potassium, vitamin A and folate.

Pineapples are native to Paraguay, South America, and are now grown in Central and South America. This fruit is a source of both soluble and insoluble dietary fiber and contains the enzyme bromelain which aids in the prevention of cancer, blood clotting and inflammation processes.

Regular consumption of pineapple has been shown to aid in the prevention of arthritis. This fruit is a source of manganese, magnesium, iron, potassium, vitamin C, vitamin A, niacin and folate.

Pine nuts, grown in Siberia and Canada, are very versatile. Rich in calories, this nut also contains phytochemicals that are heart healthy. The omega-6 fatty acid pinolenic acid has been shown to aid in weight loss by curbing appetite by suppressing the enzymes cholecystokinin and glucagon like peptide-1 (GLP-1) in the gastrointestinal tract. Pine nuts are a source of vitamin E, zinc, phosphorus, manganese, magnesium, iron, copper, potassium, niacin and folate.

Plums are grown in the United States, China, Japan and Europe. Like most fruits, plums are low in calories. This fruit contains the dietary fibers isatin and sorbitol which aid in digestion and prevent constipation. Plums contain lutein, cryptoxanthin, beta-carotene, selenium, phosphorus, magnesium, copper, potassium, vitamin K, vitamin C, vitamin A, pantothenic acid and folate.

Potatoes are a good source of starch (energy) and both soluble and insoluble fiber. These fibers slow starch absorption in the gastrointestinal tract and prevent the blood stream from being flooded with sugar. This vegetable is a source of vitamin C, lutein, phosphorus, magnesium, potassium, vitamin K, vitamin A, niacin and folate.

Pumpkin seeds are a source of energy and antioxidants. The monounsaturated fatty acids found in these are a source of oleic acid which can lower harmful low density lipoprotein (LDL) cholesterol while raising high density lipoprotein (HDL) cholesterol levels in the blood. Pumpkin seeds are a source of tryptophan and glutamate, two of the building blocks for making proteins. Glutamate participates in the synthesis of GABA which is an anti-stress neurotransmitter produced in the brain that helps to regulate anxiety. This seed is a source of zinc, lutein, beta-carotene, selenium, phosphorus, manganese, magnesium, iron, copper, potassium, vitamin E, vitamin A, niacin and folate.

Quinoa (pronounced keen-wah) is a South American plant whose seeds can be cooked like rice or ground into a flour that can be made into noodles or used in baking. It has a high protein content and is gluten free. It is not a grass, but is related to vegetables such as beets and spinach. The popularity of quinoa is increasing, particularly with increased interest in gluten free wheat substitutes. Quinoa is currently available in most grocery stores in the United States, though sometimes in blends with corn or other grains, so attention to the ingredients list is important. It can be substituted for wheat or rice in any recipe.

Sesame seeds contain monounsaturated fatty acids that reduce the risk of heart disease by lowering low density lipoprotein (LDL) cholesterol and to raising high density lipoprotein (HDL) cholesterol. These seeds contain phytochemicals including guajacol, phenylethanthiol, sesamol, furaneol, vinylguacol and decadienal which have antioxidant properties. Sesame seeds contain zinc, selenium, phosphorus, manganese, magnesium, iron, copper, potassium, niacin and folate.

Shallots are in the Allium family and are grown commercially in most countries. This vegetable is a source of flavonoids including quercetin, diallyl disulfide, kemferfol and allyl propyl disulfide. Allicin, a compound formed through enzymes from the flavonoids present in shallots, decreases the production of cholesterol and decreases blood pressure, thereby decreasing risk of heart disease and stroke. This vegetable contains phosphorus, magnesium, potassium, vitamin A and folate.

Spinach grows best during the colder seasons and is available year round. It is a source of soluble fiber which aids in the reduction of serum cholesterol. The antioxidants present in spinach include beta-carotene, zeaxanthin, lutein and vitamin C. Since the iron in spinach is bound, consuming it with foods high in vitamin C (bell peppers, oranges, strawberries, etc.) helps cleave the bound iron so that it may be absorbed. Spinach is also an excellent source of vitamin K, which is needed for the coagulation of blood and bone health. Spinach contains the essential nutrients calcium, potassium, vitamin E, Vitamin A and folate.

Squashes are a group of species that come in a variety of shapes and colors. They are grown in America, Mexico and Europe. Very low in calories and a good source of dietary fiber, squashes can contain a wide variety of vitamins and minerals including zinc, phosphorus, magnesium, iron, potassium, vitamin K, vitamin C, vitamin K, thiamin, riboflavin, vitamin B6, pantothenic acid, niacin and folate. Squashes can also contain the phytochemicals lutein and beta-carotene.

Strawberries are native to Europe and are grown commercially around the world. Full of phytochemicals, strawberries contain ellagic acid and anthocyanins which have been shown to aid in the prevention of neurological diseases, the aging process, inflammation and cancer. This fruit is a source of dietary fiber, lutein, manganese, magnesium, iron, potassium, vitamin K, vitamin E, vitamin C, vitamin A, riboflavin, niacin and folate.

Sunflower seeds are native to America and are grown in Russia, China and Argentina. A good source of energy in the form of polyunsaturated fatty acids, sunflower seeds have a healthy fatty acid ratio between monounsaturated fatty acids, polyunsaturated fatty acids and saturated fatty acids. The seeds contain the polyphenols quinic acid, caffeic acid and chlorgenic acid which are antioxidants. Sunflower seeds are a source of zinc, selenium, phosphorus, manganese, magnesium, iron, copper, potassium, vitamin E, thiamin, riboflavin, vitamin B6, pantothenic acid, niacin and folate.

Sweet potatoes come in a variety of colors including white, brown, red and purple. They contain complex carbohydrates that raise serum glucose levels slowly. Sweet potatoes are a source of beta-carotene, zinc, phosphorus, manganese, magnesium, iron, potassium, sodium, vitamin K, vitamin E, vitamin C, vitamin A, thiamin, riboflavin, vitamin B6 and folate.

Tomatoes are a very nutritious fruit that is commonly mistaken as a vegetable. This fruit comes in many shapes and colors including red, white, yellow, green, purple and pink. Very low in calories, this fruit contains the antioxidant lycopene which has been shown to prevent skin damage from ultra-violet rays and therefore reduces the risk of skin cancers. Tomatoes contain beta-carotene, lutein, phosphorus, manganese, magnesium, iron, potassium, vitamin K, vitamin E, vitamin C, vitamin A, thiamin, vitamin B6, niacin and folate.

Walnuts are available in over 30 different varieties and are grown in the United States, Europe and Central Asia. A great source of healthy dietary fatty acids, walnuts contain omega-3 fatty acids (polyunsaturated fatty acids that are considered to be essential for maintaining good health). Regular consumption of walnuts has been shown to decrease the risk of heart disease and strokes by altering a person's cholesterol profile (increasing the HDL to LDL cholesterol ratio). Walnuts contain the phytochemicals melatonin, ellagic acid and beta-carotenoid. When coupled with vitamin E, these phytochemicals provide antioxidant effects that prevent harmful inflammation, neurological diseases, cancer and the aging process. Walnuts are also a source of zinc, selenium, phosphorus, manganese, magnesium, iron, copper, potassium, vitamin K, vitamin C, thiamin, riboflavin, vitamin B6, pantothenic acid, niacin and folate.

Watermelon is a source of electrolytes, water and dietary fiber. This summer treat is grown throughout tropical countries and within the United States. Very low in calories, this fruit provides a wide variety of phytochemicals and antioxidants that aid in the prevention of multiple types of cancers including colon, breast, prostate, lung, pancreatic and endometrial. This fruit contains lycopene, lutein, beta-carotene, cryptoxanthin, magnesium, iron, copper, potassium, vitamin C, vitamin A, thiamin, vitamin B6, pantothenic acid.

Zucchini squash is grown in America, Mexico and Europe. Very low in calories and a good source of dietary fiber, zucchini also contains a wide variety of vitamins and minerals including zinc, phosphorus, magnesium, iron, potassium, vitamin K, vitamin C, vitamin K, thiamin, riboflavin, vitamin B6, pantothenic acid, niacin and folate. Zucchini squash also contains the phytochemicals lutein and beta-carotene.

Gluten

Gluten is a protein found in certain grains including wheat, barley and rye. Gluten and gluten containing food items are very troublesome for individuals with Celiac disease or other forms of gluten intolerance (See Part III). For these individuals, it is important to read food labels. Though the recipes presented here are not all gluten free, many are and have been marked as such. Please read all ingredients before making these dishes if you have been diagnosed with Celiac disease or have gluten intolerance. For more information about Celiac disease visit: www.mayoclinic.com.

Food Safety 101

One of the best ways to keep your family and yourself healthy and safe is to make sure the food you consume is fresh, cooked properly and handled in the correct way throughout the food preparation process. The majority of "stomach bugs" are not related to the common cold, flu or other ailments that may be acquired at work or the playground, but instead are food borne illnesses.

The most common causes of food borne illness are listed below.

* Campylobacter (found in poultry)
* E. coli 0157 (found in ground beef, leafy green vegetables, and raw milk)
* Listeria (found in deli meats, unpasteurized soft cheeses, fruits and vegetables)
* Salmonella (found in eggs, poultry, meat, fruits and vegetables)
* Vibrio (found in raw oysters)
* Norovirus (found in many foods including sandwiches, salads, buffet style foods)
* Toxoplasma (found in meats)
* Staphylococcus aureus (improperly refrigerated foods)

It is important to recognize and practice proper food handling techniques to reduce the possibility of eating foods that will cause a food borne illness. By using these four basic steps, you can decrease your chances of becoming sick.

Step 1: Wash your hands for 20 seconds with soap and running water. Be sure to wash all cooking and food preparation surfaces and utensils <u>before</u> you begin preparing your foods. Washing fruits and vegetables decreases the amount of bacteria on the outside, limiting the amount that is spread to the inside of the produce during cutting or peeling.

Step 2: Avoid cross contamination caused by raw meat, poultry, seafood and eggs by keeping them separate from your ready-to-eat foods. Use separate cutting boards and/or plates for produce and for meat, poultry, seafood and eggs. When storing meats, poultry, seafood and eggs, they should be kept separate from your other groceries. Place raw meats, seafood and poultry in containers or plastic Ziploc bags when storing in the refrigerator. If you do not plan to consume these in a few days, place them in the freezer. Keep eggs in their original carton and discard any that are broken or cracked. Store eggs in the main compartment of the refrigerator, not in the door of the refrigerator as the temperature in this space will fluctuate.

Step 3: Be sure to cook all foods to the correct temperature. This is not something you can visually gauge. Use a food thermometer. There are plenty on the market to choose from. Cooked foods have to be heated to a temperature high enough to kill bacteria. Place the food thermometer in the thickest part of the food when you think it is done (avoid bone, fat or gristle). Cook foods to the recommended minimum cooking temperature that is indicated on most thermometers. Some foods need to "rest" for up to 3 minutes after they have been cooked to make sure the harmful bacteria have been killed. The web site Foodsafey.gov is a valuable source for more information.

Step 4: After cooking, foods that are not going to be consumed promptly should be refrigerated. Make sure your refrigerator and freezer are set at the correct temperatures: between 32-39 degrees Fahrenheit for the refrigerator and below 0 degrees Fahrenheit for the freezer. Do not over stuff your refrigerator. It is important for the cold air to circulate. Use shallow containers to allow foods to cool rapidly. Never thaw or marinate foods on your counters. This is risky for you and your family as counters provide a perfect breeding ground for bacteria. Foods should be thawed in the refrigerator or in cold water. Some foods can be thawed in the microwave but remember these foods should be used immediately.

Remember, you cannot tell by looking or smelling a food whether it contains colonies of bacteria that can harm you. This link to the FoodSafety.gov website provides consumers with the times different foods can be safely stored in the refrigerator. http://www.foodsafety.gov/keep/charts/storagetimes.html. Remember, when in doubt, throw it out!

Recommended minimum cooking temperatures are listed below.

* **135 degrees Fahrenheit:** ready to eat, commercially processed ham and other roasts.
* **145 degrees Fahrenheit:** beef, corned beef, pork, ham (roasts), intact steaks (beef), lamb, veal, pork (steaks or chops), fish, shellfish, fresh sell eggs (broken, cooked and served immediately).
* **155 degrees Fahrenheit:** hamburger, meatloaf and other grown meats, injected meats, ground fish, fresh shell eggs (cooked and held for service such as scrambled eggs).
* **165 degrees Fahrenheit:** chicken, turkey, duck, goose, soups, stews, stuffing, casseroles, mixed dishes, stuffed meat, fish, pasta, and leftovers.
* All hot foods should be **held at 135 degrees Fahrenheit or above** once they have been cooked, until they are served.

More detailed information can be found at the following websites:
http://www.cdc.gov/foodsafety/prevention.html
www.fsis.usda.gov/thermy
http://www.cdc.gov/foodsafety/cdc-and-food-safety.html
http://www.fda.gov/Food/FoodSafety/default.htm

Vegetables

The evidence of benefits from eating a diet rich in vegetables is overwhelming. Numerous studies spanning decades have demonstrated that eating lots of vegetables and fruits reduces one's risk of a number of diseases from cancer to heart disease. Vegetables contain essential vitamins and nutrients, but studies of vitamin and nutrient supplementation to reduce risk of diseases like cancer have failed to reproduce the benefits from eating a diet high in fruits and vegetables. The reason is that vegetables and fruits contain chemicals called flavonoids that are potent antioxidants designed to protect the vegetables and fruits from oxidative stress.

Cheater's Delight (gluten free)

Serves 4

6 c baby **spinach**
2 T **sesame seeds**
½ of a sweet **onion**, diced
2-4 **garlic** cloves, minced
1 T olive oil

Step 1: Cook onion and garlic over medium heat with oil.
Step 2: Add spinach when onions are semi-transparent, cook until wilted, stirring occasionally.
Step 3: Add sesames and a pinch of salt to taste. Enjoy!

Nutrients per serving:
Calories: 30
Carbohydrate: 2g
Protein: 0g
Total Fat: 2.5g
Saturated Fat: 0g
Omega-3 fatty acids: 0.68g
Dietary Fiber: 0g
Sodium: 0mg
Cholesterol: 0mg

Green Curry Veggie Bowl

Serves 6

1 c green curry sauce (see next recipe)*
2 c cooked brown rice
4 medium red **potatoes**, cooked and diced
1 T Canola oil
1 Vidalia **onion**, diced
1 **red bell pepper**, diced
1 head of **cauliflower**, diced
1 tsp fresh **mint**, diced
1 12 oz can garbanzo beans, rinsed and drained

Step 1: Dice and cook red potatoes until tender.
Step 2: In large pan combine oil, onion, red pepper, cauliflower. Cook over medium heat for until veggies are tender.
Step 3: Add curry sauce, potatoes, mint and garbanzo beans to veggies and reduce heat to simmer.
Step 4: Serve over brown rice.

*This food item either is not naturally gluten free or may contain gluten due to preparation and processing. Read food label to ensure that food product does not contain gluten.

Nutrients per serving:
Calories: 780
Carbohydrate: 114g
Protein: 21g
Total Fat: 30g
Saturated Fat: 4.5g
Omega-3 fatty acids: 1.01g
Dietary Fiber: 9g
Sodium: 780mg
Cholesterol: 0mg

Green Curry Sauce

*6 oz Green Curry Sauce (you can buy this at your local high-end grocery store)
2 c water
1can light **coconut milk**
1 T freshly grated **ginger**

Step 1: Combine all ingredients.
Step 2: Bring to a boil and simmer 10 minutes.

*This food item either is not naturally gluten free or may contain gluten due to preparation and processing. Read food label to ensure that food product does not contain gluten.

Nutrients per serving:
Calories: 250
Carbohydrate: 22g
Protein: 4g
Total Fat: 18g
Saturated Fat: 10g
Omega-3 fatty acids: 1.36g
Dietary Fiber: 1g
Sodium: 450mg
Cholesterol: 0mg

Grilled Cheese Quesadilla

Serves 4

4 12" flour tortillas**
1 c shredded low fat cheddar cheese
¼ c salsa
½ c sour cream
½ c Guacamole Made Simple, see page 66

May add:
3 oz shrimp
3 oz chicken breast
3 oz grilled rib eye steak

Step 1: In warm skillet, place 1 flour tortilla and add cheese.
Step 2: Fold tortilla in half and lightly brown on both sides. Serve with salsa, sour cream and
guacamole.

**This food item contains gluten. You may substitute a gluten-free product for this item to make
this a gluten-free recipe.

Nutrients per serving:
Calories: 520
Carbohydrate: 71g
Protein: 18g
Total Fat: 17g
Saturated Fat: 7g
Omega-3 fatty acids: 0.08g
Dietary Fiber: 4g
Sodium: 760mg
Cholesterol: 25mg

Grilled Tofu with Cranberry Relish

Serves 4

1 package firm tofu

Tofu Marinade
4 T brown sugar
½ c canola oil
2 T **rosemary**
2 T low-sodium soy sauce*
2 tsp **black pepper**
2 **garlic** cloves, minced

Step 1: Pour marinade over 2 cups sliced firm tofu. Grill on both sides until desired color.
Step 2: Make Cranberry Relish and set aside until tofu is ready. Serve over fettuccine or favorite pasta.

Cranberry Relish
1 lb frozen **cranberries**, thawed
4 **shallots**, diced
1 T canola oil
1 tsp **thyme**
1 c brown sugar
¼ c bourbon*

Step 1: Sauté shallots in canola oil.
Step 2: Add remaining ingredients except thyme.
Step 3: Simmer until cranberries are soft.
Step 4: Add thyme.
Step 5: Blend but keep chunky. Taste and season as desired. Set aside until Tofu is cooked.

*This food item either is not naturally gluten free or may contain gluten due to preparation and processing. Read food label to ensure that food product does not contain gluten.

Nutrients per serving:
Calories: 570
Carbohydrate: 74g
Protein: 2g
Total Fat: 28g
Saturated Fat: 2g
Omega-3 fatty acids: 2.58g
Dietary Fiber: 2g
Sodium: 200mg
Cholesterol: 0mg

Homemade Mashed Potatoes (gluten free)

Serves 6

8 red **potatoes**, cut in fourths
2 T butter
½ c 2% milk, more if needed
Salt and **white pepper**, to taste

Step 1: Bring water and potatoes to a boil and then reduce temperature to simmer and cook potatoes until the potatoes are tender, drain. Set water aside.
Step 2: Add milk, butter, potatoes, salt and pepper in electric mixer and whip.
Step 3: Thin with hot potato water if needed; season as desired.

Nutrients per serving:
Calories: 330
Carbohydrate: 69g
Protein: 9g
Total Fat: 1g
Saturated Fat: 0g
Omega-3 fatty acids: 0.10g
Dietary Fiber: 6g
Sodium: 60mg
Cholesterol: 0mg

South of the Border Brown Rice Dish

Serves 6

2 c brown rice
1 medium sweet **onion**, diced
1 c **tomatoes**, diced
½ c grilled **corn** (1 ear)
1 c black beans, rinsed and drained
1 T **cumin**
½ tsp **paprika**
1 tsp **cayenne pepper**
1 c low fat sour cream
1 c guacamole
1 c salsa
tortilla chips**

May add one of the following:
3 oz shrimp
3 oz grilled chicken breast
3 oz grilled Rib-eye steak

Step 1: Cook brown rice according to package directions. Set aside.
Step 2: In medium sized pan, cook onion until tender. Add tomatoes, corn and black beans. Reduce heat to simmer. Add spices and stir well.
Step 3: Serve over brown rice with low-fat sour cream, guacamole and salsa. Add tortilla chips on the side if desired.

Note: If shrimp, chicken or steak is added, the nutritional information will need to be adjusted accordingly.

**This food item contains gluten. You may substitute a gluten-free product for this item to make this a gluten-free recipe.

Nutrients per serving:

Calories: 400
Carbohydrate: 80g
Protein: 11g
Total Fat: 7g
Saturated Fat: 0g

Omega-3 fatty acids: 0.10g
Dietary Fiber: 9g
Sodium: 720mg
Cholesterol: 0mg

Garbanzo Beans and Mushrooms

Serves 4

1 T olive oil
2 **shallots**, diced
4 **garlic** cloves, minced
1 lb **mushrooms**, sliced
½ c sundried **tomatoes**
⅔ c white wine
1 can garbanzo beans, rinsed and drained
¼ c grated Parmesan cheese
1 T **parsley**
1 tsp **oregano**
Black pepper, to taste
2 c rigatoni pasta, cooked**

Step 1: Sauté shallots in oil until soft.
Step 2: Add garlic and mushrooms and cook for 5 minutes. Stir in sun-dried tomatoes, wine and herbs.
Step 3: Add beans and cook for 5 minutes until beans are warmed.
Step 4: Add Parmesan cheese and serve over pasta.

**This food item contains gluten. You may substitute a gluten-free product for this item to make this a gluten-free recipe.

Nutrients per serving:
Calories: 590
Carbohydrate: 99g
Protein: 21g
Total Fat: 0g
Saturated Fat: 1.5g
Omega-3 fatty acids: 0.03g
Dietary Fiber: 6g
Sodium: 410mg
Cholesterol: 5mg

Black Beans and Rice (gluten free)

Serves 8

1 lb dried black beans
Vegetable cooking spray
1 tsp canola oil
1 c **onions**, chopped
½ c **red bell pepper**, chopped
½ c **yellow bell pepper**, chopped
5 **garlic** cloves, minced
5 c water
6 oz **tomato** paste
2 T seeded, minced **jalapeno pepper**
1 tsp ground **cumin**
¼ tsp **black pepper**
4 ½ jasmine rice (cooked)

Step 1: Sort and wash beans; place in a large pot. Cover with water to a depth of 2 inches above beans; let soak overnight. Drain and rinse beans. Return beans to pot and set aside.

Step 2: Coat a large, nonstick skillet with cooking spray; add oil. Place skillet over medium-high heat. Add onion, red pepper, yellow pepper, and garlic; sauté 4 to 5 minutes until tender.

Step 3: Add onion mixture, water, and next 4 ingredients to beans; bring to a boil. Cover, reduce heat, and simmer 2 hours or until beans are tender, stirring occasionally.

To serve, place ½ cup cooked rice in each individual serving bowl; spoon 1 cup bean mixture over each serving.

Nutrients per serving:

Calories: 280
Carbohydrate: 55g
Protein: 14g
Total Fat: 1.5g
Saturated Fat: 0g
Omega-3 fatty acids: 0.13g
Dietary Fiber: 12g
Sodium: 65mg
Cholesterol: 0mg

Eggplant Dip (gluten free)

Serves 4

1 **eggplant**
2 **garlic** cloves, minced
1 T tahini
2 T lemon juice
1 tsp ground **cumin**
½ tsp **cayenne pepper**
1 T **mint** leaves
Black pepper, to taste

Step 1: Broil entire eggplant, turning frequently until skin is blistered, time will vary depending on your oven. The inside of the eggplant will become tender. Remove from oven, allow to cool. Remove skin and chop into small ½ inch sections.

Step 2: Place eggplant in blender. Add garlic, tahini, lemon juice and cumin. Blend until smooth. Add mint and stir.

Step 3: Spoon into bowl. Serve with your favorite pita chips or use as a spread on sandwiches.**

**This food item contains gluten. You may substitute a gluten-free product for this item to make this a gluten-free recipe.

Nutrients per serving:
Calories: 60
Carbohydrate: 9g
Protein: 2g
Total Fat: 2.5g
Saturated Fat: 0g
Omega-3 fatty acids: 0.03g
Dietary Fiber: 5g
Sodium: 10mg
Cholesterol: 0mg

Tomato Pesto Spread (gluten free)

Serves 4

6 T cream cheese
¼ c basil pesto
2 large **tomatoes**, diced
½ red **onion**, diced
Black pepper, to taste

Step 1: Combine cream cheese and pesto in a small bowl and mix well.
Step 2: Dice the tomato and onion. Add to cheese mixture and stir well.
Step 3: Serve on your favorite bread as a sandwich spread.

Nutrients per serving:
Calories: 180
Carbohydrate: 7g
Protein: 5g
Total Fat: 15g
Saturated Fat: 7g
Omega-3 fatty acids: 0.18g
Dietary Fiber: 2g
Sodium: 190mg
Cholesterol: 30mg

Stuffed Mushrooms

Serves 4

30 white mushrooms (can use a mixed variety of mushrooms if desired)
1 T olive oil
4 c baby **spinach**
1 **red pepper,** diced
½ c **shallots**, diced
2 **garlic** cloves, minced
¼ c red wine
¼ c parmesan cheese
½ c bread crumbs**
Black pepper, to taste
Salt, to taste

Step 1: Sauté the shallots, garlic and red pepper in olive oil.
Step 2: Add red wine and reduce heat to low.
Step 3: Add spinach.
Step 4: Remove from heat and add remaining ingredients.
Step 5: Taste and season as desired with black pepper and salt.
Step 6: Stuff mushrooms and place on pre-coated cooking sheet (may use olive oil or cooking spray).
Step 7: Cook in preheated oven at 350 degrees until the mushrooms are hot and liquid forms on the top.

**This food item contains gluten. You may substitute a gluten-free product for this item to make this a gluten-free recipe.

Nutrients per serving:
Calories: 130
Carbohydrate: 17g
Protein: 5g
Total Fat: 4g
Saturated Fat: 1g
Omega-3 fatty acids: 0.01g
Dietary Fiber: 2g
Sodium: 150mg
Cholesterol: 5mg

Eggplant Wraps (gluten free)

Serves 4

1 whole **eggplant**, peeled and sliced in long strips
3 medium Roma **tomatoes**, sliced
6 oz Goat cheese
1 T **basil**
1 T olive oil

Step 1: On cookie sheet, lightly coat both sides of eggplant slices with olive oil.

Step 2: Add a medium slice of tomato and ½ an ounce of goat cheese on each slice of eggplant.

Step 3: Roll and place with end tucked under on the cookie sheet. Repeat until all of the eggplant strips are in rolls, sprinkle on basil.

Step 4: Bake at 350 for 25 minutes or until desired tenderness.

Nutrients per serving:
Calories: 150
Carbohydrate: 7g
Protein: 7g
Total Fat: 11g
Saturated Fat: 6g
Omega-3 fatty acids: 0.07g
Dietary Fiber: 3g
Sodium: 150mg
Cholesterol: 20mg

Cheesy Potato Patties

Serves 4

1 lb new **potatoes**
6 oz feta cheese
1 T **dill**
½ T **lemon juice**
¼ c skim milk
1 c all purpose flour, for dipping**
2 T olive oil
Black pepper, to taste

Step 1: Peel and rinse potatoes. Cut potatoes into 1 inch sections. Boil potatoes until soft, about 20 minutes. Drain and mash. Add feta cheese to the potatoes and add dill, lemon juice and milk. Season with salt and pepper. Mix well.

Step 2: Chill until firm. Using a spoon create 1 inch balls and then flatten. Roll potato balls in flour and place on olive oil coated baking sheet. Bake at 375 degrees for about 10 minutes. Perfect side dish to serve with baked chicken or fish and your favorite green veggies.

**This food item contains gluten. You may substitute a gluten-free product for this item to make this a gluten-free recipe.

Nutrients per serving:
Calories: 340
Carbohydrate: 45g
Protein: 14g
Total Fat: 14g
Saturated Fat: 6g
Omega-3 fatty acids: 0.01g
Dietary Fiber: 3g
Sodium: 920mg
Cholesterol: 15mg

Avocado Spread (gluten free)

2 ripe medium **avocados**
2 **garlic** cloves, minced
1 tsp **paprika**
1 tsp **cayenne pepper**
Dash of sea salt, to taste

Step 1: Slice avocados in half and remove pit and skin.
Step 2: In medium size bowl combine avocados, spices and freshly crushed garlic.
Step 3: Blend ingredients together to form a thick spread.
Step 4: Serve on toast, English muffins, or on sandwiches**.

**This food item contains gluten. You may substitute a gluten-free product for this item to make this a gluten-free recipe.

Nutrients per serving:
Calories: 160
Carbohydrate: 9g
Protein: 2g
Total Fat: 15g
Saturated Fat: 2g
Omega-3 fatty acids: 0.50g
Dietary Fiber: 7g
Sodium: 5mg
Cholesterol: 0mg

Portabello Mushrooms and Brown Rice

Serves 4

1 ½ c cooked brown rice
2 T whole **flaxseed**
1 **omega-3 egg**
¼ c skim milk
½ c grated cheddar cheese
¼ c finely chopped **celery**
½ tsp **basil**
Black pepper, to taste
4 portabello **mushrooms**
2 T canola oil
2 T balsamic vinegar*

Step 1: Preheat oven to 350 degrees.
Step 2: In medium bowl, combine cooked brown rice and flaxseed, egg and milk, beat until well mixed.
Step 3: Add cheese, celery, onion, basil, and pepper.
Step 4: Place mushroom caps, tops down, into a lightly greased 9 inch pie plate. Evenly divide rice mixture onto mushroom caps. Loosely cover with aluminum foil. Bake 45 minutes.
Step 5: Mix canola oil and balsamic vinegar and drizzle lightly over mushrooms before serving.

*This food item either is not naturally gluten free or may contain gluten due to preparation and processing. Read food label to ensure that food product does not contain gluten.

Nutrients per serving:
Calories: 350
Carbohydrate: 26g
Protein: 13g
Total Fat: 21g
Saturated Fat: 8g
Omega-3 fatty acids: 0.02g
Dietary Fiber: 4g
Sodium: 240mg
Cholesterol: 85mg

Bulgur Wheat Pilaf with Flaxseeds

Serves 4

2 T butter
1 c bulgur wheat**
¼ c **flaxseed**
1 medium **onion**, diced
1 small **tomato**, diced
2 c vegetable broth-prepackaged*
¼ tsp dried **rosemary**

Step 1: In a medium saucepan, over medium heat, melt butter. Add bulgur wheat, flax seed and onion. Stir until bulgur wheat is golden brown and flax is turning dark.
Step 2: Turn off heat and cool for about 10 minutes before serving.

*This food item either is not naturally gluten free or may contain gluten due to preparation and processing. Read food label to ensure that food product does not contain gluten.

**This food item contains gluten. You may substitute a gluten-free product for this item to make this a gluten-free recipe.

Nutrients per serving:
Calories: 160
Carbohydrate: 21g
Protein: 5g
Total Fat: 6g
Saturated Fat: 2g
Omega-3 fatty acids: 0.1g
Dietary Fiber: 7g
Sodium: 200mg
Cholesterol: 5mg

Vegetarian Burgers

Serves 6

¾ c dry lentils
1 ½ c water
2 T balsamic vinegar*
1 T canola oil
1 c large **onion**, finely diced
4-5 **garlic** cloves, minced
About 10 large **mushrooms**, minced
½ c **walnuts,** finely chopped
1 bunch fresh **spinach**, finely chopped
1 tsp dry **mustard**
Black pepper, to taste
½ c Italian bread crumbs**

Step 1: Place lentils and water in a small pan and bring to a boil. Lower heat and simmer, for 30 minutes. Transfer to a medium-sized bowl, add vinegar and mash well.

Step 2: Heat oil in skillet. Add onions and sauté over medium heat until clear. Add all remaining ingredients except or bread crumbs, and sauté until vegetables are tender. Add the vegetables to the lentils and mix well.

Step 3: Chill for 1 hour before patties.

Step 4: For 3-inch burgers; brown shaped patties in a small amount of hot canola oil on both sides until heated through and crispy on the outside.

*This food item either is not naturally gluten free or may contain gluten due to preparation and processing. Read food label to ensure that food product does not contain gluten.

**This food item contains gluten. You may substitute a gluten-free product for this item to make this a gluten-free recipe.

Nutrients per serving:

Calories: 250	Omega-3 fatty acids: 1.03g
Carbohydrate: 30g	Dietary Fiber: 6g
Protein: 12g	Sodium: 300mg
Total Fat: 10g	Cholesterol: 0mg
Saturated Fat: 1g	

Garlicky Refried Beans (gluten free)

Serves 6

2 c dried pinto beans, soaked
2 T canola oil
2 c minced onion
6 medium **garlic** cloves, minced
1 T **cumin**
Black pepper
1 **red bell pepper**, finely chopped

Step 1: Sort and soak beans in large pot with cold water overnight (at least 8 hours).

Step 2: Rinse beans, place back in large pot and water until beans are covered by 2 inches of water. Bring to a soft boil and then reduce heat and simmer until beans are very tender. Drain and set aside.

Step 3: Heat canola oil in a large skillet. Add onion, garlic, cumin and salt. Sauté over medium heat until the onions are soft. Add red bell pepper, and sauté 5 minutes. Add black pepper.

Step 4: Reduce heat to low, add beans, and mix well. Mash with a potato masher, and cook until warm. Serve with brown rice or eat plain.

Nutrients per serving:

Calories: 260
Carbohydrate: 42g
Protein: 13g
Total Fat: 5g
Saturated Fat: 0g
Omega-3 fatty acids: 0.12g
Dietary Fiber: 0.18g
Sodium: 5mg
Cholesterol: 0mg

Walnuts and Wild Rice (gluten free)

Serves 6

1 T canola oil
¾ c **walnuts,** chopped
2 large **onions,** diced
2 T **tarragon**
Black pepper, to taste
3 c cooked wild rice

Step 1: Heat oil in a medium skillet over high heat.
Step 2: Add walnuts, onions, and tarragon. Season with pepper and sauté until the onions are
caramelized.
Step 3: Mix with rice and serve.

Nutrients per serving:
Calories: 220
Carbohydrate: 25g
Protein: 6g
Total Fat: 12g
Saturated Fat: 1g
Omega-3 fatty acids: 1.45g
Dietary Fiber: 3g
Sodium: 5mg
Cholesterol: 0mg

Quinoa with Pine Nuts (gluten free)

Serves 4

1 large **onion**, diced
3 **garlic** cloves, minced
1 T canola oil
1 **red bell pepper**
2 tsp ground **cumin**
2 tsp ground **coriander**
1 c **quinoa**
2 c water
½ c fresh **basil**, chopped
2 c frozen **corn**
Black pepper, to taste
1 ½ T toasted **pine nuts***

* To toast, spread on a baking sheet and bake at 300 degrees for about 8 minutes.

Step 1: In a heavy saucepan, sauté onions and garlic in canola oil for 5 minutes.
Step 2: Add red bell pepper, cumin, and coriander and continue to sauté for 5 more minutes.
Step 3: Rinse quinoa in a fine sieve under cold water. Add the quinoa and water to the saucepan, cover tightly, and simmer for 15 minutes.
Step 4: Stir in basil and corn; cook until the quinoa is tender. Add black pepper to taste, and serve topped with the toasted pine nuts.

Nutrients per serving:
Calories: 290
Carbohydrate: 45g
Protein: 9g
Total Fat: 9g
Saturated Fat: 1g
Omega-3 fatty acids: 0.14g
Dietary Fiber: 5g
Sodium: 10mg
Cholesterol: 0mg

Red Lentil Dal (gluten free)

Serves 4

1 c red lentils
1 medium **onion**, diced
4 **garlic** cloves, minced
2 **jalapeno peppers**, chopped with seeds
3 T butter
1 tsp **turmeric**
1 15-oz can light coconut milk*
2 **shallots**, sliced
1 tsp red pepper flakes
1 tsp **mustard seed**

* Can substitute the coconut milk with evaporated skim milk for a lower fat version.

Step 1: Wash lentils. In saucepan over medium heat, sauté onions, garlic, and jalapenos in 2 tablespoons of butter for 1 minute. Add turmeric, lentils, and 3 cups of water. Bring to a boil, then lower heat and simmer, covered, for about 30 minutes. Add coconut milk and simmer 5 additional minutes, stirring occasionally. Remove from heat.

Step 2: Heat remaining butter in a small skillet over high heat. Add shallots, red pepper flakes, and mustard. Fry until mustard seeds begin to turn grayish. Stir this into the lentils and serve.

Nutrients per serving:
Calories: 352
Carbohydrate: 37g
Protein: 17g
Total Fat: 15g
Saturated Fat: 8g
Omega-3 fatty acids: 1.03g
Dietary Fiber: 9g
Sodium: 25mg
Cholesterol: 10mg

Three-Bean Medley

Serves 6-8

1 (15-oz) can white kidney beans, drained and rinsed
1 (15-oz) can black beans, drained and rinsed
1 (15 oz) can red kidney beans, drained and rinsed
1 T canola oil
2 Roma **tomatoes**, diced
4 **garlic** cloves, minced
¼ c fresh **cilantro,** chopped
1 ½ tsp chili powder
1 **zucchini** and 1 **yellow squash**
1 15 oz can spicy **tomatoes**
Tortilla chips**
Shredded reduced fat cheddar cheese

Step 1: Combine beans, tomatoes, garlic, cilantro, and chili powder in a large pot over low heat with canola oil.
Step 2: Dice zucchini and squash and stir into beans. Stir in canned spicy tomatoes.
Step 3: Cover and cook on LOW about 1 hour. Serve with tortilla shells and top with cheese.

**This food item contains gluten. You may substitute a gluten-free product for this item to make this a gluten-free recipe.

Nutrients per serving:
Calories: 320
Carbohydrate: 56g
Protein: 20g
Total Fat: 4g
Saturated Fat: 1.5g
Omega-3 fatty acids: 0.14g
Dietary Fiber: 16g
Sodium: 360mg
Cholesterol: 5mg

Garden Vegetables with Brown Rice

Serves 4

1 T canola oil
1 c **onion,** diced
4-6 **garlic** cloves, minced
1 c water
½ c vegetable broth*
1 c instant brown rice, uncooked**
1 c diced **carrot**
¾ c Roma **tomatoes,** chopped
1 tsp **thyme**
½ tsp **oregano**
¼ tsp **black pepper**
1 c **broccoli,** chopped
1 c **zucchini,** sliced
1 (15-oz) can garbanzo beans, rinse and drained
¼ c grated Asiago cheese

**May substitute white or jasmine rice if desired.

Step 1: Heat oil in a large saucepan over medium-high heat. Add onion and garlic, sauté until onion is clear. Add water and broth to onion mixture, and bring to a boil.

Step 2: Stir in rice and carrots, tomatoes, thyme, oregano, black pepper and broccoli. Cover, reduce heat, and simmer 10 minutes or until rice is tender and liquid is absorbed (~10 minutes). Let stand, covered, 5 minutes. Add beans and cheese; toss gently.

*This food item either is not naturally gluten free or may contain gluten due to preparation and processing. Read food label to ensure that food product does not contain gluten.

Nutrients per serving:
Calories: 310
Carbohydrate: 49g
Protein: 12g
Total Fat: 8g
Saturated Fat: 1.5g
Omega-3 fatty acids: 0.04g
Dietary Fiber: 9g
Sodium: 190mg
Cholesterol: 5mg

Canadian Bacon with Baked Beans

Serves 8

1 lb dried small navy beans, sorted and rinsed
4 c water
⅓ c honey
¼ c packed light brown sugar
1 **onion**, diced
1 T Dijon **mustard***
2 oz sliced Canadian bacon

Step 1: Thoroughly combine beans, water, molasses, brown sugar, onion, and mustard, in a 3 quart slow cooker. Place Canadian bacon on top of mixture.

Step 2: Cover and cook on HIGH about 5 hours. Stir mixture; cover and cook on HIGH 1 to 2 additional hours or until beans are tender.

*This food item either is not naturally gluten free or may contain gluten due to preparation and processing. Read food label to ensure that food product does not contain gluten.

Nutrients per serving:
Calories: 140
Carbohydrate: 27g
Protein: 6g
Total Fat: 1g
Saturated Fat: 0g
Omega-3 fatty acids: 0.06g
Dietary Fiber: 3g
Sodium: 380mg
Cholesterol: 5mg

Hearty Bean Dish with Lentils

Serves 6

1 ½ T canola oil
1 **onion**, diced
1 **bell pepper**, finely chopped (green, yellow, red or orange)
1 T **tarragon**
¾ c green lentils, sorted and rinsed
2 c cooked bulgur wheat**
1 (15 oz) can chickpeas, rinsed and drained
Black pepper, to taste

Step 1: Heat oil in a medium sized pan. Add onion, pepper, and tarragon, cook over medium heat stirring frequently, until the onion begins to color, about 7 minutes.

Step 2: Add the lentils, 5 cups water, and bring to a boil. Lower heat and simmer, covered, until tender.

Step 3: Add the bulgur wheat and chickpeas; cooking about 5 minutes. Drain and taste for salt, season with pepper.

**This food item contains gluten. You may substitute a gluten-free product for this item to make this a gluten-free recipe.

Nutrients per serving:
Calories: 290
Carbohydrate: 49g
Protein: 13g
Total Fat: 6g
Saturated Fat: 0g
Omega-3 fatty acids: 0.03g
Dietary Fiber: 12g
Sodium: 35mg
Cholesterol: 0mg

Ginger Chickpeas (gluten free)

Serves 6

4 T canola oil
1 large **onion**, finely chopped
1 **bay leaf**
4-6 **garlic** cloves, minced
3 T grated **ginger**
2 T ground **coriander**
2 T ground **cumin**
½ tsp ground **cardamom**

Black pepper

2 Roma **tomatoes**, diced
2 15-oz cans chickpeas, rinsed and drained
Juice of ½ a **lemon** (more if desired)
1 minced jalapeno with seeds

Step 1: Heat oil in large skillet over medium heat. Add onion and cook until caramelized, about 12 to 15 minutes.

Step 2: Lower heat and add the bay leaf, garlic, ginger, spices, pepper, and tomatoes. Cook 5 minutes, add chickpeas. Simmer until liquid is reduced to a sauce-like consistency. Taste and season with lemon juice. Serve with jalapenos on top.

Nutrients per serving:

Calories: 270
Carbohydrate: 30g
Protein: 8g
Total Fat: 14g
Saturated Fat: 1g
Omega-3 fatty acids: 0.01g
Dietary Fiber: 7g
Sodium: 260mg
Cholesterol: 0mg

Spring Rolls

Serving size: 1 spring roll

4 oz rice noodles*
1 c **onions**
1 c shredded **lettuce**
1 c **bell peppers**
1 c **mung bean sprouts**
1 c plain tofu*
⅓ c **peanuts**, chopped
12 rice wrappers
Sauce

Step 1: Cook rice noodles and set aside.

Step 2: Cut onions, peppers, and tofu into thin strips. Mix onions, peppers, tofu, sprouts and crushed peanuts in a bowl.

Step 3: Place 1 wrapper on a large cutting board and add about 2 tablespoons of noodles then add 1 large spoonful of veggie/tofu mix to the middle of the wrapper. Fold the outside edges of the wrapper over the mixture and roll up. Set aside, seam down, and continue making the rest of the spring rolls. Chill for 1 hour or until ready to serve.

*This food item either is not naturally gluten free or may contain gluten due to preparation and processing. Read food label to ensure that food product does not contain gluten.

Nutrients per serving:
Calories: 120
Carbohydrate: 19g
Protein: 4g
Total Fat: 3g
Saturated Fat: 0g
Omega-3 fatty acids: 0.01g
Dietary Fiber: 1g
Sodium: 20mg
Cholesterol: 0mg

Beans and Rice

Serves 6

1 T olive oil
1 sweet **onion**, diced
2 **carrots**, peeled and diced
1 each **red and green bell peppers**, diced
4 **garlic** cloves, minced
½ tsp **fennel**
1 **jalapeno pepper**, diced with seeds
1 medium can diced **tomatoes**
4 **shallots**, diced
2 c cooked white rice
1 c water
1 tsp **thyme**
1 tsp **oregano**
½ tsp salt
1 tsp **black pepper**
1 tsp hot sauce*
1 tsp Cajun seasoning*
2 cans kidney beans, rinsed and drained.

Step 1: Sauté onion, carrots, garlic, fennel, and bell peppers in olive oil.
Step 2: Add remaining ingredients except rice and beans.
Step 3: Bring to boil and add rice and beans. Reduce heat and simmer for 20 minutes, stirring occasionally. May add more water if needed or desired.
Step 4: Taste and season with salt and pepper.

*This food item either is not naturally gluten free or may contain gluten due to preparation and processing. Read food label to ensure that food product does not contain gluten.

Nutrients per serving:

Calories: 420
Carbohydrate: 83g
Protein: 14g
Total Fat: 3.5g
Saturated Fat: 0.5g

Omega-3 fatty acids: 0.18g
Dietary Fiber: 8g
Sodium: 390mg
Cholesterol: 0mg

Hummus and Couscous Wrap

Serves 6

1 c black bean hummus* (see next page)
1 c cooked couscous**
1 medium **tomato**, sliced
1 **cucumber**, sliced in rounds
¼ of a red **onion**, sliced
romaine lettuce, washed and patted dry
6 flour tortillas, warmed if desired**

On individual plates, place 1 flour tortilla and add a spoonful of black bean hummus, 1 spoonful of couscous, tomatoes, cucumber, onion and lettuce leafs. Serve and enjoy!

*This food item either is not naturally gluten free or may contain gluten due to preparation and processing. Read food label to ensure that food product does not contain gluten.

**This food item contains gluten. You may substitute a gluten-free product for this item to make this a gluten-free recipe.

Nutrients per serving:
Calories: 140
Carbohydrate: 28g
Protein: 5g
Total Fat: 2g
Saturated Fat: 0g
Omega-3 fatty acids: 0.01g
Dietary Fiber: 5g
Sodium: 110mg
Cholesterol: 0mg

Black Bean Hummus

Serving size: 2 T

This hummus recipe can be used as a dip or a spread for sandwiches.

4 – 6 **garlic** cloves, minced
2 T **parsley**
¼ c sweet **onions**, diced
3 c cooked black beans (2 15½ oz cans, rinsed and drained)
2 T tahini*
1 whole **lemon**, squeezed and seeds removed
1 T cayenne pepper (more if desired)
2 T **cumin**
Pinch of salt, to taste

Step 1: Place all ingredients in either a food processor or a blender. Blend until creamy. May add a pinch of water, if needed.
Step 2: Place hummus in a tightly covered container and chill until ready to serve.

Note: You can make this hummus more or less spicy by adjusting the parsley, cumin, and cayenne pepper to you desired taste.

*This food item either is not naturally gluten free or may contain gluten due to preparation and processing. Read food label to ensure that food product does not contain gluten.

Nutrients per serving:
Calories: 180
Carbohydrate: 32g
Protein: 10g
Total Fat: 5g
Saturated Fat: 0.5g
Omega-3 fatty acids: 0.04g
Dietary Fiber: 11g
Sodium: 400mg
Cholesterol: 0mg

Quesadillas from the Garden

Serves 6

1 of each **red, yellow and green bell peppers**
1 large sweet **onion**
3 large **tomatoes**
2 **jalapeño peppers**
1 T olive oil
1 package low fat cheese
1 package burrito shells**

Step 1: Dice bell peppers and onion and sauté in large skillet with 1 T olive oil until onion and peppers are caramelized.

Step 2: Dice tomatoes and add to the onions and bell peppers. Next add the jalapeno peppers, finely chopped. Cook 5 minutes to let flavors blend together.

Step 3: In a non-stick skillet, lightly coat with non-stick spray and place 1 burrito shell in skillet. Add pepper mixture and 1 ounce of cheese to half of the burrito shell and fold in half using a spatula. Cook until light brown on one side and then flip to allow other side to brown. May serve with black bean salsa over top or on the side (see next page).

**This food item contains gluten. You may substitute a gluten-free product for this item to make this a gluten-free recipe.

Nutrients per serving:
Calories: 230
Carbohydrate: 31g
Protein: 11g
Total Fat: 8g
Saturated Fat: 2.5g
Omega-3 fatty acids: 0.18g
Dietary Fiber: 2g
Sodium: 490mg
Cholesterol: 5mg

Black Bean Salsa (gluten free)

1 15 oz can black beans, rinsed and drained
1 12 oz can spicy **tomatoes**
1 ½ tsp **cumin**
1 tsp **paprika**
1 tsp **cayenne pepper**
½ c chopped **cilantro**

Step 1: In medium size bowl add all of the above ingredients. Mix well. You may add more cumin, paprika, cayenne pepper and/or cilantro for more flavor if you desire, without adding additional calories or sodium.

Step 2: Chill until ready to serve.

Nutrients per serving:
Calories: 140
Carbohydrate: 24g
Protein: 8g
Total Fat: 1.5g
Saturated Fat: 0g
Omega-3 fatty acids: 0.05g
Dietary Fiber: 9g
Sodium: 500mg
Cholesterol: 0mg

Guacamole Made Simple (gluten free)

Serves 4

2 ripe **avocados**
3 medium Roma **tomatoes**
½ purple **onion**
1 **jalapeno pepper** (add more if you like more spice, omit for those who don't tolerate hot chilies)
1 **garlic** clove, minced
½ c **cilantro,** chopped
1 **lime**

Step 1: In medium sized bowl add all ingredients. Cut avocados in half and scoop out the middle, discarding the seed.
Step 2: Dice tomatoes, onion, and jalapeno pepper.
Step 3: Press the garlic clove and add to mixture.
Step 4: Rinse and drain the cilantro, chop well. Add ½ cup of chopped cilantro to the bowl.
Step 5: Squeeze the juice from the lime into the bowl and mix. Chill for 1 hour and serve.

Nutrients per serving:
Calories: 120
Carbohydrate: 10g
Protein: 2g
Total Fat: 10g
Saturated Fat: 1.5g
Omega-3 fatty acids: 0.51g
Dietary Fiber: 5g
Sodium: 5mg
Cholesterol: 0mg

Spinach and Toasted Pine Nuts

Serves 4

16 oz cooked pasta**
2 medium **tomatoes**, diced
½ c toasted **pine nuts**
1 bunch fresh baby **spinach**
1 8 oz evaporated skim milk
4 oz shaved Parmesan cheese

Step 1: In large saucepan over medium heat, warm evaporated milk for 6-8 minutes.
Step 2: Add Parmesan cheese and stir occasionally until melted.
Step 3: Add tomatoes, spinach, and pine nuts.
Step 4: Serve over your favorite pasta and stir to coat. Serve warm.

**This food item contains gluten. You may substitute a gluten-free product for this item to make this a gluten-free recipe.

Nutrients per serving:

Calories: 470
Carbohydrate: 65g
Protein: 22g
Total Fat: 14g
Saturated Fat: 4g
Omega-3 fatty acids: 0.33g
Dietary Fiber: 3g
Sodium: 350mg
Cholesterol: 15mg

Sundried Tomato Sauce

Serves 4

2 T butter
2 T flour**
2 c 2% milk
2 c sundried **tomatoes,** not packed in oil
1 T roasted **garlic**
2 **shallots**, chopped
Salt and **black pepper**, to taste
¼ tsp sugar

Step 1: In medium sized pan, melt butter.
Step 2: Add flour and stir into melted butter.
Step 3: Add milk to make a roux, stirring with a whisk for several minutes.
Step 4: When thick, add remaining ingredients, mix well.
Step 5: Cook for about 5 minutes over low heat and then serve over favorite pasta.

**This food item contains gluten. You may substitute a gluten-free product for this item to make this a gluten-free recipe.

Nutrients per serving:
Calories: 120
Carbohydrate: 18g
Protein: 7g
Total Fat: 2.5g
Saturated Fat: 1.5g
Omega-3 fatty acids: 0.10g
Dietary Fiber: 2g
Sodium: 130mg
Cholesterol: 10mg

Vegetable Barley

Serving size: 1 cup

1 T olive oil
1 **onion**, diced
3 **celery** stalks, diced
2 **carrots**, peeled and diced
1 tsp **fennel**
1 **yellow squash**, diced
1 **zucchini**, diced
¼ c **corn**
¼ c **green beans**
2 c barley**
2 c water, more if needed
Salt and **black pepper,** to taste

Step 1: In large pan sauté onion, carrots, celery in olive oil.
Step 2: Add remaining ingredients and bring to boil.
Step 3: Simmer for 20 minutes or until barley is done.
Step 4: Taste and season as desired.

**This food item contains gluten. You may substitute a gluten-free product for this item to make this a gluten-free recipe.

Nutrients per serving:
Calories: 210
Carbohydrate: 41g
Protein: 7g
Total Fat: 3g
Saturated Fat: 0.5g
Omega-3 fatty acids: 0.07g
Dietary Fiber: 10g
Sodium: 150mg
Cholesterol: 0mg

Lentil Loaf

Serves 6

1 T olive oil
1 **onion**, diced
3 **celery** stalks, diced
¼ c **mushrooms**, diced
2-3 **garlic** cloves, minced
½ c lentils, cooked
1 c **walnuts**, chopped
½ c all-purpose flour**
½ c white cheddar cheese, grated
¼ c skim milk
1 T **oregano**
1 T **basil**
½ T **parsley**
½ tsp **thyme**
Black pepper, to taste
¼ c fresh **chives**

Step 1: Sauté onion, celery, mushrooms and garlic in oil. Stir occasionally and cook until vegetables are soft.
Step 2: Add lentils, walnuts, flour, cheese, milk and herbs. Mix well.
Step 3: Spoon into loaf pan (lightly grease bottom and sides – best if baked in a 9x5x3 inch pan and lined with waxed paper). Bake in preheated oven at 375 degrees until lightly brown on top and the center is firm to the touch (about 60 minutes, depending on oven).
Step 4: Cool for about 15 minutes and then turn out onto serving plate. Serve with your favorite vegetable side dishes. This dish goes well with asparagus or fresh garden vegetables.

**This food item contains gluten. You may substitute a gluten-free product for this item to make this a gluten-free recipe.

Nutrients per serving:

Calories: 300
Carbohydrate: 18g
Protein: 11g
Total Fat: 21g
Saturated Fat: 6g
Omega-3 fatty acids: 1.82g
Dietary Fiber: 5g
Sodium: 290mg
Cholesterol: 20mg

Potato Casserole with Mushrooms

Serves 6

1 lb **potatoes**, peeled	1 c vegetable stock*
½ c 1% milk	½ c light cream
1 T **chives**	1 tsp spicy **mustard**
Black pepper, to taste	1 T wine vinegar
1 T canola oil	1 tsp **caraway seeds**
1 sweet **onion**, diced	2 c **mushrooms**, sliced
3 T all-purpose flour**	1 T **parsley**

Step 1: Preheat oven to 375 degrees. Prepare a 9-inch round baking dish with cooking spray and set aside.

Step 2: Sauté onion in canola oil and cook until tender. Add flour, stir and remove from heat. Add stock and stir until well mixed.

Step 3: Return pan to heat, stir mixture and simmer until thickened. Add light cream, mushrooms, mustard, vinegar, and caraway seeds. Remove from heat and set aside.

Step 4: Cover cut potatoes in large pot with water and bring to a boil. Cook for 20 minutes. Drain water and return to pot. Mash potatoes and add milk. Add dill and season to taste with salt and black pepper.

Step 5: Spoon potatoes into prepared dish and make a well in the center. Spoon the mushroom mixture into the well and set aside.

Step 6: Cover dish and bake for about 30 minutes.

*This food item either is not naturally gluten free or may contain gluten due to preparation and processing. Read food label to ensure that food product does not contain gluten.

**This food item contains gluten. You may substitute a gluten-free product for this item to make this a gluten-free recipe.

Nutrients per serving:

Calories: 200	Omega-3 fatty acids: 0.08g
Carbohydrate: 29g	Dietary Fiber: 2g
Protein: 5g	Sodium: 250mg
Total Fat: 7g	Cholesterol: 15mg
Saturated Fat: 3g	

Asian Eggplant Wraps

Serves 4-6

2 medium eggplants, peeled and sliced lengthwise
½ c **snow peas**
½ c **shallots**, peeled and diced
2 **carrots**, diced
1 **red bell pepper**, sliced
1 **yellow bell pepper**, sliced
½ c **leeks**, diced

Ginger Sauce
4 T low sodium soy sauce*
2 T olive oil
2 T water
2 T freshly grated **ginger**
6 roasted garlic **cloves**

Step 1: To roast the garlic cloves, take 1 full garlic bulb, cover with 1 T olive oil and tightly wrap it with aluminum foil. Bake at 400 degrees for about 30 minutes. The individual cloves should be soft. Allow to cool and use a small spoon to scoop out the roasted garlic cloves. You can use the remaining cloves for other dishes as the leftover garlic cloves will keep well in a tightly sealed container in the refrigerator for several days.

Step 2: Combine all vegetables in a large bowl.

Step 3: Peel and slice eggplant. Spoon vegetable mixture onto 1 slice of the eggplant and roll in half, securing the eggplant together with a toothpick. Place eggplant wrap into a greased shallow baking pan. Repeat until all of the eggplant and vegetable mixture has been used.

Step 4: Pour the Ginger Sauce over the eggplant, cover and bake at 375 degrees for 20 minutes or until the vegetables are tender.

*This food item either is not naturally gluten free or may contain gluten due to preparation and processing. Read food label to ensure that food product does not contain gluten.

Nutrients per serving:
Calories: 280
Carbohydrate: 43g
Protein: 8g
Total Fat: 6g
Saturated Fat: 1g
Omega-3 fatty acids: 0.06g
Dietary Fiber: 6g
Sodium: 220mg
Cholesterol: 0mg

Barbecue Flavored Beans

Serves 6

2 c dried navy beans, soaked overnight in water to cover by 2 inches
4 **garlic** cloves, minced
1 large **onion**, diced
½ c nonfat barbecue sauce*
½ c Dijon **mustard***
¼ c molasses
1 T cider vinegar*
Tabasco*, to taste
Black pepper, to taste

Step 1: Drain beans and combine with garlic and onions in large pot. Cover with water and bring to a rapid boil. Lower heat, cover and simmer for 1 ½ hours or until tender. Be sure to add water as necessary to maintain water level above beans throughout the cooking process.

Step 2: When beans are tender, drain and add barbecue sauce, mustard, molasses or maple syrup, and vinegar. Add Tabasco, salt and pepper to taste.

*This food item either is not naturally gluten free or may contain gluten due to preparation and processing. Read food label to ensure that food product does not contain gluten.

Nutrients per serving:
Calories: 320
Carbohydrate: 64g
Protein: 16g
Total Fat: 1g
Saturated Fat: 0g
Omega-3 fatty acids: 2.26g
Dietary Fiber: 18g
Sodium: 270mg
Cholesterol: 0mg

Roasted Garlic Potatoes (gluten free)

Serves 6

1 ½ lb red **potatoes**
1 roasted **garlic** <u>bulb</u>
2 T canola oil
4 tsp **sage**
pinch of **thyme**
Black pepper, to taste

Step 1: To roast the garlic cloves, take 1 full garlic bulb, cover with 1 T olive oil and tightly wrap it with aluminum foil. Bake at 400 degrees for about 30 minutes. The individual cloves should be soft. Allow to cool and use a small spoon to scoop out the roasted garlic cloves. You can use the remaining cloves for other dishes as the leftover garlic cloves will keep well in a tightly sealed container in the refrigerator for several days.

Step 2: Cut and wash potatoes. Mix potatoes with garlic cloves, oil, herbs and black pepper.

Step 3: Preheat oven to 400 degrees and lightly spray a shallow baking pan with cooking spray. Pour the potato mixture into the baking pan and bake about 40 minutes (baking time will vary).

Nutrients per serving:

Calories: 200
Carbohydrate: 35g
Protein: 3g
Total Fat: 6g
Saturated Fat: 0g
Omega-3 fatty acids: 0.01g
Dietary Fiber: 4g
Sodium: 10mg
Cholesterol: 0mg

Stir-fried Vegetables

Serves 4

1 T canola oil
1 medium **onion**, sliced
7 small **zucchini**, sliced
1 ½ c **cauliflower**
1 ½ c **broccoli**
1 c fresh **mushrooms**, sliced
½ c **carrots**, peeled and thinly sliced
½ **green bell pepper**, sliced
½ **red bell pepper**, sliced

Sauce:
1 T ground **flaxseed**
1 **garlic** clove, minced
1 T grated fresh **ginger**
¼ c water
2 T low sodium soy sauce*
1 T balsamic vinegar*
1 tsp granulated sugar
1 T whole **flaxseed**, toasted

Step 1: In large frying pan add oil, onions, zucchini, cauliflower, broccoli, mushrooms, carrots, and peppers and sauté over medium heat for 5 minutes.

Step 2: Place lid over vegetables and cook an additional 2 minutes.

Step 3: In separate bowl combine ground flaxseed, garlic, ginger, water, soy sauce, vinegar and sugar. Pour over vegetables. Cook and stir until heated. Sprinkle with 1 T toasted flaxseed. Serve and enjoy!

*This food item either is not naturally gluten free or may contain gluten due to preparation and processing. Read food label to ensure that food product does not contain gluten.

Nutrients per serving:
Calories: 160
Carbohydrate: 23g
Protein: 7g
Total Fat: 6g
Saturated Fat: 0.5g

Omega-3 fatty acids: 0.13g
Dietary Fiber: 8g
Sodium: 260mg
Cholesterol: 0mg

Vegetable Pilaf (gluten free)

Serves 4

1 c basmati rice
1 T canola oil
½ tsp **cumin seeds**
1 **bay leaf**
2 green **cardamom pods**
1 sweet **onion**, diced
1 **carrot**, peeled and diced
½ c **peas**, rinsed and drained
½ c **corn**, rinsed and drained
½ c unsalted **peanuts**
1 tsp ground **cumin**

Step 1: Put rice in a medium size bowl and cover with cold water. Soak for about 30 minutes.

Step 2: In large frying pan, sauté the cumin seeds for 2 minutes over medium heat, stirring to prevent them from burning. Add bay leaf (more if desired) and cardamom, sautéing for 2 additional minutes. *Remember to remove the bay leaf and cardamom pods before serving.*

Step 3: Add onion and cook until tender.

Step 4: Stir in carrot and cook for 4 minutes.

Step 5: Drain rice and rinse under cold water. Add rice to pan with peas, corn and the peanuts. Cook for 5 minutes over medium heat.

Step 6: Add 2 cups water and ground cumin. Bring to a boil, cover and simmer for 15 minutes over low heat. Let stand for 10 minutes before serving. Enjoy!

Nutrients per serving:

Calories: 340
Carbohydrate: 48g
Protein: 9g
Total Fat: 13g
Saturated Fat: 1.5g
Omega-3 fatty acids: 0.06g
Dietary Fiber: 4g
Sodium: 480mg
Cholesterol: 0mg

Provencal Stuffed Peppers (gluten free)

Serves 6

1 T olive oil
1 red **onion**, diced
2 **garlic** cloves, minced
1 8-oz can petite diced **tomatoes**
1 **yellow squash**, diced
1 **zucchini**, diced
6 oz **mushrooms**, sliced
½ c **pine nuts**
1 T dried **basil**
6 large **bell peppers**, different colors
Parmesan cheese, optional

Step 1: Heat olive oil in medium saucepan. Add onion and cook for 3 minutes over medium heat. Add garlic, squash, zucchini and mushrooms, cooking until tender.

Step 2: Add tomatoes and stir well. Continue to cook while you add the pine nuts, basil and seasoning. Remove from heat and set aside.

Step 3: Cut off the tops of the peppers and remove seeds. Place peppers in greased ovenproof dish and fill each one with the vegetable mixture.

Step 5: Preheat oven to 375 degrees. Cover dish with foil and bake for 30 minutes. May top with freshly grated Parmesan cheese before serving.

Nutrients per serving:

Calories: 200
Carbohydrate: 17g
Protein: 5g
Total Fat: 14g
Saturated Fat: 2g
Omega-3 fatty acids: 0.16g
Dietary Fiber: 5g
Sodium: 120mg
Cholesterol: 0mg

Pasta Dishes

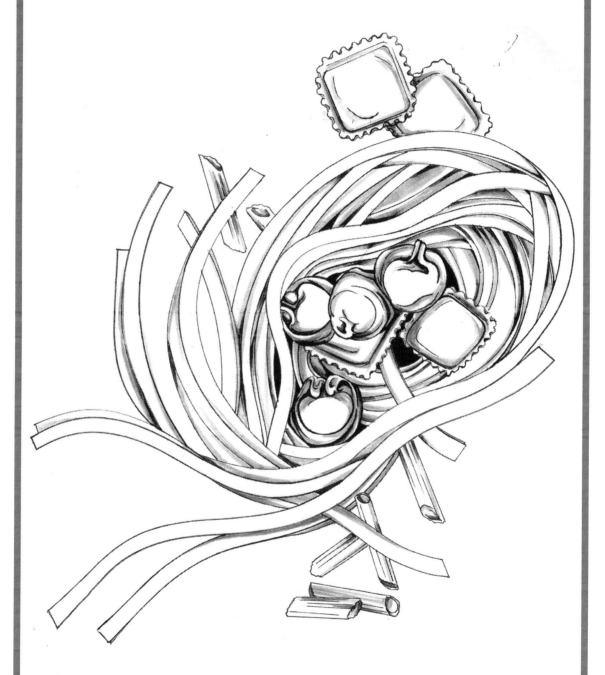

When accompanied with vegetables, lean meats or beans, pasta dishes can be very healthy and filling. By adding other healthy ingredients to pasta dishes, it is possible to incorporate the vitamins, minerals, dietary fiber and protein necessary for good health.

Quinoa Spaghetti with Spinach and Oyster Sauce (gluten free)

Serves 4

8 oz of thin **quinoa** spaghetti style pasta
1 medium **onion**, chopped finely
2 **garlic** cloves, minced
2 T of olive oil
1 lb fresh **spinach**
Black pepper, to taste

Step 1: Sautee the onion in olive oil over low heat, until the onion becomes translucent. Add garlic and continue to cook on low for 1-2 minutes.
Step 2: Add the spinach and cook covered for five minutes, season with salt and pepper to taste.
Step 3: In a separate pot, add the quinoa noodles to boiling water and cook to tender.
Step 4: Combine the spinach mixture and quinoa noodles. Serve with oyster sauce (see next page).

Nutrients per serving:
Calories: 570
Carbohydrate: 54g
Protein: 25g
Total Fat: 27g
Saturated Fat: 7.5g
Omega-3 fatty acids: 0.24g
Dietary Fiber: 7g
Sodium: 545mg
Cholesterol: 90mg

Oyster Sauce for Quinoa Spaghetti with Spinach Dish

Serves 4

2 oz lean prosciutto ham, finely diced.
1 **shallot**, thinly diced
2 T olive oil
½ c dry white wine
2 tsp **turmeric**
2 T dry vermouth*
½ c light cream
1 pint (approximately 20) shucked oysters

Step 1: Sauté shallot and ham in olive oil until the shallot is translucent.
Step 2: Add the white wine, reduce to half volume. Stir in the oysters, oyster liquor, turmeric, vermouth, and light cream.
Step 3: Cook over low heat, stirring constantly, until the desired serving temperature is reached. Ladle over the spaghetti mixture and serve immediately.

*This food item either is not naturally gluten free or may contain gluten due to preparation and processing. Read food label to ensure that food product does not contain gluten.

Nutrients per serving:
Calories: 260
Carbohydrate: 10g
Protein: 13g
Total Fat: 16g
Saturated Fat: 6g
Omega-3 fatty acids:
Dietary Fiber: 0g
Sodium: 450mg
Cholesterol: 90mg

Broccoli Stuffed Shells

Serves 4

20 shells, cooked**
2 c **broccoli** florets and stems, chopped
¼ c skim milk
1 c low-fat Ricotta cheese
¼ tsp **nutmeg**
½ c grated Parmesan cheese
½ c **pine nuts**
Black pepper, to taste
2 c favorite homemade **tomato** sauce

Step 1: Preheat the oven to 375 degrees. Lightly grease large ovenproof dish with cooking spray.

Step 2: Boil water in large pot and cook shells according to directions on package. Drain pasta, rinse under cold water and set aside.

Step 3: Boil broccoli until tender, about 10 minutes. Drain broccoli and let it cool. Place in food processor and process until smooth. Set aside.

Step 4: In medium size bowl mix together milk, Ricotta cheese, broccoli, nutmeg and grated Parmesan cheese. Set aside.

Step 5: Spoon the cheese mixture into each of the shells, setting them in the large dish. Be careful not to overfill the shells. Cover the shells with your favorite tomato sauce and bake for about 30 minutes. Dish and top with pine nuts. Serve and enjoy.

**This food item contains gluten. You may substitute a gluten-free product for this item to make this a gluten-free recipe.

Nutrients per serving:
Calories: 690
Carbohydrate: 82g
Protein: 34g
Total Fat: 29g
Saturated Fat: 9g
Omega-3 fatty acids: 0.25g
Dietary Fiber: 8g
Sodium: 820mg
Cholesterol: 40mg

Spinach and Ricotta Pasta

Serves 6

1 ½ c large pasta shells**, cooked
1 c crushed **tomatoes** (canned)
1 package frozen chopped **spinach**, thawed
½ c skim milk
2 T olive oil
2 c low fat Ricotta cheese
2 **garlic** cloves, minced
½ c shaved Parmesan cheese
½ c pitted black **olives**

Step 1: Preheat oven to 350 degrees.
Step 2: Boil water in a large pot. Add pasta and cook according to package directions. Drain and rinse under cold water. Set aside.
Step 3: Place spinach in sieve and press out excess liquid.
Step 3: In medium bowl combine spinach, Ricotta, Parmesan cheese and milk. Add mixture to pasta and set aside.
Step 4: Mix together crushed tomatoes and garlic. Spread the sauce evenly over bottom of a large greased baking dish.
Step 5: Add spinach and pasta mixture evenly over the sauce. Top with pine nuts and olives, if desired.
Step 6: Heat for 20 minutes. Serve and enjoy.

**This food item contains gluten. You may substitute a gluten-free product for this item to make this a gluten-free recipe.

Nutrients per serving:
Calories: 460
Carbohydrate: 54g
Protein: 26g
Total Fat: 17g
Saturated Fat: 6g
Omega-3 fatty acids: 0.18g
Dietary Fiber: 4g
Sodium: 760mg
Cholesterol: 40mg

Vegetable Lasagna

Serves 8

1 package lasagna noodles**, cooked and drained
1 T dry sherry*
1 medium **onion**, finely diced
½ c **mushrooms**, sliced
1 c **zucchini**, coarsely grated
1 **red bell pepper,** seeded & chopped
2 c fresh **spinach**
1 tsp **basil**
½ tsp **oregano**
15 oz light Ricotta cheese
¼ c grated Parmesan cheese
8 oz of your favorite **tomato** sauce (homemade or store bought)
1 c shredded low moisture part-skim Mozzarella cheese

Step 1: In large bowl combine onion, mushrooms, zucchini, pepper and spinach. Add dry sherry and stir.

Step 2: Cook pasta and then create layers in a lasagna pan by alternating sauce, noodles cheese and vegetables within each layer. On top layer, sprinkle with leftover veggies and cheese.

Step 3: Bake at 375 degrees covered for 30 minutes. Remove aluminum foil and bake for an additional 10 minutes until the top is bubbling. Serve and enjoy!

*This food item either is not naturally gluten free or may contain gluten due to preparation and processing. Read food label to ensure that food product does not contain gluten.

**This food item contains gluten. You may substitute a gluten-free product for this item to make this a gluten-free recipe.

Nutrients per serving:
Calories: 300
Carbohydrate: 43g
Protein: 22g
Total Fat: 5g
Saturated Fat: 1.5g
Omega-3 fatty acids: 0.04g
Dietary Fiber: 9g
Sodium: 400mg
Cholesterol: 15mg

Quinoa Noodles with Tomato Sauce (gluten free)

Serves 4

4 T olive oil
1 medium **onion**, finely chopped
4 **garlic** gloves, minced
4 lb ripe **tomatoes**, peeled, seeded, and chopped
1 T fresh **basil**, chopped
1 T fresh **parsley**, chopped
8 oz thin **quinoa** noodles
1 c finely grated Parmesan cheese

Step 1: Gently sauté the onions until translucent. Add the garlic and cook for 2 minutes.

Step 2: Add the basil, parsley, and tomatoes. Season with black pepper to taste, stir and simmer over low heat for 25 minutes until cooked down.

Step 3: Add the quinoa noodles to boiling water, cook until tender. Drain and rinse.

Step 4: Ladle the sauce over the quinoa noodles. Serve hot with Parmesan cheese.

Substitutions:
- Up to a pound of quinoa noodles can be used, for those who prefer a higher starchy dish.
- Canned tomatoes can be used and are preferred when fresh tomatoes are out of season.
- If canned tomatoes are used, the sauce may require longer simmering to reduce the liquid unless the liquid is drained prior to adding to the dish.

Nutrients per serving:
Calories: 480
Carbohydrate: 58g
Protein: 17g
Total Fat: 22g
Saturated Fat: 5g
Omega-3 fatty acids: 0.34g
Dietary Fiber: 10g
Sodium: 330mg
Cholesterol: 20mg

Pasta Primavera

Serves 4

1 bunch **asparagus** spears, cut in half and discard ends
6 oz **snow peas**
1 c baby **carrots**, cut in half
1 **red bell pepper**, diced
1 ½ c cooked pasta**
½ c Ricotta cheese
½ c fat-free Greek yogurt
½ T **lemon juice**
1 tsp **parsley**
Black pepper, to taste

Step 1: Cook asparagus, snow peas, carrots and peppers in a pan of boiling water for 5 minutes. Drain and rinse.
Step 2: Cook pasta in large pan with boiling water until tender. Drain and set aside.
Step 3: Put the Ricotta cheese, yogurt, lemon juice and parsley into food processor. Season and process until smooth.
Step 4: Combine sauce with pasta and vegetables, stir well. Serve and enjoy!

**This food item contains gluten. You may substitute a gluten-free product for this item to make this a gluten-free recipe.

Nutrients per serving:
Calories: 150
Carbohydrate: 25g
Protein: 7g
Total Fat: 2g
Saturated Fat: 1g
Omega-3 fatty acids: 0.01g
Dietary Fiber: 5g
Sodium: 55mg
Cholesterol: 5mg

Chinese Noodles and Vegetables

Serves 6

12 oz Chinese egg noodles**
1 T olive oil
4 **garlic** cloves, minced
1 large **onion**, diced
1 each **red and yellow bell peppers**, diced
2 **zucchinis**, diced
1 c roasted unsalted **peanuts**

Step 1: Cook noodles according to the package instructions and drain well.
Step 2: Sauté onion in olive oil on medium heat until onion is transparent. Add garlic and cook for an additional 1-2 minutes.
Step 3: Add peppers and zucchini and cook on medium heat until tender.
Step 4: Add peanuts, stir and serve over Chinese noodles.

**This food item contains gluten. You may substitute a gluten-free product for this item to make this a gluten-free recipe.

Nutrients per serving:
Calories: 410
Carbohydrate: 44g
Protein: 17g
Total Fat: 21g
Saturated Fat: 3g
Omega-3 fatty acids: 0.01g
Dietary Fiber: 5g
Sodium: 310mg
Cholesterol: 5mg

Quinoa Noodles with Asparagus (gluten free)

Serves 4

1 lb fresh **asparagus**
½ c olive oil
1 **onion**, finely diced
4 **garlic** cloves, minced
1 tsp **lemon juice**
10 fresh **basil** leaves
8 oz thin **quinoa** noodles
6 oz prosciutto ham, cut into ½ inch squares

Step 1: Chop off and discard the tough ends of the asparagus. Chop asparagus into 1 inch pieces.
Step 2: Sauté onions on medium heat until translucent. Add garlic and cook for 1 to 2 minutes.
Step 3: Reduce heat to low and add asparagus. Cook until tender.
Step 4: Add lemon juice, black pepper and basil, to taste.
Step 5: Add quinoa noodles to boiling water, cook until tender. Drain and rinse.
Step 6: Combine noodles, asparagus mixture, and prosciutto. Serve and enjoy.

Substitutions:
• Up to a pound of quinoa noodles can be used, for those who prefer a higher starchy dish.

Nutrients per serving:
Calories: 510
Carbohydrate: 35g
Protein: 17g
Total Fat: 35g
Saturated Fat: 6g
Omega-3 fatty acids: 0.24g
Dietary Fiber: 4g
Sodium: 650mg
Cholesterol: 25mg

Vegetable Curry with Basmati Rice

Serves 4

2 c basmati rice
4 oz curry **roasted peppers,** 1 jar drained*
½ bunch **cauliflower**
1 can garbanzo beans, rinsed and drained
4 **shallots**, diced
2 medium **tomatoes**, diced
½ c **green peas**
6 oz green curry sauce, canned*

Step 1: Cook basmati rice and set aside.
Step 2: In medium sized pan, combine the remaining ingredients and cook on medium-low heat
for 15 minutes (until cauliflower is just tender).
Step 3: Add vegetable mixture to rice, stir well and serve warm.

*This food item either is not naturally gluten free or may contain gluten due to preparation and processing. Read food label to ensure that food product does not contain gluten.

Nutrients per serving:
Calories: 520
Carbohydrate: 113g
Protein: 17g
Total Fat: 2g
Saturated Fat: 0g
Omega-3 fatty acids: 0.07g
Dietary Fiber: 10g
Sodium: 160mg
Cholesterol: 0mg

Vegetables and Pasta

Serves 6

12 meatballs*, cooked (either use frozen or make your own from scratch)
3 c cooked pasta**
1 T olive oil
1 **onion**, diced
1 **celery** stalk, diced
1 **carrot**, peeled and diced
2 **garlic** cloves, minced
2 T flour**
2 c water
1 15 oz can crushed **tomatoes**
1 15 oz can petite diced **tomatoes**
1 15 oz can navy beans, rinsed and drained
1 bunch fresh **spinach**
1 c fresh green beans, sliced
1 green and 1 yellow **squash**, diced
½ c basil pesto
1 T **black pepper**
¼ c Parmesan cheese, freshly grated

Step 1: Sauté onion, carrot, celery, and garlic in olive oil.
Step 2: Add all ingredients except Parmesan cheese, meatballs, and pasta.
Step 3: Bring to boil and simmer on low for 10 minutes, stirring occasionally.
Step 4: Add remaining ingredients.

*This food item either is not naturally gluten free or may contain gluten due to preparation and processing. Read food label to ensure that food product does not contain gluten.

**This food item contains gluten. You may substitute a gluten-free product for this item to make this a gluten-free recipe.

Nutrients per serving:

Calories: 550   Omega-3 fatty acids: 0.14g
Carbohydrate: 64g   Dietary Fiber: 14g
Protein: 30g   Sodium: 560mg
Total Fat: 21g   Cholesterol: 55mg
Saturated Fat: 6g

Peppers and Pasta

Serves 4

2 c pasta**
1 **red bell pepper**
1 **yellow bell pepper**
1 medium **onion**
1 small bunch **spinach**
½ c **olives**

Step 1: Sauté peppers, onion, and olives. Add spinach last and stir occasionally until the spinach wilts.

Step 2: Cook 2 cups of your favorite pasta. Add cooked, drained pasta to the pepper mixture and serve with a garden salad.

**This food item contains gluten. You may substitute a gluten-free product for this item to make this a gluten-free recipe.

Nutrients per serving:

Calories: 530
Carbohydrate: 82g
Protein: 20g
Total Fat: 14g
Saturated Fat: 2g
Omega-3 fatty acids: 0.00g
Dietary Fiber: 19g
Sodium: 550mg
Cholesterol: 0mg

Penne Pasta with Light Tomato Sauce

Serves 4

5 Roma **tomatoes,** diced
¼ c fresh **basil,** chopped
¼ c halved ripe **olives**
3-4 **garlic** cloves, minced
1 ½ T olive oil
1 T balsamic vinegar*
⅛ tsp coarsely ground **black pepper**
1 c penne pasta**, uncooked
½ c crumbled Feta cheese

Step 1: Combine first 7 ingredients in a medium sized bowl; toss well. Cover and let stand 15 minutes.

Step 2: Cook pasta according to package directions, rinse and drain. Add pasta to tomato mixture; toss. Sprinkle with Feta cheese and serve.

*This food item either is not naturally gluten free or may contain gluten due to preparation and processing. Read food label to ensure that food product does not contain gluten.

**This food item contains gluten. You may substitute a gluten-free product for this item to make this a gluten-free recipe.

Nutrients per serving:
Calories: 140
Carbohydrate: 19g
Protein: 5g
Total Fat: 5g
Saturated Fat: 1.5g
Omega-3 fatty acids: 0.03g
Dietary Fiber: 2g
Sodium: 190mg
Cholesterol: 5mg

Shrimp and Pasta

Serves 4

8 oz uncooked penne pasta**
2 T olive oil
⅓ c low fat sour cream
¼ c crumbled Feta cheese
¼ c water
3-4 **garlic** cloves, minced
12 oz frozen shrimp, peeled, de-veined and uncooked
1 **red bell pepper**, diced
4 c fresh **spinach**, coarsely chopped

Step 1: Cook pasta as directed on package.
Step 2: In a small bowl combine: oil, sour cream and Feta cheese.
Step 3: In a large skillet combine water, garlic, shrimp and bell pepper. Cook over medium high heat until shrimp is pink and bell peppers are tender.
Step 4: Add spinach and cook an additional 2 minutes. Remove from heat and stir in sour cream mixture. Add pasta and toss well. Serve and enjoy!

**This food item contains gluten. You may substitute a gluten-free product for this item to make this a gluten-free recipe.

Nutrients per serving:
Calories: 420
Carbohydrate: 49g
Protein: 28g
Total Fat: 13g
Saturated Fat: 4.5g
Omega-3 fatty acids: 0.01g
Dietary Fiber: 5g
Sodium: 360mg
Cholesterol: 195mg

Clam Sauce and Pasta

Serves 4

1 ½ c minced clams with liquid
2 T canola oil
⅓ c flour*
1 pt clam juice
1 **green bell pepper**, diced
2 medium sweet **onions**, diced
2-4 **garlic** cloves, minced
1 **celery** stalk, diced
1 tsp **tarragon**
¼ tsp **white pepper**
Favorite pasta for four**

Step 1: Heat oil in a medium saucepan. Add flour, stirring vigorously with wire whisk.
Step 2: Add clam juice; stirring constantly. Stir in diced pepper, onions, garlic, celery, tarragon, and pepper. Simmer over low heat for 45-50 minutes, stirring often.
Step 3: Add clams and simmer for about 5 minutes. Pour over pasta and enjoy.

*This food item either is not naturally gluten free or may contain gluten due to preparation and processing. Read food label to ensure that food product does not contain gluten.

**This food item contains gluten. You may substitute a gluten-free product for this item to make this a gluten-free recipe.

Nutrients per serving:
Calories: 276
Carbohydrate: 30g
Protein: 21g
Total Fat: 8g
Saturated Fat: 1g
Omega-3 fatty acids: 0.02g
Dietary Fiber: 5g
Sodium: 400mg
Cholesterol: 20mg

Orzo with Roasted Shallots

Serves 4

½ c peeled **shallots**
2 T olive oil, to coat
2 c cooked orzo**

Step 1: Coat shallots with olive oil and place in a baking dish. Bake covered at 300 degrees for 1 hour.
Step 2: Strain and blend in food processor.
Step 3: Follow the directions on the package for the orzo. Cook 2 cups and set aside until the shallots are done. Then combine and serve.

**This food item contains gluten. You may substitute a gluten-free product for this item to make this a gluten-free recipe.

Nutrients per serving:
Calories: 500
Carbohydrate: 91g
Protein: 16g
Total Fat: 9g
Saturated Fat: 1.5g
Omega-3 fatty acids: 0.00g
Dietary Fiber: 4g
Sodium: 10mg
Cholesterol: 0mg

Penne Pasta with a Spicy Sauce

Serves 6

16 oz cooked penne pasta**

Spicy Tomato Sauce
8 **tomatoes**, diced
1 **onion**, diced
4 **shallots**, diced
1 each **red** and **green bell pepper**, diced
½ c **mushrooms**, diced
½ tsp **fennel**
2 **garlic** cloves, minced
¼ c red wine
1 tsp **basil**
1 tsp **oregano**
1 tsp crushed **red pepper**, more if desired
¼ c **tomato juice**
½ c fresh Parmesan cheese, for top of dish if desired

Step 1: Sauté onions, shallots, and peppers in pan with oil.

Step 2: Add tomatoes, garlic, mushrooms, wine and spices. Simmer for 15 minutes. Serve over pasta and top with Parmesan cheese.

**This food item contains gluten. You may substitute a gluten-free product for this item to make this a gluten-free recipe.

Nutrients per serving:
Calories: 140
Carbohydrate: 19g
Protein: 5g
Total Fat: 5g
Saturated Fat: 1.5g
Omega-3 fatty acids:
Dietary Fiber: 2g
Sodium: 190mg
Cholesterol: 5mg

Ratatouille with Pasta

Serves 6

2 c cooked penne pasta**
1 **eggplant**, diced into 1-inch chunks
1 **green bell pepper**, cut into 1-inch squares
1 **zucchini**, sliced
2 **tomatoes**, diced
1 large **onion**, diced
2 **garlic** cloves, minced
¼ c dry white wine
½ tsp **lemon juice**
1 T olive oil
1 tsp **thyme**
1 tsp **basil**
1 **bay leaf**
1 tsp black pepper
½ c fresh Parmesan cheese, for top of dish if desired

Step 1: Sauté onions, garlic, eggplant, zucchini and peppers in pan with olive oil.
Step 2: Add tomatoes, white wine, lemon juice and spices. Simmer for 15 minutes. Serve over pasta and top with parmesan cheese.

**This food item contains gluten. You may substitute a gluten-free product for this item to make this a gluten-free recipe.

Nutrients per serving:
Calories: 350
Carbohydrate: 68g
Protein: 12g
Total Fat: 4g
Saturated Fat: 0.5g
Omega-3 fatty acids: 0.03g
Dietary Fiber: 7g
Sodium: 340mg
Cholesterol: 0mg

Three Ravioli Pastas

Serves 6

6 oz cooked cheese ravioli**
6 oz cooked meat ravioli**
6 oz cooked vegetable ravioli**
½ c basil pesto
½ c marinara sauce
½ c Alfredo sauce*
1 c **broccoli**, steamed
1 c **cauliflower**, steamed
1 T olive oil
¼ c Kalamata **olives**
½ c diced **yellow squash**
¼ c diced **onion**
4-6 **garlic** cloves, minced
¼ c Parmesan cheese

Step 1: Cook pasta and set aside.
Step 2: Steam broccoli, cauliflower and set aside.
Step 3: Sauté onions, garlic, squash and olives in pan with olive oil.
Step 4: Combine veggies and serve alongside the pasta topped with 1 T of each: basil pesto, marinara sauce and Alfredo sauce. Serve topped with Parmesan cheese.

*This food item either is not naturally gluten free or may contain gluten due to preparation and processing. Read food label to ensure that food product does not contain gluten.

**This food item contains gluten. You may substitute a gluten-free product for this item to make this a gluten-free recipe.

Nutrients per serving:
Calories: 410
Carbohydrate: 45g
Protein: 17g
Total Fat: 19g
Saturated Fat: 6g
Omega-3 fatty acids: 0.08g
Dietary Fiber: 5g
Sodium: 890mg
Cholesterol: 50mg

Teriyaki Tofu with Vegetables and Lo Mein Noodles

Serves 4

16 oz cooked lo mein noodles**
Marinated tofu

Teriyaki Marinade
¼ c light soy sauce*
¼ c hoisin sauce*
2 tsp **ginger**
1 **garlic** clove, minced
1 tsp sugar
1 tsp **sesame** oil

Stir Fry Vegetables
2 **carrots**, peeled and sliced
1 **onion**, diced
½ c **snow peas**
½ c mung bean sprouts
1 **red bell pepper**, diced
½ c baby **corn**
½ c bamboo shoots

Step 1: Make Teriyaki Marinade sauce and set aside.
Step 2: In large bowl combine vegetables and tofu. Cover with Teriyaki Marinade. Stir to coat.
Step 3: In wok or large skillet, cook over medium high heat until veggies and tofu are cooked (about 8-10 minutes), stirring often.
Step 4: Serve over lo mein noodles.

*This food item either is not naturally gluten free or may contain gluten due to preparation and processing. Read food label to ensure that food product does not contain gluten.

**This food item contains gluten. You may substitute a gluten-free product for this item to make this a gluten-free recipe.

Nutrients per serving:
Calories: 360
Carbohydrate: 71g
Protein: 13g
Total Fat: 2.5g
Saturated Fat: 0.5g

Omega-3 fatty acids: 0.02g
Dietary Fiber: 5g
Sodium: 450mg
Cholesterol: 0mg

Green and Gold Pasta

Serves 4

2 c **spinach** fettuccine**
1 c yellow **tomato** marinara
¼ c Parmesan cheese
2 T fresh **basil**

Yellow Tomato Marinara Sauce

6 medium yellow **tomatoes**, diced
1 **yellow bell pepper**, diced
4 **shallots**, diced
3 roasted **garlic** cloves, minced
2 T olive oil
¼ c white wine
¼ tsp **white pepper**
1 tsp sugar

Step 1: Sauté shallots and garlic in olive oil.
Step 2: Add remaining ingredients and simmer 30 minutes.
Step 3: Blend until smooth; season as desired.
Step 4: Serve over cooked spinach fettuccine.

**This food item contains gluten. You may substitute a gluten-free product for this item to make this a gluten-free recipe.

Nutrients per serving:

Calories: 430
Carbohydrate: 63g
Protein: 18g
Total Fat: 13g
Saturated Fat: 3.5g
Omega-3 fatty acids: 0.01g
Dietary Fiber: 6g
Sodium: 300mg
Cholesterol: 10mg

Cheese Tortellini with Red Pepper Pesto

Serves 4

2 c roasted **red peppers**
6 **shallots**, chopped
5-6 roasted **garlic** cloves
1 T olive oil
1 T chopped **almonds**
2 T fresh parmesan cheese
1 T **basil**
1 tsp sugar
½ tsp salt
1 tsp **black pepper**
2 T heavy cream
2 c cooked cheese tortellini**

Step 1: Slice red pepper and place in greased baking pan with garlic cloves. Cover in olive oil and bake at 450 degrees for 10-15 minutes or until slightly roasted. Let cool.

Step 2: Place all ingredients except the cooked cheese tortellini into a food processor and blend well. May add a dash of water, if needed. Serve over cooked cheese tortellini or favorite pasta.

**This food item contains gluten. You may substitute a gluten-free product for this item to make this a gluten-free recipe.

Nutrients per serving:
Calories: 280
Carbohydrate: 41g
Protein: 11g
Total Fat: 13g
Saturated Fat: 4g
Omega-3 fatty acids: 1.49g
Dietary Fiber: 9g
Sodium: 170mg
Cholesterol: 25mg

Penne with Beef Bolognese

Serves 4-6

2 c cooked whole wheat penne pasta**
2 medium **onions,** diced
4-6 **garlic** cloves, minced
2 T olive oil
1 large **carrot**, diced
1 **celery** stalk, diced
2 **shallots**, chopped
½ lb lean ground beef, cooked
1 16 oz can diced **tomatoes**
1 15 oz can crushed **tomatoes**
½ c dry red wine
1 T **basil**
1 T **oregano**
1 tsp **black pepper**
½ tsp crushed **red pepper**

Step 1: In a large cooking pot, sauté onions, garlic, carrot, celery, and shallots in olive oil until tender.
Step 2: Add cooked ground beef, tomatoes, and wine.
Step 3: Cook on low heat for 1 hour.
Step 4: Add spices, stir and serve over ½ cup of cooked whole wheat penne.

**This food item contains gluten. You may substitute a gluten-free product for this item to make this a gluten-free recipe.

Nutrients per serving:
Calories: 320
Carbohydrate: 49g
Protein: 14g
Total Fat: 6g
Saturated Fat: 1g
Omega-3 fatty acids: 0.24g
Dietary Fiber: 3g
Sodium: 220mg
Cholesterol: 15mg

Homemade Marinara for Beef Ravioli

Serves 4

2 medium **onions**, diced
6 large **tomatoes**, diced
4-6 **garlic** cloves, minced
½ c red wine
½ T crushed **red pepper**
1 tsp **oregano**
½ tsp **cumin**
Serve over beef ravioli.

**This food item contains gluten. You may substitute a gluten-free product for this item to make this a gluten-free recipe.

Nutrients per serving:

Calories: 460
Carbohydrate: 68g
Protein: 18g
Total Fat: 11g
Saturated Fat: 3g
Omega-3 fatty acids: 0.07g
Dietary Fiber: 8g
Sodium: 520mg
Cholesterol: 60mg

Rice Noodles with Fresh Veggies

Serves 4

8 oz package rice noodles
1 small head **broccoli**
1 **bell pepper (red, yellow or green)**
1 small purple **onion**
1 tsp of freshly grated **ginger** (add more for stronger taste)
3 **garlic** cloves, minced
6 large **tomatoes**
1 T canola oil
Low sodium soy sauce*

Step 1: Follow directions for noodles on the package (you have to soak them in hot water for at least 20 minutes – so be sure to read the directions before starting).
Step 2: Cook onions, ginger, garlic and peppers in canola oil over medium heat in skillet.
Step 3: Dice tomatoes and add to skillet when onions and peppers are tender.
Step 4: Blanch broccoli and add to skillet.
Step 5: Add cooked rice noodles to the skillet, stir and warm for 5 minutes on low heat. Add low sodium soy sauce and black pepper (if desired) to taste. Enjoy!

*This food item either is not naturally gluten free or may contain gluten due to preparation and processing. Read food label to ensure that food product does not contain gluten.

Nutrients per serving:
Calories: 160
Carbohydrate: 34g
Protein: 2g
Total Fat: 2g
Saturated Fat: 0g
Omega-3 fatty acids: 1.35g
Dietary Fiber: 3g
Sodium: 15mg
Cholesterol: 0mg

Shrimp Fra Diavolo Pasta

Serves 4

2 T olive oil
1 medium sweet **onion**, diced
½ c **celery**, diced
2 **garlic** cloves, minced
¼ c red wine
2 c Roma **tomatoes**, diced
¼ c **tomato** paste
¼ tsp **thyme**
¼ tsp **oregano**
¼ tsp crushed **red pepper**
Black pepper, to taste
26-30 shrimp, shelled and de-veined
2 c cooked pasta**

Step 1: Sauté onion, celery and garlic in olive oil until tender.
Step 2: Add wine and reduce heat, cook for 5 minutes.
Step 3: Add tomatoes, tomato paste, herbs and spices. Simmer for about 30 minutes.
Step 4: Boil shrimp, drain and add to tomato sauce. Serve over pasta.
Step 5: Garnish with parsley and freshly grated Parmesan cheese.

**This food item contains gluten. You may substitute a gluten-free product for this item to make this a gluten-free recipe.

Nutrients per serving:
Calories: 380
Carbohydrate: 62g
Protein: 17g
Total Fat: 6g
Saturated Fat: 1g
Omega-3 fatty acids: 0.14g
Dietary Fiber: 3g
Sodium: 60mg
Cholesterol: 45mg

Three Cheese Cappelleti

Serves 6

2 T butter
1 T all purpose flour**
2 c 2% milk
¼ c Parmesan cheese
¼ c Asiago cheese
¼ c Mozzarella cheese
Salt and **black pepper,** to taste
3 **garlic** cloves, minced
4 c cooked cappelleti pasta**

Step 1: In medium sauce pan, melt butter. Add garlic and stir well.
Step 2: Add flour and make a roux.
Step 3: Add milk and whisk until milk begins to thicken.
Step 4: Whisk in cheese, stir until cheese is melted.
Step 5: Taste and season as desired.
Step 6: May thin with more milk if too thick.
Step 7: Serve over cooked cappelleti pasta or favorite other pasta.

**This food item contains gluten. You may substitute a gluten-free product for this item to make this a gluten-free recipe.

Nutrients per serving:
Calories: 600
Carbohydrate: 104g
Protein: 26g
Total Fat: 9g
Saturated Fat: 4g
Omega-3 fatty acids: 0.08g
Dietary Fiber: 4g
Sodium: 370mg
Cholesterol: 20mg

Salad Creations

There are no downsides to eating salads except that some commercial salads may contain fungicides and preservatives such as sulfites, which are poorly tolerated by some. Salad greens are rich in fiber and low in calories. Salad dressings must be chosen with care because they can contain high levels of salt and unwanted fat calories.

Simple Greek Salad

Serves 4

6 c Romaine lettuce
1 medium **cucumber**
4 Roma **tomatoes**
¼ c black **olives,** pitted
6 oz low fat Feta cheese
2 T white wine vinegar*
¼ c olive oil
Black pepper and salt, to taste

Step 1: Combine shredded lettuce, sliced cucumber, diced tomatoes, and olives in a large salad bowl.

Step 2: Add crumbled Feta cheese.

Step 3: In salad dressing container combine vinegar, olive oil, salt and pepper. Shake well. Pour dressing lightly over salad and toss well. Serve and enjoy!

*This food item either is not naturally gluten free or may contain gluten due to preparation and processing. Read food label to ensure that food product does not contain gluten.

Nutrients per serving:

Calories: 250
Carbohydrate: 9g
Protein: 11g
Total Fat: 20g
Saturated Fat: 5g
Omega-3 fatty acids: 0.06g
Dietary Fiber: 2g
Sodium: 570g
Cholesterol: 15mg

Strawberry and Watermelon Salad (gluten free)

Serves 6

3 cups **strawberries**, washed and tops removed

3 cups **watermelon**, diced in 1 inch cubes, seeded

2 T freshly grated **ginger**

1 T sugar

1 T freshly grated **black pepper**

2 T **cilantro**, chopped

In a large serving bowl combine all ingredients, mix well, cover and place in the refrigerator for 2 hours. Serve and enjoy!

Nutrients per serving:

Calories: 45

Carbohydrate: 13g

Protein: 1g

Total Fat: 0g

Saturated Fat: 0g

Omega-3 fatty acids: 0.06g

Dietary Fiber: 2g

Sodium: 0mg

Cholesterol: 0mg

Mom's Hearty Black Bean Salad

Serves 6

1 can black beans, rinsed and drained
1 cup **corn**, fresh or frozen
3 T red **onion**, diced
½ c **cucumber**, diced
1 c cherry **tomatoes**, halved
½ c fresh **basil**, chopped
1 **avocado**, diced
¼ c balsamic dressing* (see page 128)

Step 1: In large bowl, add all ingredients and mix well.
Step 2: Toss with balsamic vinaigrette. Serve and enjoy!

*This food item either is not naturally gluten free or may contain gluten due to preparation and processing. Read food label to ensure that food product does not contain gluten.

Nutrients per serving:

Calories: 160
Carbohydrate: 18g
Protein: 5g
Total Fat: 8g
Saturated Fat: 0.5g
Omega-3 fatty acids: 0.10g
Dietary Fiber: 6g
Sodium: 180mg
Cholesterol: 0mg

Garden Vegetable Salad

Serves 6

3 medium **carrots**, diced
1 head **broccoli**, chopped
1 head **cauliflower**, chopped
1 medium red **onion**
1 **red bell pepper**, diced
1 **yellow squash**, diced
1 T olive oil
1 T white vinegar*
½ t salt
½ t **black pepper**

In large salad bowl combine all of the ingredients and toss well.

*This food item either is not naturally gluten free or may contain gluten due to preparation and processing. Read food label to ensure that food product does not contain gluten.

Nutrients per serving:
Calories: 130
Carbohydrate: 25g
Protein: 9g
Total Fat: 2.5g
Saturated Fat: 0g
Omega-3 fatty acids: 0.17g
Dietary Fiber: 10g
Sodium: 400mg
Cholesterol: 0mg

Lentil Salad

Serves 6

4 c water
1 c dried lentils
1 medium **onion**, chopped
¾ c bulgur (cracked wheat), uncooked**
⅓ c **lemon juice**
¼ c vegetable stock*
1 T canola oil
¼ tsp **black pepper**
3 **garlic** cloves, minced
¾ c fresh **parsley**, chopped
¼ c fresh **mint**, chopped
2 c diced **tomatoes**
green leaf lettuce
¾ c plain Greek nonfat yogurt

Step 1: Combine first 3 ingredients in a large saucepan; bring to a boil. Cover, reduce heat, and simmer 10 minutes. Stir in bulgur; cover and simmer 15 minutes or until lentils are tender. Drain well; spoon into a large bowl.

Step 2: Combine lemon juice and next 5 ingredients; stir with wire whisk. Add to lentil mixture; toss well. Cover and let stand at room temperature 1 hour, stirring occasionally.

Step 3: Stir in parsley and mint. Cover and chill 2 hours. Stir in tomato. Serve on lettuce-lined plates; top with yogurt.

*This food item either is not naturally gluten free or may contain gluten due to preparation and processing. Read food label to ensure that food product does not contain gluten.

**This food item contains gluten. You may substitute a gluten-free product for this item to make this a gluten-free recipe.

Nutrients per serving:

Calories: 201
Carbohydrate: 35g
Protein: 16g
Total Fat: 3g
Saturated Fat: 0.29g

Omega 3 fatty acids: 0.23g
Dietary Fiber: 12g
Sodium: 80mg
Cholesterol: 5mg

Black Bean Salad (gluten free)

Serves 4

1 c water
1 tsp canola oil
4 tsp fresh **lime juice**, or more to taste
½ tsp ground **cumin**
½ tsp ground **coriander**
3 T fresh **cilantro,** chopped
2 T minced scallions
15-oz can black beans, rinsed & drained
2 c diced **tomatoes**
1 c diced **bell peppers** (red, green, yellow, or a mixture)
1 fresh **green chilie,** minced
Black pepper, to taste

Step 1: In a large mixing bowl combine oil, lime juice, cumin, coriander, cilantro, and scallions.
Step 2: Add beans, tomatoes, bell peppers, and chilies. Stir well.
Step 3: Add black pepper to taste, and combine thoroughly. Refrigerate until ready to serve. Garnish with lemon or lime wedges.

Nutrients per serving:
Calories: 150
Carbohydrate: 25g
Protein: 6g
Total Fat: 6g
Saturated Fat: 0.5g
Omega-3 fatty acids: 0g
Dietary Fiber: 5g
Sodium: 320mg
Cholesterol: 0mg

Garden Salad

Serves 6

1 **red pepper**
3 T balsamic vinegar*
2 T water
1 T canola oil
¼ tsp ground red pepper
1 T fresh **basil**
2 c red leaf lettuce
2 c green leaf lettuce
2 c Romaine lettuce
1 c **tomatoes**, diced
1 c **cucumber**, diced

Step 1: Cut pepper in half lengthwise; remove seeds. Place pepper, skin side up, on a greased baking sheet. Bake at 425 degrees for 20 minutes. Let cool and then peel and discard skin.

Step 2: Place roasted pepper, vinegar, water, canola oil, ground red pepper and basil in an electric blender. Blend mixture until smooth and transfer to a small bowl. Cover and chill at least 1 hour.

Step 3: Combine lettuces, tomato, and cucumber in a large bowl; toss gently. Arrange lettuce mixture evenly on individual plates. Sprinkle salad with red pepper mixture.

*This food item either is not naturally gluten free or may contain gluten due to preparation and processing. Read food label to ensure that food product does not contain gluten.

Nutrients per serving:
Calories: 50
Carbohydrate: 6g
Protein: 1g
Total Fat: 2.5g
Saturated Fat: 0g
Omega-3 fatty acids: 0.03g
Dietary Fiber: 1g
Sodium: 75mg
Cholesterol: 0mg

Salmon Salad (gluten free)

Serves 6

2 cans cannelloni beans, rinsed & drained
1 small **fennel** bulb, finely chopped or sliced
1 small red **onion**, chopped
3 large **carrots**, peeled and sliced
2 T fresh **dill,** chopped
¼ c canola oil
2 T fresh **lemon juice**
½ tsp **black pepper**
½ lb fresh salmon fillets

Step 1: In a large bowl, combine beans, fennel, onion, carrots, dill, canola oil, lemon juice, and pepper.
Step 2: Preheat broiler. Rinse salmon and place on broiler rack. Broil salmon until it starts to flake when pierced with a fork, about 10 minutes.
Step 3: Break salmon into chunks and remove bones. Sprinkle salmon over bean mixture.

Nutrients per serving:
Calories: 310
Carbohydrate: 30g
Protein: 18g
Total Fat: 15g
Saturated Fat: 2g
Omega-3 fatty acids: 0.81g
Dietary Fiber: 9g
Sodium: 450mg
Cholesterol: 20mg

Mushroom Salad

Serves 6-8

¼ c canola oil
4 T red vinegar*
4 T freshly squeezed **lemon juice**
¼ tsp salt
¼ tsp **black pepper**
12 large fresh **mushrooms**
1 bunch watercress
¼ c fresh **chives**, chopped

Step 1: Make dressing by thoroughly mixing oil, vinegar, lemon juice, salt and pepper.

Step 2: Wash mushrooms and cut into thin slices. Pour dressing over mushrooms, refrigerate and soak for 4 hours.

Step 3: Before serving, place mushrooms and dressing in salad bowl. Wash and drain watercress and add to bowl. Top with cut chives

*This food item either is not naturally gluten free or may contain gluten due to preparation and processing. Read food label to ensure that food product does not contain gluten.

Nutrients per serving:
Calories: 90
Carbohydrate: 3g
Protein: 1g
Total Fat: 8g
Saturated Fat: 0.5g
Omega-3 fatty acids: 0g
Dietary Fiber: 1g
Sodium: 85mg
Cholesterol: 0mg

Broccoli Salad

Serves 6

6 c **broccoli**, chopped
¼ c red **onion,** finely chopped
¾ c sweetened dried **cranberries**
½ c **pumpkin seeds**
¼ c **flaxseeds**

Dressing:
¾ c light mayonnaise
2 T balsamic vinegar*
2 T granulated sugar

Step 1: Mix broccoli, onions, cranberries, pumpkin seeds and flaxseeds in large bowl.
Step 2: Combine mayonnaise, vinegar and sugar in small mixing bowl, and then pour over salad, toss well. For best results, chill before serving.

*This food item either is not naturally gluten free or may contain gluten due to preparation and processing. Read food label to ensure that food product does not contain gluten.

Nutrients per serving:
Calories: 254
Carbohydrate: 37g
Protein: 13g
Total Fat: 6g
Saturated Fat: 1g
Omega-3 fatty acids: 0g
Dietary Fiber: 11g
Sodium: 330mg
Cholesterol: 5mg

Chinese Noodle Salad

Serves 10

2 T canola oil
2 packages Ramen noodles, omit seasoning packet
¼ c **sesame seeds**
5 ½ oz **almonds**, chopped
1 head **cabbage**, chopped
1 bunch **green onions**, diced

Sauce:

¾ c canola oil
½ c vinegar*
2 tsp low sodium soy sauce*
⅔ c sugar

Step 1: In large pan heat oil and add noodles, almonds, and sesame seeds. Brown until golden; put in a separate bowl and place in refrigerator to cool.
Step 2: On medium heat, cook chopped cabbage and green onions until cabbage is crisp-tender; mix with noodles when cooled.
Step 3: Combine ingredients for sauce in small bowl. Combine cabbage and sauce mixture 10 minutes before serving. Cover and shake well to mix.

*This food item either is not naturally gluten free or may contain gluten due to preparation and processing. Read food label to ensure that food product does not contain gluten.

Nutrients per serving:

Calories: 410
Carbohydrate: 35g
Protein: 8g
Total Fat: 29g
Saturated Fat: 2g
Omega-3 fatty acids: 0g
Dietary Fiber: 7g
Sodium: 180mg
Cholesterol: 0mg

Lentil Salad

Serves 6

1 c dry lentils	**Black pepper**, to taste
2 c water	2 T fresh **parsley**
1 c dry bulgur wheat**	1 red **onion**, minced
1 c boiling water	1 **bell pepper** (any color), diced
¼ c canola oil	1 **celery** stalk, finely chopped
¼ c **lemon juice**	½ c crumbled low-fat feta cheese
2 **garlic** cloves, minced	½ c **olives**
½ tsp **oregano**	1 Roma **tomato**, diced
2 T fresh **mint**	½ c **walnuts**, chopped
2 T fresh **dill**	6 lemon wedges

Step 1: Place lentils in medium-sized saucepan, cover with water, and bring to a boil. Turn the heat to simmer, partially cover, and cook for 20 to 25 minutes, or until tender but not mushy. Drain well and transfer to a large bowl.

Step 2: Place bulgur wheat in a small bowl. Add boiling water, cover, and let stand for 15 minutes or until the water is absorbed.

Step 3: Add all ingredients to the lentils, except tomatoes, walnuts, and lemon wedges. Mix thoroughly. Cover and refrigerate.

Step 4: Just before serving, add tomatoes and walnuts. Serve with lemon wedges on the side.

**This food item contains gluten. You may substitute a gluten-free product for this item to make this a gluten-free recipe.

Nutrients per serving:
Calories: 180
Carbohydrate: 31g
Protein: 10g
Total Fat: 3g
Saturated Fat: 0g
Omega-3 fatty acids: 0.03g
Dietary Fiber: 7g
Sodium: 65mg
Cholesterol: 0mg

Yummy Portobello Mushrooms

Serves 6

1 ½ T olive oil
10 Portobello **mushrooms,** washed with caps and stalks separated
1 sweet **onion**, diced
3 Roma **tomatoes**, diced
½ tsp **basil**
½ tsp **oregano**
½ tsp hot sauce*
½ c **pine nuts**
½ c shaved Parmesan cheese

Step 1: Sauté onion, garlic and mushroom stalks until lightly browned. Add tomatoes, basil, oregano and hot sauce.

Step 2: Arrange mushrooms caps in large greased baking dish. Stuff mushrooms with onions and tomato mixture.

Step 3: Sprinkle pine nuts and cheese over the stuffed mushrooms. Bake at 375 degrees for 25 minutes, until mushrooms are tender.

*This food item either is not naturally gluten free or may contain gluten due to preparation and processing. Read food label to ensure that food product does not contain gluten.

Nutrients per serving:
Calories: 250
Carbohydrate: 13g
Protein: 10g
Total Fat: 18g
Saturated Fat: 4.5g
Omega-3 fatty acids: 0.02g
Dietary Fiber: 4g
Sodium: 135mg
Cholesterol: 5mg

Summer Sensation (gluten free)

Serves 1

½ c Greek yogurt
½ c skim milk
1 c fresh or frozen fruit of choice*
½ tsp **vanilla**
1 tsp honey

In a blender, add all ingredients and purée. Pour into 1 glass and serve.

*Select your favorite fresh or frozen fruit. This recipe was analyzed using 1 cup of fresh strawberries.

Nutrients per serving:

Calories: 180
Carbohydrate: 28g
Protein: 15g
Total Fat: 0.5g
Saturated Fat: 0g
Omega-3 fatty acids: 0.13g
Dietary Fiber: 4g
Sodium: 100mg
Cholesterol: 5mg

Walnut-Raisin Quinoa Salad (gluten free)

Serves 4

1 c **quinoa**
¼ c English **walnuts***
2 T olive oil
2 **garlic** cloves, minced
½ c fresh **parsley**, chopped
⅓ c **raisins**
1 T **lemon juice**

Step 1: Toast the quinoa lightly in a frying pan over medium heat, then add 2 cups water, bring to a boil, then cover and simmer over medium heat. When the water is absorbed, keep the cover in place and let it cool for at least 2 minutes.

Step 2: Chop the walnuts and toast lightly in a small frying pan over medium heat. Cook the garlic in olive oil over medium heat until yellow, after approximately 2 minutes. Remove the garlic from the oil before it turns brown.

Step 3: Combine all ingredients except the olive oil in a bowl and gently toss. Add salt and pepper to taste.

*To increase the omega-3 fatty acid content of this dish, try substituting Black Walnuts for the English Walnuts.

Substitutions

- Organic raisins are readily available and preferred over conventional raisins, which also can be used.
- Vegetable or other broth can be substituted for the water, leading to a tastier dish.
  Be sure to check food label for broths, they can be high in sodium and may contain gluten.

Nutrients per serving:

Calories: 340
Carbohydrate: 47g
Protein: 8g
Total Fat: 15g
Saturated Fat: 2g
Omega-3 fatty acids:
Dietary Fiber: 5g
Sodium: 10mg
Cholesterol: 0mg

Caprese Salad

Serves 4

1 c fresh Mozzarella, sliced
1 c cherry **tomatoes**, cut in half
¼ c red **onions**, diced
Fresh **basil**-washed and chopped
Cracked **black pepper**, to taste
Olive oil
Balsamic vinegar*

Step 1: On individual small serving plates place 2 slices of Mozzarella cheese.
Step 2: Place tomatoes and onions on the Mozzarella cheese and sprinkle with dressing.
Step 3: Add fresh basil, salt, pepper, olive oil and balsamic vinegar, to taste.

*This food item either is not naturally gluten free or may contain gluten due to preparation and processing. Read food label to ensure that food product does not contain gluten.

Nutrients per serving:
Calories: 150
Carbohydrate: 14g
Protein: 9g
Total Fat: 7g
Saturated Fat: 4g
Omega-3 fatty acids: 0.06g
Dietary Fiber: 1g
Sodium: 560mg
Cholesterol: 20mg

Marinated Green Bean Salad

Serves 4

2 c **green beans**, steamed
3-4 **shallots**, diced
½ c Balsamic Vinaigrette* (see next page)

Step 1: Steam green beans and shallots until tender.
Step 2: Place green beans and shallots in a serving bowl and cover lightly with balsamic dressing. Serve and enjoy!

*This food item either is not naturally gluten free or may contain gluten due to preparation and processing. Read food label to ensure that food product does not contain gluten.

Nutrients per serving:

Calories: 70
Carbohydrate: 16g
Protein: 2g
Total Fat: 0g
Saturated Fat: 0g
Omega-3 fatty acids: 0.01g
Dietary Fiber: 2g
Sodium: 460mg
Cholesterol: 0mg

Balsamic Vinaigrette

Serving size 2 T

4 oz olive oil
8 oz balsamic vinegar*
2 **garlic** cloves, minced
1 tsp Dijon **mustard***
1 tsp **basil**
1 tsp shaved Parmesan cheese
¼ tsp salt
1 tsp **black pepper**
1 tsp sugar

Step 1: In small bowl, combine all ingredients and stir well.
Step 2: Pour into salad bottle to serve and store in refrigerator up to 1 week.

*This food item either is not naturally gluten free or may contain gluten due to preparation and processing. Read food label to ensure that food product does not contain gluten.

Nutrients per serving:
Calories: 200
Carbohydrate: 8g
Protein: 0g
Total Fat: 19g
Saturated Fat: 2.5g
Omega-3 fatty acids: 0.00g
Dietary Fiber: 0g
Sodium: 130mg
Cholesterol: 0mg

Blue Cheese Dressing

Serving size 1 T

1 T mayonnaise
¼ c blue cheese
1 T **lemon juice**
¼ c buttermilk
¼ tsp **black pepper**
¼ tsp salt
¼ tsp **celery seed**
¼ tsp Worcestershire*
dash of Tabasco sauce*

Mix all ingredients in a salad dressing container. Refrigerate after preparation.

*This food item either is not naturally gluten free or may contain gluten due to preparation and processing. Read food label to ensure that food product does not contain gluten.

Nutrients per serving:
Calories: 35
Carbohydrate: 2g
Protein: 2g
Total Fat: 2.5g
Saturated Fat: 1.5g
Omega-3 fatty acids: 0.04g
Dietary Fiber: 0g
Sodium: 200mg
Cholesterol: 5mg

Old Family Recipe Red Wine Vinaigrette

Serving size 1 T

¼ c olive oil
¼ c red wine vinegar*
2 **garlic** cloves, minced
½ T red **onion**, diced
1 T Dijon **mustard***
2 T **oregano**
2 T sugar
Pinch of salt
Black pepper

Combine all ingredients in a salad dressing container and shake well. Refrigerate between uses.

*This food item either is not naturally gluten free or may contain gluten due to preparation and processing. Read food label to ensure that food product does not contain gluten.

Nutrients per serving:
Calories: 120
Carbohydrate: 10g
Protein: 0g
Total Fat: 10g
Saturated Fat: 1.5g
Omega-3 fatty acids: 0.11g
Dietary Fiber: 1g
Sodium: 60mg
Cholesterol: 0mg

Cilantro Lime Dressing

Serving size 1 T

1 T **cilantro**, chopped
2 **garlic** cloves, minced
1 tsp chili powder
¼ c olive oil
1 T **lime juice**
1 T **orange juice**
¼ c rice wine vinegar*
1 T sugar
1 tsp salt
1 tsp **black pepper**

Step 1: Combine all ingredients in salad dressing container. Shake well.
Step 2: Serve over your favorite fresh from the garden greens for a light citrus flavor.

*This food item either is not naturally gluten free or may contain gluten due to preparation and processing. Read food label to ensure that food product does not contain gluten.

Nutrients per serving:
Calories: 60
Carbohydrate: 3g
Protein: 0g
Total Fat: 6g
Saturated Fat: 1g
Omega-3 fatty acids: 0g
Dietary Fiber: 0g
Sodium: 290mg
Cholesterol: 0mg

Light Honey Mustard Dressing

Serving size 1 T

1 c light mayonnaise
1 T Dijon **mustard***
1 tsp **lemon juice**
2 T honey
½ tsp salt
1 tsp **black pepper**

Combine all ingredients in a salad dressing container. Shake well and refrigerate in between uses.

*This food item either is not naturally gluten free or may contain gluten due to preparation and processing. Read food label to ensure that food product does not contain gluten.

Nutrients per serving:
Calories: 35
Carbohydrate: 9g
Protein: 0g
Total Fat: 0g
Saturated Fat: 0g
Omega-3 fatty acids: 1.15g
Dietary Fiber: 0g
Sodium: 290mg
Cholesterol: 0mg

Sun-dried Tomato Vinaigrette

Serving size 1 T

½ c diced sundried **tomatoes,** packaged without oil
¼ c sugar
2 T **basil** pesto
1 **garlic** clove, minced
1 T Dijon **mustard***
¼ c apple cider vinegar*
2 T olive oil
1 tsp salt
1 tsp **black pepper**

Step 1: Combine all ingredients and mix well. Serve over favorite salad or fresh summer vegetables.

*This food item either is not naturally gluten free or may contain gluten due to preparation and processing. Read food label to ensure that food product does not contain gluten.

Nutrients per serving:
Calories: 150
Carbohydrate: 14g
Protein: 1g
Total Fat: 11g
Saturated Fat: 1.5g
Omega-3 fatty acids: 0.00g
Dietary Fiber: 1g
Sodium: 740mg
Cholesterol: 5mg

Chipotle Herb Dressing

Serving size 1 T

1 T **cilantro**, chopped
1 **garlic** clove, minced
¼ c canned chipotle pepper, pureed
1 T apple cider vinegar*
1 ½ T sugar
1 tsp **black pepper**

Combine all ingredients in salad dressing container. Shake well and use on chicken as marinade or pour over your favorite salad and toss to mix.

*This food item either is not naturally gluten free or may contain gluten due to preparation and processing. Read food label to ensure that food product does not contain gluten.

Nutrients per serving:
Calories: 50
Carbohydrate: 13g
Protein: 0g
Total Fat: 0g
Saturated Fat: 0g
Omega-3 fatty acids:
Dietary Fiber: 0g
Sodium: 230mg
Cholesterol: 0mg

Sandwiches

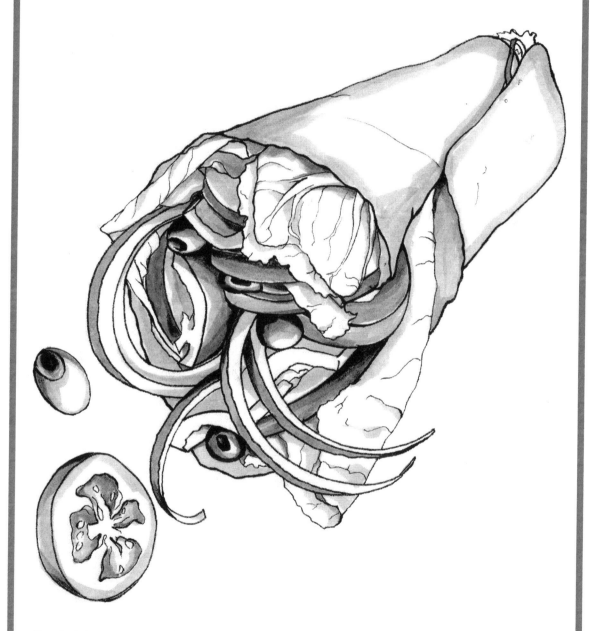

Sandwiches are one of the most convenient foods for picnics, lunches, and travels. They can range from wholesome to junk foods, depending on one's choice of breads and what is between them. A wholesome variety of sandwiches are presented here.

Zesty Mozzarella Sandwiches

Serves 4

1 T olive oil
¼ c chopped **onion**
2-3 **garlic** cloves, minced
2 tsp fresh **parsley**
½ tsp dried **oregano**
½ tsp dried **thyme**
Dash of **black pepper**, to taste
½ (14.5 oz) can diced petite **tomatoes**, drained
½ c dry red wine
1 **bay leaf**
8 (1-oz) slices part-skim Mozzarella cheese
16 (½-oz) slices French bread**

Step 1: Pour olive oil into small saucepan and place over medium-high heat until hot. Add onion and garlic; sauté until tender.

Step 2: Add tomato, wine, and bay leaf, mix well. Reduce heat, and simmer, uncovered for 30 minutes stirring frequently. *Remove and discard bay leaf.*

Step 3: Place 1 slice of cheese on each of 8 bread slices; top with remaining 8 bread slices.

Step 4: Place sandwiches on a large baking sheet coated with cooking spray. Bake at 400 degrees for 3 minutes; turn sandwiches, and bake an additional 4 to 6 minutes or until crisp and golden. Serve immediately with warm marinara sauce.

**This food item contains gluten. You may substitute a gluten-free product for this item to make this a gluten-free recipe.

Nutrients per serving:
Calories: 410
Carbohydrate: 43g
Protein: 22g
Total Fat: 14g
Saturated Fat: 7g
Omega-3 fatty acids: 0.14g
Dietary Fiber: 2g
Sodium: 560g
Cholesterol: 35mg

Greek Salad Wrap

Serves 4

2 **cucumbers**, peeled and sliced
1 Roma **tomato**, sliced
4 oz low-fat Feta cheese
1 c Romaine lettuce
¼ c **banana peppers,** diced
3 oz black **olives**
4 3 oz flour tortilla shells**

Step 1: Prepare ingredients and place in mixing or salad bowl.
Step 2: Toss well.
Step 3: Spoon mixture into tortilla shells and serve.

**This food item contains gluten. You may substitute a gluten-free product for this item to make this a gluten-free recipe.

Nutrients per serving:
Calories: 350
Carbohydrate: 50g
Protein: 15g
Total Fat: 11g
Saturated Fat: 3.5g
Omega-3 fatty acids: 0.05g
Dietary Fiber: 6g
Sodium: 600mg
Cholesterol: 10mg

Tangy Burgers

Serves 6

1 15-oz can light red kidney beans, drained
1 small bunch **green onions**, including tops, rinsed and chopped
½ pound extra-lean ground beef, crumbled into small pieces
1 8-oz can crushed **tomatoes**
1 T honey
¼ tsp **lemon juice**
6 whole wheat hamburger buns**

Step 1: Add drained beans into a 3 ½-quart slow cooker. Add green onions, ground beef, crushed tomatoes, honey, and lemon peel. Stir until mixed. Cover and cook on LOW for 4 hours.

Step 2: Preheat oven to 350. Split buns and place, cut sides up, on a baking sheet. Toast until lightly browned. Serve tangy beef and bean mixture on toasted buns.

**This food item contains gluten. You may substitute a gluten-free product for this item to make this a gluten-free recipe.

Nutrients per serving:
Calories: 170
Carbohydrate: 25g
Protein: 13g
Total Fat: 2g
Saturated Fat: 0.5g
Omega-3 fatty acids: 0.02g
Dietary Fiber: 5g
Sodium: 240mg
Cholesterol: 20mg

Eggplant Parmesan Club Sandwich

Serves 4

1 medium **eggplant**, sliced in long sections, grilled
4 oz Mozzarella cheese
4 oz marinara sauce
4 Ciabatta rolls**

Step 1: Slice eggplant in long sections and grill on both sides until golden brown.
Step 2: Place in baking pan and cover with marinara sauce until ready to serve.
Step 3: Place 1 slice of eggplant on sliced Ciabatta roll with marinara sauce and 1 slice of Mozzarella cheese. Serve warm.

**This food item contains gluten. You may substitute a gluten-free product for this item to make this a gluten-free recipe.

Nutrients per serving:
Calories: 500
Carbohydrate: 80g
Protein: 21g
Total Fat: 13g
Saturated Fat: 5g
Omega-3 fatty acids: 0.24g
Dietary Fiber: 15g
Sodium: 910mg
Cholesterol: 15mg

Sloppy Joe Remake

Serves 8

1 T canola oil
½ c **onions**, diced
½ c **celery**, diced
½ c **carrots**, diced
½ c **bell pepper**, any color, diced
2 **garlic** cloves, minced
1-14 oz can diced **tomatoes**, drained
2 T chili powder
1 T balsamic vinegar*
1 – 15 ½ oz can red kidney beans, rinsed and drained
8 Whole wheat rolls**

Step 1: Pour canola oil into a large nonstick skillet and place over medium-high heat until hot. Add onion, celery, carrot, bell pepper, and garlic; sauté until tender.

Step 2: Stir in diced tomato, chili powder, balsamic vinegar. Cover, reduce heat, and simmer 10 minutes.

Step 3: Add kidney beans, and cook an additional 5 minutes.

Step 4: Toast buns and spoon bean mixture evenly and enjoy!

*This food item either is not naturally gluten free or may contain gluten due to preparation and processing. Read food label to ensure that food product does not contain gluten.

**This food item contains gluten. You may substitute a gluten-free product for this item to make this a gluten-free recipe.

Nutrients per serving:
Calories: 260
Carbohydrate: 47g
Protein: 10g
Total Fat: 5g
Saturated Fat: 0.5g
Omega-3 fatty acids: 0.09g
Dietary Fiber: 9g
Sodium: 570mg
Cholesterol: 0mg

Soups

The fantastic combination of flavors that can be incorporated into soups makes them a culinary delight. Unfortunately, most commercially available soups have unacceptable levels of salt and may contain hidden unhealthy ingredients such as trans-fats at levels that do not require reporting on the Food Label. The soup recipes presented here blend rich flavors with healthy ingredients.

Potato Soup (gluten free)

Serves 4

2 medium sweet **onions**
8 medium **potatoes**
1 bunch **celery**
1 T canola oil
2 c 1% low fat milk

Step 1: Dice celery and onions.

Step 2: In medium pan, sauté onions and celery in canola oil over medium heat until tender. Peel, rinse and dice the potatoes. Place the potatoes in a large pot, cover with water and bring to a boil and then lower to medium-low heat and cook for 20 minutes or until potatoes are soft.

Step 3: Drain potatoes. Set in ⅓ of cooked potatoes aside in a small bowl. Mash the remaining potatoes in the large pot. Add the cooked celery, onions and remaining potatoes to the pot. Add milk to your desired thickness.

* Note, nutritional information provided is for soup prepared with 2 cups of 1% milk. Adding more or less milk and/or changing the type of milk will alter nutritional content of soup; adjust accordingly.

Nutrients per serving:

Calories: 140
Carbohydrate: 28g
Protein: 6g
Total Fat: 2g
Saturated Fat: 0g
Omega-3 fatty acids: 1.29g
Dietary Fiber: 3g
Sodium: 45mg
Cholesterol: 5mg

Gazpacho

Serves 4

8-10 large **tomatoes**
1 **red bell pepper**, diced
3 **garlic** cloves, minced
2 T olive oil
juice from 1 **lime** and 1 **lemon**, seeds remove seeded
Tabasco sauce, to taste*
Black pepper, to taste
1 tsp **basil**

Avocado Salsa
1 ripe **avocado**
½ **lemon**, freshly squeezed
½ red **chile**, finely chopped
2 tsp **cumin**
1 tsp **paprika**

Step 1: Place tomatoes in a bowl and cover with boiling water. Leave for 30 seconds, then peel, seed, and chop the flesh.

Step 2: Place tomatoes, red pepper, chile, garlic, olive oil, lime and lemon juice in food processor with 2 cups water; blend until mixed but still chunky. Season to taste and chill for 2-3 hours.

Step 3: Make avocado salsa 30 minutes before serving. Cut the avocado in half, remove the pit, then peel and dice. Toss avocado in the lemon juice to prevent browning, then mix chile.

Step 4: Ladle soup into bowls (1 cup each) and top with Avocado Salsa. Garnish with basil.

*This food item either is not naturally gluten free or may contain gluten due to preparation and processing. Read food label to ensure that food product does not contain gluten.

Nutrients per serving:

Calories: 260
Carbohydrate: 29g
Protein: 7g
Total Fat: 16g
Saturated Fat: 2g

Omega-3 fatty acids: 0.09g
Dietary Fiber: 9g
Sodium: 60mg
Cholesterol: 0mg

Navy Bean Soup

Serves 6

1 **onion**, diced
1 **celery** stalk, diced
2 **carrots**, peeled and diced
1 T olive oil
1 c white wine
3 c vegetable stock*
6 large Roma **tomatoes,** diced
1 ½ c pasta, cooked**
2 medium cans navy beans, rinsed and drained
16 oz baby **spinach**, washed
Black pepper, to taste
¼ c freshly grated Parmesan cheese, to serve

Step 1: Sauté onion, celery and carrots in a large saucepan with olive oil over medium heat until tender.

Step 2: Add wine, vegetable stock and tomatoes. Bring to a boil. Reduce heat and simmer for 15 minutes.

Step 3: Add cooked pasta and beans and simmer for 10 minutes.

Step 4: Add spinach and cook until spinach begins to wilt. Serve sprinkled with Parmesan cheese.

*This food item either is not naturally gluten free or may contain gluten due to preparation and processing. Read food label to ensure that food product does not contain gluten.

**This food item contains gluten. You may substitute a gluten-free product for this item to make this a gluten-free recipe.

Nutrients per serving:
Calories: 420
Carbohydrate: 72g
Protein: 17g
Total Fat: 4.5g
Saturated Fat: 1g
Omega-3 fatty acids: 0.01g
Dietary Fiber: 12g
Sodium: 450mg
Cholesterol: 5mg

Old Fashioned Beef Stew

Serves 6

½ lb sirloin, cut into 2" cubes
1 T olive oil
1 **onion**, diced
3 **carrots**, peeled and diced
2-3 **celery** stalks, diced
1 15 oz can petite diced **tomatoes**
½ c beef broth*
3 c water, may add more if desired
3 c **potatoes**, peeled and diced
2 **garlic** cloves, minced
1 tsp **thyme**
1 tsp **rosemary**
1 tsp **cayenne pepper**
½ tsp **black pepper**

Step 1: Brown beef in olive oil.

Step 2: Add vegetables and cook for about 8 minutes.

Step 3: Add remaining ingredients, stir well. Reduce heat and simmer until beef is tender, about 40 minutes or so.

Step 4: Taste and season as desired. Serve and enjoy!

*This food item either is not naturally gluten free or may contain gluten due to preparation and processing. Read food label to ensure that food product does not contain gluten.

Nutrients per serving:
Calories: 150
Carbohydrate: 12g
Protein: 13g
Total Fat: 6g
Saturated Fat: 1.5g
Omega-3 fatty acids: 0.01g
Dietary Fiber: 3g
Sodium: 200mg
Cholesterol: 30mg

Crab Bisque

Serves 4

1 T canola oil
2 T butter
2 medium **onions**, diced
1 T **thyme**
3 **garlic** cloves, minced
1 T flour*
1 ½ c half-and-half cream
3 6-oz cans crab meat, drained, flaked and cartilage removed
1½ c 2% milk
2 T sherry*
¼ tsp **black pepper**
¼ tsp **lemon juice**
¼ tsp **dill**
¼ tsp **parsley**

Step 1: Sauté vegetables in canola oil and butter over medium heat.
Step 2: Add remaining ingredients.
Step 3: Mix well and simmer on low heat; season as desired.

*This food item either is not naturally gluten free or may contain gluten due to preparation and processing. Read food label to ensure that food product does not contain gluten.

Nutrients per serving:
Calories: 300
Carbohydrate: 23g
Protein: 24g
Total Fat: 11g
Saturated Fat: 4g
Omega-3 fatty acids: 0.31g
Dietary Fiber: 1g
Sodium: 680mg
Cholesterol: 95mg

Chicken Noodle Soup

Serves 6

2 T canola oil
1 **onion**, diced
3 **celery** stalks, diced
2 medium **carrots**, diced
2-3 **garlic** cloves, minced
1 ½ c diced chicken, cooked
2 c chicken stock*
2 c water
¼ tsp **thyme**
1 tsp **oregano**
1 tsp salt
1 tsp **black pepper**
1 tsp **lemon juice**
2 c cooked pasta**
1 T **chives**, chopped

Step 1: Sauté onions, carrot, celery, and garlic in canola oil over medium heat.
Step 2: Add chicken, chicken stock, water and spices.
Step 3: Bring to a boil and simmer 15 minutes. Reduce heat.
Step 4: Add cooked pasta and chives. Taste and season, as desired.

*This food item either is not naturally gluten free or may contain gluten due to preparation and processing. Read food label to ensure that food product does not contain gluten.

**This food item contains gluten. You may substitute a gluten-free product for this item to make this a gluten-free recipe.

Nutrients per serving:
Calories: 430
Carbohydrate: 65g
Protein: 25g
Total Fat: 9g
Saturated Fat: 1g
Omega-3 fatty acids: 0.01g
Dietary Fiber: 4g
Sodium: 820mg
Cholesterol: 30mg

Curry Carrot Soup

Serves 4-6

1 T canola oil
2 **onions**, diced
3 **carrots**, diced
2 c water
1 c vegetable base*
1 tsp **ginger**, grated
1 tsp curry powder
½ tsp hot sauce*
½ tsp sugar
¼ tsp **cinnamon**
¼ c **orange juice**
¼ c half-and-half
2 T **chives**

Step 1: Combine all ingredients in a large pot. Bring to a boil then simmer for 30 minutes.
Step 2: Cool and then blend in a food processor or blender until smooth; taste and season as desired.

*This food item either is not naturally gluten free or may contain gluten due to preparation and processing. Read food label to ensure that food product does not contain gluten.

Nutrients per serving:
Calories: 160
Carbohydrate: 22g
Protein: 5g
Total Fat: 6g
Saturated Fat: 0.5g
Omega-3 fatty acids: 0.22g
Dietary Fiber: 4g
Sodium: 1120mg
Cholesterol: 0mg

Egg Drop Soup with Shrimp

Serves 4

1 T **sesame oil**
4 **shallots**, sliced
1 T freshly grated **ginger**
3 **garlic** cloves, minced
2 **celery** stalks, diced
2 c water
1 T shrimp base, store bought*
½ lb shrimp, diced
2 T low sodium soy sauce*
1 tsp **lemon juice**
¼ c **green onions,** chopped
¼ tsp **white pepper**
2-3 drops yellow food coloring*
4 **omega-3 eggs,** beaten

Step 1: Sauté shallots, ginger, garlic, celery and leeks in sesame oil on low heat. Add remaining ingredients except green onion, food color, and omega-3 eggs.
Step 2: Bring to a boil and simmer 10 minutes.
Step 3: Add food color and green onion. Taste and season.
Step 4: Just before serving, bring to high simmer (not a boil).
Step 5: Put omega-3 eggs into squeeze bottle and whisk them into the soup slowly to allow strands to form. Serve and enjoy!

*This food item either is not naturally gluten free or may contain gluten due to preparation and processing. Read food label to ensure that food product does not contain gluten.

Nutrients per serving:
Calories: 225
Carbohydrate: 16g
Protein: 21
Total Fat: 9g
Saturated Fat: 2g
Omega-3 fatty acids: 0.29g
Dietary Fiber: 1g
Sodium: 480mg
Cholesterol: 230mg

Lentil Soup (gluten free)

Serves 4

1 T olive oil
1 red **onion**, diced
1 **jalapeno pepper**, finely diced with seeds
3 **garlic** cloves, minced
1 ½ c red lentils, rinsed
1 tsp ground **coriander**
1 tsp **paprika**
1 ⅔ c **light coconut milk**
Juice of 1 **lime**, seeds removed
4-5 **green onions**, diced
Black pepper, to taste

Step 1: Heat oil in large pan. Add onion, jalapeno pepper, and garlic. Cook until onions soften, stirring occasionally.

Step 2: Add lentils and spices. Add coconut milk and 4 cups of water. Stir well. Bring to a boil and stir. Reduce heat and cook for about 45 minutes (lentils will be soft).

Step 3: Add lime juice. Ladle into bowls. Top with green onions.

Nutrients per serving:
Calories: 540
Carbohydrate: 54g
Protein: 23g
Total Fat: 29g
Saturated Fat: 22g
Omega-3 fatty acids:
Dietary Fiber: 14g
Sodium: 30mg
Cholesterol: 0mg

Eggplant Soup

Serves 6

1 ½ T olive oil
1 large **onion**, diced
2 **shallots**, diced
4 **garlic** cloves, minced
2 c lentils
1 medium **eggplant**, peeled and diced
1 c vegetable broth*
3 c water
1 T **curry powder**
½ tsp salt
1 tsp **black pepper**

Step 1: Sauté onion, shallots, and garlic in olive oil until tender.
Step 2: Add eggplant to onion mixture and simmer for 5 minutes on medium-low heat.
Step 3: Add remaining ingredients and simmer on low for 15 minutes.
Step 4: Taste and season, as desired.

*This food item either is not naturally gluten free or may contain gluten due to preparation and processing. Read food label to ensure that food product does not contain gluten.

Nutrients per serving:
Calories: 80
Carbohydrate: 12g
Protein: 3g
Total Fat: 3g
Saturated Fat: 0g
Omega-3 fatty acids: 0.02g
Dietary Fiber: 3g
Sodium: 210mg
Cholesterol: 0mg

Butternut Squash Soup

Serves 6

1 T olive oil
1 sweet **onion**, diced
1 **carrot**, diced
4 c **butternut squash**, peeled, seeded and diced
¼ c brown sugar
2 tsp maple syrup
¼ tsp hot peppers, minced
1 tsp **cumin**
¼ tsp **cinnamon**
1 tsp chili powder
1 tsp **lime juice**
1 tsp **orange juice**
¼ c 2% milk
2 c water, more if needed
1 T apple cider vinegar*
Salt and **black pepper**, to taste

Step 1: Sauté onion, carrot, and hot peppers in olive oil.
Step 2: Add remaining ingredients and simmer until squash is tender when poked with a fork.
Step 3: In food processor or blender, blend until smooth.
Step 4: Taste and season, and then serve.

*This food item either is not naturally gluten free or may contain gluten due to preparation and processing. Read food label to ensure that food product does not contain gluten.

Nutrients per serving:
Calories: 120
Carbohydrate: 24g
Protein: 2g
Total Fat: 2.5g
Saturated Fat: 0g
Omega-3 fatty acids: 0.03g
Dietary Fiber: 3g
Sodium: 25mg
Cholesterol: 0mg

Vegetarian Chili (gluten free)

Serves 8

2 large **onions**
3-4 **garlic** cloves, minced
2 T canola oil
1 c water (may need more depending on desired thickness)
2 T **cumin**
1 T **paprika**
1 can black beans (rinsed and drained)
1 can red kidney beans (rinsed and drained)
1 can (14.5 oz) spicy **tomatoes** with chili peppers
½ can (7 oz) chipotle peppers, blended in food processor
1 medium yellow **squash**
1 medium **zucchini**
1 **red, yellow or green bell pepper**
1 c frozen or fresh **corn**

Step 1: In large pot sauté onions and garlic in oil over medium heat until tender. Add diced pepper, squash and zucchini. Continue to cook over medium heat for 5 minutes, stirring occasionally.

Step 2: Add beans, tomatoes, corn and spices. Stir slowly adding water to chili until desired thickness is obtained. May substitute kidney beans for black beans, if desired.

Nutrients per serving:

Calories: 210
Carbohydrate: 38g
Protein: 9g
Total Fat: 5g
Saturated Fat: 0g
Omega-3 fatty acids: 0.46g
Dietary Fiber: 11g
Sodium: 620mg
Cholesterol: 0mg

Broccoli Soup

Serves 4

1 bunch fresh **broccoli**
2 c 1% milk
2 T all purpose flour**
1 T butter
White pepper, to taste
Pinch of salt

Step 1: Wash and cut broccoli into small sections. In blender or food processor puree ⅔ of broccoli and set aside.

Step 2: In medium sauce pan, melt butter over medium-low heat. Add flour and mix well. Add milk and whip with a whisk until thick, about 8 minutes.

Step 3: Add broccoli to milk mixture, and cook on low heat for 5 minutes or until desired tenderness. Add salt and pepper to taste and serve.

**This food item contains gluten. You may substitute a gluten-free product for this item to make this a gluten-free recipe.

Nutrients per serving:
Calories: 100
Carbohydrate: 16g
Protein: 7g
Total Fat: 1.5g
Saturated Fat: 0.5g
Omega-3 fatty acids: 0.05g
Dietary Fiber: 3g
Sodium: 125mg
Cholesterol: 5mg

Spicy Tomato Soup with Chipotle (gluten free)

Serves 6

1 T canola oil
1 **onion**, diced
¼ c **leeks**, diced
2 **garlic** cloves, minced
1 15 oz can diced **tomatoes**
1 15 oz can crushed **tomatoes**
1 c water
½ can chipotle peppers, blended in food processor
1T **cilantro**
1 tsp sugar
1 tsp **parsley**, chopped
Salt and **black pepper**, to taste

Step 1: Sauté onion, leeks, and garlic in canola oil.
Step 2: add remaining ingredients.
Step 3: Simmer 30 minutes, stirring occasionally.
Step 4: In food processor, blend until smooth.
Step 5: Taste and season, as desired.
Step 6: Garnish with additional cilantro and serve.

Nutrients per serving:
Calories: 80
Carbohydrate: 11g
Protein: 2g
Total Fat: 3g
Saturated Fat: 0g
Omega-3 fatty acids: 0.26g
Dietary Fiber: 1g
Sodium: 210mg
Cholesterol: 0mg

Mint Spinach Soup (gluten free)

Serves 6

1 T olive oil
2 **onions**, diced
2 **celery** stalks, diced
¼ c **shallots**, diced
2 **garlic** cloves, minced
2 c water
1 c 2% milk
6 c **spinach**
1 T **lemon juice**
1 T dried **mint** leafs
1 tsp **black pepper**
1 tsp salt
1 T **parsley**
¼ c **green onions**, chopped

Step 1: Sauté onions, celery, shallots and garlic in olive oil until tender.
Step 2: Add remaining ingredients except herbs.
Step 3: Simmer about 10 minutes, stirring occasionally.
Step 4: Add herbs and blend.
Step 5: Taste and season.

Nutrients per serving:
Calories: 90
Carbohydrate: 13g
Protein: 3g
Total Fat: 3g
Saturated Fat: 1g
Omega-3 fatty acids: 0.02g
Dietary Fiber: 2g
Sodium: 460mg
Cholesterol: 5mg

Hearty Fish Chowder

Serves 8

2 medium **potatoes**, peeled and diced
2 medium **carrots**, peeled and sliced
1 **celery** stalk, thinly sliced
2-3 **garlic** cloves, minced
3 c water
½ c dry white wine
½ tsp ground **white pepper**
½ tsp ground **thyme**
1 tsp low-sodium Worcestershire sauce*
½ tsp hot sauce*
⅓ c dry nonfat powdered milk
¼ c flour**
½ c water
¾ pound firm white fish, cut into ½-inch cubes
1 (2-oz) jar chopped **pimientos**, drained

Step 1: Combine potatoes, carrots, celery, garlic, water, wine, salt, pepper, thyme, Worcestershire sauce, and hot sauce in a 3 ½-quart slow cooker. Cover and cook on LOW 8 hours or until potatoes are tender.

Step 2: Turn to HIGH. In a small bowl, combine dry powdered milk and flour. Gradually whisk in water; stir into mixture in slow cooker.

Step 3: Add fish and pimientos. Cover and cook on HIGH 15 to 20 minutes or until fish flakes easily and chowder begins to thicken.

*This food item either is not naturally gluten free or may contain gluten due to preparation and processing. Read food label to ensure that food product does not contain gluten.

**This food item contains gluten. You may substitute a gluten-free product for this item to make this a gluten-free recipe.

Nutrients per serving:

Calories: 220
Carbohydrate: 23g
Protein: 18g
Total Fat: 4.5g
Saturated Fat: 1g

Omega-3 fatty acids: 0.18g
Dietary Fiber: 2g
Sodium: 230mg
Cholesterol: 40mg

Vegetable Soup with Corn Tortillas (gluten free)

Serves 8

8 corn tortillas
1 T canola oil
2 sweet **onions**, diced
4 **garlic** cloves, minced
1 tsp chili powder
1 15 oz can petite diced **tomatoes**
1 can salsa
1 **orange bell pepper**, seeded and diced
1 **yellow squash**, diced
½ c **corn**
4 c water, more if desired
1 T **cumin**
1tsp **oregano**
Black pepper, to taste
1 tsp **lime juice**
¼ c **cilantro,** chopped

Step 1: Sauté onion, garlic, and celery in canola oil.
Step 2: Add remaining ingredients except cilantro and tortillas. Bring to boil and then add tortillas and simmer 10 minutes.
Step 3: Add cilantro, stir well and then serve.

Nutrients per serving:
Calories: 140
Carbohydrate: 26g
Protein: 3g
Total Fat: 3g
Saturated Fat: 0g
Omega-3 fatty acids: 0.17g
Dietary Fiber: 4g
Sodium: 220mg
Cholesterol: 0mg

Sweet Potato Soup (gluten free)

Serves 6

2 T olive oil
1 **onion**, diced
2 **celery** stalks, diced
½ c **leeks**, diced
2-4 **garlic** cloves, minced
6 c **sweet potatoes**, peeled, washed and diced
4 c 2% milk
1 tsp **thyme**
½ c brown sugar
1 tsp **cinnamon**
1 tsp maple syrup
*Garnish with **pecans** (optional)

Step 1: Sauté onion, celery, leeks, and garlic in olive oil.
Step 2: Add remaining ingredients.
Step 3: Simmer until potatoes are soft to touch.
Step 4: Blend in food processor or blender until smooth. Serve and enjoy!

Nutrients per serving:
Calories: 200
Carbohydrate: 36g
Protein: 5g
Total Fat: 4g
Saturated Fat: 1.5g
Omega-3 fatty acids: 0.03g
Dietary Fiber: 4g
Sodium: 115mg
Cholesterol: 5mg

Lentil Soup

Serves 8

2 tsp canola oil
2 c **onions**, diced
6 **garlic** cloves, minced
¾ c dried lentils
1 19 oz can garbanzo beans, rinsed and drained
4 c water
1 14 ½ oz can vegetable broth*
1 ½ T freshly grated **ginger**
2 tsp ground **cumin**
1 ½ tsp ground **coriander**
½ tsp dried crushed **red pepper** (more if desired)
½ tsp curry powder
1 c **tomatoes**, diced
½ c low fat sour cream

Step 1: In a large cooking pot add canola oil and place over medium heat until hot. Add onion and sauté 5 minutes or until tender. Add garlic and cook an additional 1-2 minutes.

Step 2: Add lentils, garbanzo beans, gingerroot, cumin, coriander, crushed red pepper, tomatoes, water and vegetable broth; stir well. Bring to a boil; cover, reduce heat to low, and simmer 25 to 35 minutes, until lentils are tender.

Step 3: Serve warm with 1 tablespoon sour cream on top.

*This food item either is not naturally gluten free or may contain gluten due to preparation and processing. Read food label to ensure that food product does not contain gluten.

Nutrients per serving:
Calories: 180
Carbohydrate: 31g
Protein: 10g
Total Fat: 3g
Saturated Fat: 0g
Omega-3 fatty acids: 0.01g
Dietary Fiber: 7g
Sodium: 65mg
Cholesterol: 0mg

White Bean Soup

Serves 6

1 ½ c **onions**, diced
4 **garlic** cloves, pressed
2 T olive oil
1 T ground **fennel seed**
1 tsp **thyme**
1 c **cabbage**, chopped into thin strips
4 **celery** stalks, sliced
1 **butternut squash**, peeled, seeded, and cubed
1 **red bell pepper**, diced
3 c low sodium vegetable stock*
1 15 oz can navy beans, rinsed and drained
Pinch of **saffron**, or more to taste
Ground **black pepper,** to taste

Step 1: In a soup pot or large cooking pot, sauté onions and garlic in olive oil until caramelized. Stir in the fennel and thyme.
Step 2: Add cabbage and celery, cover and cook about 5 minutes.
Step 3: Add squash and bell peppers. Pour in the stock and bring to a boil, and cook until the squash softens (about 5 minutes).
Step 4: Stir in beans and saffron. When the soup is hot, add pepper to taste.

*This food item either is not naturally gluten free or may contain gluten due to preparation and processing. Read food label to ensure that food product does not contain gluten.

Nutrients per serving:
Calories: 260
Carbohydrate: 38g
Protein: 9g
Total Fat: 8g
Saturated Fat: 1.5g
Omega-3 fatty acids: 0.12g
Dietary Fiber: 10g
Sodium: 350mg
Cholesterol: 5mg

Miso Soup

Serves 6

1 T sesame oil
1 sweet **onion**, diced
1 **celery** stalk, diced
3 **shallots**, chopped
1 medium **carrot**, diced
1 head of **cabbage**, diced
2 **garlic** cloves, minced
2 cooked chicken breasts, diced
¼ c canned bamboo shoots, sliced
1 T miso paste*
1 tsp light soy sauce*
1 tsp brown sugar
1 tsp hot sauce*
¼ c rice wine vinegar*
4 c water
1 tsp cornstarch, more if desired*
Salt and **black pepper**, to taste

Step 1: Sauté onion, celery, carrot, shallots, and garlic in sesame seed oil over medium heat until tender.
Step 2: Add remaining ingredients and bring to boil and simmer 20 minutes.
Step 3: Taste and season, as desired.

*This food item either is not naturally gluten free or may contain gluten due to preparation and processing. Read food label to ensure that food product does not contain gluten.

Nutrients per serving:
Calories: 70
Carbohydrate: 10g
Protein: 5g
Total Fat: 1.5g
Saturated Fat: 0g
Omega-3 fatty acids: 0.00g
Dietary Fiber: 2g
Sodium: 190mg
Cholesterol: 10mg

Traditional Southern Black Eyed Pea Soup (gluten free)

Serves 4-6

2 T canola oil
1 **onion**, diced
4 **celery** stalks, diced
2 **carrots**, diced
5-6 **shallots**, diced
3-4 **garlic** cloves, minced
1 12 oz can black eyed peas, rinsed and drained
½ c cooked ham, diced
2 c water (add more if desired)
¼ tsp **thyme**
¼ tsp **rosemary**
½ tsp **basil**
Black pepper, to taste

Step 1: Sauté onion, celery, carrots, shallots, and garlic in canola oil.
Step 2: Add black-eyed peas, ham, water and seasonings except black pepper.
Step 3: Cook on medium-low heat for ~20 minutes.
Step 4: Season with black pepper, to taste.

Nutrients per serving:
Calories: 150
Carbohydrate: 14g
Protein: 10g
Total Fat: 7g
Saturated Fat: 1g
Omega-3 fatty acids: 0.38g
Dietary Fiber: 3g
Sodium: 300mg
Cholesterol: 0mg

Chicken Dishes

Lean cuts of chicken are a great source of protein while limiting exposure to saturated fats and cholesterol.

Mushroom Stuffed Chicken Breast

Serves 4

4 6 oz chicken breasts halves

Mushroom Stuffing for Chicken Breasts
1 T olive oil
1 sweet **onion**, diced
1 **celery** stalk, diced
1 **carrot**, peeled and diced
1 **garlic** clove, minced
1 c **mushrooms,** finely diced
½ c breadcrumbs**
¼ c grated Parmesan cheese
1 tsp **chives**
1 tsp **parsley**
1 T sherry*
Salt and **black pepper**

Step 1: Pound chicken breasts with a meat mallet until evenly flattened. Set aside.
Step 2: Sauté vegetables in olive oil until tender. Add sherry and stir well.
Step 3: Add remaining ingredients, mix and remove from heat. Cool and fill chicken breasts with the mixture by placing vegetable mixture in the center of each flattened chicken breast. Roll up each chicken breast and secure with toothpicks (may take more than 1 or 2).
Step 4: Arrange chicken breasts on a lightly greased baking sheet and cover with foil.

Bake chicken at 400 degrees until internal temperature reaches 165 degrees (about 20 minutes).

*This food item either is not naturally gluten free or may contain gluten due to preparation and processing. Read food label to ensure that food product does not contain gluten.

**This food item contains gluten. You may substitute a gluten-free product for this item to make this a gluten-free recipe.

Nutrients per serving:
Calories: 180
Carbohydrate: 11g
Protein: 23g
Total Fat: 6g
Saturated Fat: 1g

Omega-3 fatty acids: 0.01g
Dietary Fiber: 1g
Sodium: 550mg
Cholesterol: 50mg

Chicken Parmesan

Serves 4

4 5 oz breaded chicken breasts**
12 oz cooked pasta**
4 oz Mozzarella cheese

Breading for Chicken
1 loaf French bread, sliced and toasted**
½ c grated Parmesan cheese
3 T **oregano**
3 T **basil**
1 T **black pepper**

Marinade for Chicken
2 T canola oil
1 T fresh **basil**, chopped
1 T **oregano,** chopped
4 **garlic** cloves, minced

Marinara Sauce
2 Vidalia **onions**, chopped and caramelized
1 16.5 oz can crushed **tomatoes**
1 12 oz can petite diced **tomatoes**
4 **garlic** cloves, minced

1 T dried **basil**
½ tsp **black pepper**
1 tsp sugar
½ tsp crushed **red pepper**

Step 1: Soak chicken breasts in marinade for at least 2 hours, covered in the refrigerator.

Step 2: Prepare breading for chicken by following recipe above.

Step 3: Dip marinated chicken in breading mix, coat well. Place chicken in a greased baking dish. Bake chicken at 375 degrees until internal temperature reaches 165 degrees (about 30 minutes).

Step 4: Prepare marinara sauce while the chicken is baking.

Step 5: Cook pasta. Serve with baked chicken, marinara and top with Mozzarella cheese.

**This food item contains gluten. You may substitute a gluten-free product for this item to make this a gluten-free recipe.

Nutrients per serving:
Calories: 910
Carbohydrate: 128g
Protein: 55g
Total Fat: 21g
Saturated Fat: 7g

Omega-3 fatty acids: 0.95g
Dietary Fiber: 13g
Sodium: 410mg
Cholesterol: 70mg

Chipotle Marinated Chicken with Fresh Salsa

Serves 4

4 4 oz chicken breasts
2 c cooked pasta**

Chipotle Marinade

¼ c chipotle peppers in adobe sauce
3 **garlic** cloves, minced
1 T **lime juice**
1 tsp **cumin**
1 tsp brown sugar
¼ c water

Step 1: Marinate chicken for 1 hour before baking at 375 degrees until internal temperature reaches 165 degrees (about 45 minutes).

Fresh Salsa

2 c **tomatillos**
1 c **Poblano peppers**
¼ c Vidalia **onions**
8 **garlic** cloves, minced
1 T **lime juice**
¼ c **cilantro**
¼ c **green onions**
½ tsp **black pepper**

Step 2: Combine and chill these ingredients. Serve over chicken with pasta.

**This food item contains gluten. You may substitute a gluten-free product for this item to make this a gluten-free recipe.

Nutrients per serving:

Calories: 450
Carbohydrate: 64g
Protein: 37g
Total Fat: 10g
Saturated Fat: 0.5g

Omega-3 fatty acids: 0.10g
Dietary Fiber: 18g
Sodium: 360mg
Cholesterol: 60mg

Chicken Marinade (gluten free)

Serves 6

6 – 4 oz chicken breast
2 T olive oil
¼ c fresh **parsley**
¼ c fresh **basil**
¼ c fresh **oregano**
3 **garlic** cloves, minced
1 small **onion**, chopped
2 T **black pepper**
2 T water

Step 1: In large greased baking pan, place chicken.
Step 2: In small bowl combine all remaining ingredients and stir well. Pour over chicken and cover with foil.
Step 2: Bake at 350 degrees until internal temperature reaches 165 degrees (about 45 minutes).

Nutrients per serving:
Calories: 250
Carbohydrate: 9g
Protein: 29g
Total Fat: 13g
Saturated Fat: 1g
Omega-3 fatty acids: 1.01g
Dietary Fiber: 4g
Sodium: 550mg
Cholesterol: 60mg

Chicken Marsala (gluten free)

Serves 4

4 chicken breasts, baked

Marsala Sauce
½ c marsala wine
2-4 **shallots**, chopped
1 c **mushrooms**, diced
½ tsp **thyme**
½ tsp **basil**
¼ c water
¼ tsp **black pepper**
1 **garlic** clove, minced
¼ canola oil

Step 1: Sauté shallots and garlic in canola oil over medium heat.

Step 2: Add mushrooms, water, wine, and basil; simmer until reduced by half.

Step 3: Remove from heat and add thyme and black pepper.

Step 4: Blend in food processor or blender until smooth; taste and season. Serve over baked chicken and garnish with sliced mushrooms.

Nutrients per serving:
Calories: 320
Carbohydrate: 15g
Protein: 22g
Total Fat: 17g
Saturated Fat: 1g
Omega-3 fatty acids: 1.36g
Dietary Fiber: 1g
Sodium: 710mg
Cholesterol: 45mg

Sweet Chili Chicken Breast

Serves 4

4 5 oz marinated chicken breasts

Sweet Chili Marinade Sauce

¼ c sweet chili sauce (your favorite brand)*
1 T light soy sauce*
1 T fresh **cilantro**
½ tsp sugar
½ tsp **sesame** oil
1 T **green onions**, diced
1 **garlic** clove, minced

Step 1: Make Sweet Chili Marinade Sauce and set aside.

Step 2: Place chicken breasts on sprayed cooking pan. Cover with marinade and place in refrigerator for at least 1 hour.

Step 3: Preheat oven at 400 degrees.

Step 4: Bake chicken breasts until internal temperature reaches 165 degrees (about 18 minutes).

Step 5: Serve with your favorite side dishes.

*This food item either is not naturally gluten free or may contain gluten due to preparation and processing. Read food label to ensure that food product does not contain gluten.

Nutrients per serving:

Calories: 190
Carbohydrate: 6g
Protein: 34g
Total Fat: 3.5g
Saturated Fat: 0g
Omega-3 fatty acids: 0.00g
Dietary Fiber: 0g
Sodium: 780mg
Cholesterol: 75mg

Coriander Chicken

Serves 4

4 chicken breasts

Coriander Marinade
2 T **sesame seed** oil
½ c brown sugar
2 **garlic** cloves, minced
1 T vinegar*
1 T **turmeric**
2 T **coriander**

Step 1: In small pan combine sesame seed oil and brown sugar, stir until caramelized.
Step 2: Add garlic, vinegar, and turmeric and season if needed.
Step 3: Add coriander last and remove from heat. Brush Coriander Marinade over chicken breasts and bake at 350 degrees covered until internal temperature reaches 165 degrees.

*This food item either is not naturally gluten free or may contain gluten due to preparation and processing. Read food label to ensure that food product does not contain gluten.

Nutrients per serving:
Calories: 310
Carbohydrate: 10g
Protein: 29g
Total Fat: 20g
Saturated Fat: 7g
Omega-3 fatty acids: 0.06g
Dietary Fiber: 0g
Sodium: 85mg
Cholesterol: 105mg

Grilled Chicken Teriyaki Wrap

Serves 4

4 4 oz chicken breasts, grilled and sliced
4 flour tortillas**
1 c low fat cheddar cheese, grated
1 Roma **tomatoes**, sliced
1 head of lettuce
1 red **onion**, diced
4 oz low sodium teriyaki sauce*
4 oz mung bean sprouts
1 T pickled **ginger**

Step 1: In medium size bowl, combine tomatoes, onion teriyaki sauce, mung bean sprouts and ginger. Stir well.
Step 2: In warm skillet, place 1 flour tortilla and add the grilled chicken, cheese, and the vegetable mixture.
Step 3: Fold tortilla in half and lightly brown on both sides. Serve and enjoy.

This dish can also be served cold.

*This food item either is not naturally gluten free or may contain gluten due to preparation and processing. Read food label to ensure that food product does not contain gluten.

**This food item contains gluten. You may substitute a gluten-free product for this item to make this a gluten-free recipe.

Nutrients per serving:
Calories: 310
Carbohydrate: 51g
Protein: 15g
Total Fat: 6g
Saturated Fat: 1.5g
Omega-3 fatty acids: 0.05g
Dietary Fiber: 4g
Sodium: 700mg
Cholesterol: 15mg

Chicken and Vegetables (gluten free)

Serves 6

1 lb boneless chicken breasts, cut into 1 inch pieces
1 small **onion**, chopped
1 c fresh **mushrooms**, sliced
2 medium new **potatoes**, peeled and diced into ½ inch cubes
1 (16-oz) package frozen, **mixed vegetables**
1 ½ c water
1 T fresh **lemon juice**
1 tsp ground **black pepper**
¼ tsp ground **mustard**
¼ crushed **sage**
⅛ tsp **garlic** powder
⅛ tsp **turmeric**
⅓ c nonfat dry milk powder
Fresh **parsley**

Step 1: Rinse chicken and pat dry with paper towels.
Step 2: Combine chicken, mixed vegetables, onion, mushrooms, and potatoes in a 3 ½ quart slow cooker.
Step 3: In medium sized bowl combine water, lemon juice, white pepper, mustard, sage, garlic powder, and turmeric.
Step 4: Add to chicken and vegetables, mix well. Cover and cook on LOW 6 to 7 hours.

Nutrients per serving:
Calories: 200
Carbohydrate: 26g
Protein: 21g
Total Fat: 1g
Saturated Fat: 0g
Omega-3 fatty acids: 0.03g
Dietary Fiber: 4g
Sodium: 105mg
Cholesterol: 45mg

Baked Chicken with Herbs (gluten free)

Serves 4

4 - 4 oz boneless chicken breasts

Herb Rub
½ T **parsley**
½ T **chives**
½ T dry **basil**
½ T **oregano**
1 ½ tsp dry **mustard**
1 T granulated **garlic**
1 T **white pepper**
1 T **dill**
½ c olive oil

Step 1: Combine all ingredients.
Step 2: Toss chicken in herb mix.
Step 3: Place chicken on a greased baking pan and cover chicken. Bake at 350 degrees until internal temperature reaches 165 degrees (about 45 minutes).

Nutrients per serving:
Calories: 390
Carbohydrate: 5g
Protein: 28g
Total Fat: 31g
Saturated Fat: 4g
Omega-3 fatty acids: 0.03g
Dietary Fiber: 1g
Sodium: 590mg
Cholesterol: 60mg

Egg Dishes

Eggs are the gold standard for protein. They contain all of the essential and non-essential amino acids in the right combinations to promote growth and development. Due to the protein content of eggs and the vitamin and mineral composition available present in eggs, eggs are a great choice for dietary protein. It is possible to consume an egg a day and be within the recommended cholesterol guidelines. Recommendations for egg consumption have a varied history because they are high in cholesterol. When the initial epidemiological studies found a high correlation with the amount of cholesterol in a person's blood and the risk of a heart attack, many health care specialists recommended eliminating cholesterol from the diet. Egg consumption plummeted. As our knowledge evolved and further research studies were conducted, scientists realized that the internal production and regulation of cholesterol are very complex and not a direct reflection of dietary cholesterol, so recommendations were changed. Eggs are a very versatile food. Eating an average of one egg each day is now considered harmless. When selecting eggs, try to purchase the functional omega-3 (n-3) eggs from your local grocery store as these will provide you and your family the nutritional benefits of regular eggs and add heart healthy omega-3 fatty acids.

Frittata (gluten free)

Serves 4

2 Roma **tomatoes**, diced
1 T olive oil
1 sweet **onion**, finely chopped
½ tsp **thyme**
6 **omega-3 eggs**
¼ c 2% milk
½ c shaved Parmesan cheese
Black pepper, to taste

Step 1: Sauté onion over medium heat until almost caramelized. Add tomatoes and thyme.

Step 2: In medium size bowl beat eggs lightly with a fork. Stir in Parmesan cheese and 2% milk.

Step 3: Add egg and cheese mixture to pan with the tomatoes and onions. Stir into the tomatoes and onions and then stop stirring. Cook for about 5 minutes. The frittata should be puffed and golden brown on the bottom.

Step 4: Turn out onto a large plate and then slide the frittata back into the pan and continue cooking until golden brown on the second side. Remove from heat and slice into wedges to serve.

Omega-3 fatty acid content will vary depending on the brand of egg you select.

Nutrients per serving:

Calories: 200
Carbohydrate: 6g
Protein: 14g
Total Fat: 0g
Saturated Fat: 4.5g
Omega-3 fatty acids: 0.03g
Dietary Fiber: 1g
Sodium: 260mg
Cholesterol: 355mg

Feta Frittata (gluten free)

Serves 4

1 T olive oil
8 **omega-3 eggs**, beaten
1 c low fat Feta cheese, crumbled
½ c **mushrooms**, diced
Black pepper, to taste

Step 1: Season eggs and add Feta and mushrooms. Cook over a moderate heat for 5 minutes or until eggs are lightly golden.

Step 2: Place the pan under the broiler and cook the top for 3 minutes until lightly golden. Serve and enjoy.

The amount of omega-3 fatty acids will vary depending on the brand of eggs you purchase. Adjust the nutritional information according to the amount of omega-3 fatty acids listed on the box of eggs selected.

Nutrients per serving:

Calories: 270
Carbohydrate: 4g
Protein: 24g
Total Fat: 19g
Saturated Fat: 7g
Omega-3 fatty acids: 0.3g
Dietary Fiber: 0g
Sodium: 670mg
Cholesterol: 380mg

Omega-3 Omelet (gluten free)

Serves 4

1 T olive oil
1 sweet **onion**, diced
1 **red bell pepper**, diced
½ c cannellini beans, rinsed and drained
½ c Feta cheese
6 **omega-3 eggs** (your favorite brand)
Pinch of salt and **black pepper**, to taste

Step 1: Sauté onion and pepper in olive oil.
Step 2: Add beans, mixing well and cook for 5 minutes on medium-low heat.
Step 3: In medium sized bowl, beat eggs and add in Feta cheese.
Step 4: Stir egg mixture with a flat wooden spoon and allow to firm over low heat.
Step 5: Slice omelet into pie shape sections and serve.

Omega-3 fatty acid content will vary depending on the brand of egg you select.

Nutrients per serving:
Calories: 240
Carbohydrate: 11g
Protein: 16g
Total Fat: 15g
Saturated Fat: 6g
Omega-3 fatty acids: 0.01g
Dietary Fiber: 2g
Sodium: 520mg
Cholesterol: 330mg

Salmon Quiche

6 servings

1 c whole wheat flour**
⅔ c Cheddar cheese
¼ t salt
¼ t paprika
6 T canola oil
8 oz cooked salmon
3 omega-3 eggs
1 c low fat sour cream
2 T low fat mayonnaise
½ c cheddar cheese
1 T onion, diced
¼ t dill
Tabasco sauce, to taste*

Step 1: For the crust, combine flour, ⅔ c cheddar cheese, salt and paprika. Stir in oil and set aside ½ c of crust mixture for the top. Press the remaining crust into the bottom and sides of a 9 inch pie pan. Bake at 400 degrees for 10 minutes. Remove from oven and let cool. Reduce oven temperature to 325 degrees.

Step 2: To create the quiche filling, in a medium size mixing bowl combine salmon, ½ c water, eggs, sour cream, low fat mayonnaise, ½ c Cheddar cheese, onion, dill and Tabasco sauce. Stir well and then spoon into baked crust. Sprinkle the remaining pie crust over the top of the quiche. Bake at 325 degrees for 45 minutes.

*This food item either is not naturally gluten free or may contain gluten due to preparation and processing. Read food label to ensure that food product does not contain gluten.

**This food item contains gluten. You may substitute a gluten-free product for this item to make this a gluten-free recipe.

Nutrients per serving:

Calories: 460
Carbohydrate: 19g
Protein: 23g
Total Fat: 33g
Saturated Fat: 10g

Omega-3 fatty acids: 1.03g
Dietary Fiber: 2.5g
Sodium: 385mg
Cholesterol: 154mg

Impossible Quiche (gluten free)

Serves 6

1 c Swiss cheese
2 c skim milk
½ c onion
½ c Bisquick
4 omega-3 eggs
¼ t salt
⅛ t black pepper

Step 1: Preheat oven to 350 degrees. Grease a 9 inch pie pan with cooking spray. Sprinkle pan with the cheese and onion. Place the remaining ingredients into the blender and mix on high for 1 minute. Add mixture to the pie pan. Bake until golden brown, about 50 minutes. Allow to cool for 5 minutes before cutting.

Nutrients per serving:
Calories: 270
Carbohydrate: 13g
Protein: 17g
Total Fat: 16g
Saturated Fat: 9g
Omega-3 fatty acids: 0.10g
Dietary Fiber: 0.4g
Sodium: 447mg
Cholesterol: 155mg

Quick Crabby Eggs Benedict

Serves 4

10 oz baby mustard greens
2 T olive oil
4 lightly toasted high fiber English muffins**
8 omega-3 eggs
1 c of cooked crab meat
1 package of McCormick's Hollandaise sauce*

Step 1: Poach the eggs.

Step 2: Lightly toast the English muffins.

Step 3: Sautee the mustard greens in olive oil over medium heat until wilted. Prepare the Hollandaise sauce according to package directions, substituting Smart Balance® spread for the butter.

Step 4: Layer the mustard greens over each English muffin, place 2 T of cooked crab meat over the greens and then add the poached egg. Top with Hollandaise sauce and garnish with capers or fresh dill if desired.

Note: Fresh baby arugala or sautéed spinach can be substituted for the mustard greens.

*This food item either is not naturally gluten free or may contain gluten due to preparation and processing. Read food label to ensure that food product does not contain gluten.

**This food item contains gluten. You may substitute a gluten-free product for this item to make this a gluten-free recipe.

Nutrients per serving:
Calories: 620
Carbohydrate: 37g
Protein: 34g
Total Fat: 37g
Saturated Fat: 7g
Omega-3 fatty acids: 0.30g
Dietary Fiber: 2g
Sodium: 720mg
Cholesterol: 420mg

Turmeric Deviled Eggs (gluten free)

Makes 12 deviled egg halves (serving size 1 egg half)

6 omega-3 eggs
3 tsp turmeric
4 T olive oil
2 garlic cloves, minced

Step 1: Hard boil the eggs. Shell the eggs and cut into halves along the long axis, remove the yolks and set them aside.

Step 2: Lightly sauté the garlic over low heat, until the garlic is translucent.

Step 3: Blend the yolks, turmeric, and garlic. Fill the cavities in the egg white halves with the mixture.

Nutrients per serving:

Calories: 78
Carbohydrate: 1g
Protein: 3g
Total Fat: 7g
Saturated Fat: 1g
Omega-3 fatty acids: 0.08g
Dietary Fiber: 0.13g
Sodium: 33mg
Cholesterol: 90mg

Meats

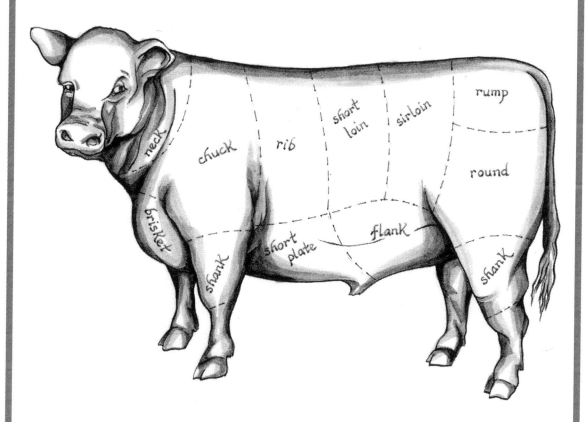

The Inflammation Cure Food Choices recommends limiting consumption of red meats. Hence, recipes for meat dishes are limited and spiked with vegetables and fruits that deliver an antioxidant punch. A glass of red wine paired with a meat dish might be regarded as an antidote to the toxic effects of red meats.

Mushrooms and Pepper Steak

Serves 4

½ lb sirloin steak, cut into 1" cubes
1 **green bell pepper**, diced
1 yellow **onion**, diced
2 **garlic** cloves, minced
2 T olive oil
1 T flour**
Salt and **black pepper**, to taste
1 c **mushrooms**, sliced
½ c beef broth*
2 c egg noodles, cooked**

Step 1: Sauté onions, mushrooms, and pepper in olive oil.
Step 2: Add steak cubes (cook until internal temperature reaches 145 degrees).
Step 3: Add flour to make a roux.
Step 4: Add salt and pepper, to taste.
Step 5: Add beef broth and bring to a boil.
Step 6: Reduce heat and simmer until thickened (add corn starch if needed).
Step 7: Serve over egg noodles.

*This food item either is not naturally gluten free or may contain gluten due to preparation and processing. Read food label to ensure that food product does not contain gluten.

**This food item contains gluten. You may substitute a gluten-free product for this item to make this a gluten-free recipe.

Nutrients per serving:
Calories: 730
Carbohydrate: 76g
Protein: 37g
Total Fat: 32g
Saturated Fat: 7g
Omega-3 fatty acids: 0.01g
Dietary Fiber: 9g
Sodium: 980mg
Cholesterol: 35mg

Country Vegetable Soup with Grilled Beef

Serves 6

1 T canola oil
1 sweet **onion**, diced
2 **celery** stalks, diced
2 **carrots**, diced
3 **garlic** cloves, minced
1 T flour**
½ c **yellow squash**, diced
½ c **corn**
½ c **cabbage**, shredded
1 medium can diced **tomatoes**
1 medium can **tomatoes**, crushed
8 oz grilled beef, cut into small ½ inch cubes, set aside
2 c water
1 tsp **thyme**
1 tsp **basil**
1 tsp **rosemary**
1 tsp **oregano**
1 T **black pepper**

Step 1: Sauté beef, onion, carrots, celery, and garlic in canola oil.
Step 2: Add flour to make roux.
Step 3: Add remaining ingredients and bring to a boil. Simmer for 15 minutes.
Step 4: Taste and season as desired.

**This food item contains gluten. You may substitute a gluten-free product for this item to make this a gluten-free recipe.

Nutrients per serving:
Calories: 70
Carbohydrate: 13g
Protein: 2g
Total Fat: 2g
Saturated Fat: 0g
Omega-3 fatty acids: 0.18g
Dietary Fiber: 4g
Sodium: 190mg
Cholesterol: 0mg

Rib-Eye with Mango Salsa

Serves 4

4 6 oz Rib-Eye Steaks, cut 1 inch thick

Mango Salsa
1 c **mango**, diced
¼ c red **onion**, diced
1 **red bell pepper**
1 **yellow bell pepper**
1 jalapeno pepper, finely diced
2 T fresh **cilantro**, chopped
¼ c **green onion**, chopped
½ tsp salt
½ tsp **white pepper**
½ tsp brown sugar
¼ tsp rice wine vinegar*

Step 1: Prepare Mango Salsa and set aside.
Step 2: Preheat grill for medium-high heat, and lightly oil the grate.
Step 3: Lightly coat both sides of the Rib-Eye with olive oil and cook Rib-Eye on the grill for 7 minutes, then turn over and cook second side for 7 minutes. Continue cooking 7 minutes more for medium-well, or longer if desired (internal temperature must reach 145 degrees).

*This food item either is not naturally gluten free or may contain gluten due to preparation and processing. Read food label to ensure that food product does not contain gluten.

Nutrients per serving:
Calories: 250
Carbohydrate: 9g
Protein: 24g
Total Fat: 13g
Saturated Fat: 5g
Omega-3 fatty acids: 0.10g
Dietary Fiber: 1g
Sodium: 250mg
Cholesterol: 95mg

Pepper Steak

Serves 6

1 (1 ¼ lb) beef flank steak
1 **yellow bell pepper**
1 **red bell pepper**
½ tsp red pepper flakes
3 **green onions**, chopped
2 T low-sodium soy sauce*
3 Roma **tomatoes**, chopped

Step 1: Trim visible fat from steak. Place steak in a 3 ½ - quart slow cooker. Cut peppers into strips. Arrange bell peppers on steak.

Step 2: Top with red pepper flakes, green onions, soy sauce, and tomatoes.

Step 3: Cover and cook on LOW 6 hours or until steak is tender (internal temperature must reach 145 degrees). Serve and enjoy!

*This food item either is not naturally gluten free or may contain gluten due to preparation and processing. Read food label to ensure that food product does not contain gluten.

Nutrients per serving:

Calories: 170
Carbohydrate: 5g
Protein: 22g
Total Fat: 6g
Saturated Fat: 2.5g
Omega-3 fatty acids: 0.06g
Dietary Fiber: 1g
Sodium: 190mg
Cholesterol: 40mg

Spicy Meat Loaf

Serves 6

1 lb lean ground beef
¼ lb pork sausage
1 **omega-3 egg**, lightly beaten
¾ c **onion**, diced
½ c fine dry bread crumbs**
2 T hot sauce*
⅛ tsp ground **black pepper**
1 tsp **basil**
1 large **zucchini**, shredded

Step 1: In a large bowl combine beef, sausage, Omega-3 egg, onion, bread crumbs, hot sauce, pepper, basil, and zucchini.

Step 2: Shape into a 5 ½- inch flattened round loaf. Place loaf on a trivet in a 3 ½-quart slow cooker. Cover and cook on LOW about 4 hours or until done.

Step 3: Remove and cut into 6 slices.

*This food item either is not naturally gluten free or may contain gluten due to preparation and processing. Read food label to ensure that food product does not contain gluten.

**This food item contains gluten. You may substitute a gluten-free product for this item to make this a gluten-free recipe.

Nutrients per serving:

Calories: 220
Carbohydrate: 12g
Protein: 21g
Total Fat: 9g
Saturated Fat: 3g
Omega-3 fatty acids: 0.05g
Dietary Fiber: 2g
Sodium: 270mg
Cholesterol: 90mg

Fish and Seafood

Fish are a healthy source of protein and are high in omega 3 fatty acids. Persons with multiple food intolerances find that different species of fish are well-tolerated. Mercury in fish is a concern, but the species in these recipes are low in mercury. No more than two servings a week are recommended for pregnant women, nursing mothers, and small children, while avoiding those species that are high in mercury. Others may choose to eat four servings a week. Many of these recipes combine fish with vegetables to provide the added benefits of phytochemicals.

Grilled Red Snapper with Pineapple Salsa

Serves 4

4 4 oz servings of Red Snapper fillets
3 c rice pilaf, cooked

Pineapple Salsa
2 c **pineapple**, diced
¼ c sweet **onions**, diced
¼ c **red bell peppers,** diced
¼ c **green bell peppers**, diced
1 **garlic** clove, minced
1 T **hot peppers**, minced
1 T honey
½ T rice wine vinegar*
1 tsp **black pepper**
¼ c **cilantro**, chopped

Step 1: Make the Pineapple Salsa and place in the refrigerator until ready to serve.
Step 2: Grill fish and set aside, be sure that internal temperature reaches 145 degrees.

*This food item either is not naturally gluten free or may contain gluten due to preparation and processing. Read food label to ensure that food product does not contain gluten.

Vegetable Rice Pilaf (gluten free)

1 Vidalia **onion**, diced
2 **celery** stalks, diced
1 **carrot**, diced
1 T canola oil
1 c fresh **tomatoes**, diced
6 oz **tomato juice**
¼ c white rice
1 tsp **white pepper**

Step 3: Sauté vegetables in canola oil. Add rice and toast.
Step 4: Add remaining ingredients and cover with water.
Step 5: Simmer until rice is done. Season as desired.

Nutrients per serving:

Calories: 620
Carbohydrate: 110g
Protein: 32g
Total Fat: 11g
Saturated Fat: 1.5g
Omega-3 fatty acids: 2.32g
Dietary Fiber: 7g
Sodium: 730mg
Cholesterol: 60mg

Grilled Salmon with Carbonara Sauce

Serves 4

4 4 oz Salmon fillet, grilled
1 package Spinach fettuccine, cooked**
Carbonara sauce

Carbonara Sauce (gluten free)

2 T canola oil
4 oz bacon, cooked
4 **omega-3 egg** yolks
4 large **omega-3 eggs**
1 T milk
½ c Parmesan cheese
black pepper, to taste

Step 1: Grill Salmon, cook until internal temperature reaches 145 degrees and set aside.

Step 2: Cook Spinach fettuccine, rinse and drain.

Step 3: In medium sauce pan make Carbonara Sauce by heating canola oil and cook the bacon for 3-4 minutes until crisp. In small bowl mix together eggs, egg yolk, milk and Parmesan cheese. Add mixture to sauce pan with the bacon and reduce heat. Stir as it cooks until eggs are thoroughly cooked but not scrambled.

Step 4: Place pasta on a serving platter, top with Salmon and cover with Carbonara Sauce. Serve and enjoy!

**This food item contains gluten. You may substitute a gluten-free product for this item to make this a gluten-free recipe.

Nutrients per serving:

Calories: 740
Carbohydrate: 62g
Protein: 67g
Total Fat: 25g
Saturated Fat: 12g
Omega-3 fatty acids: 0.75g
Dietary Fiber: 4g
Sodium: 920mg
Cholesterol: 540mg

Salmon with Ginger and Brown Rice

Serves 4

2 Salmon steaks, with skins removed
2 T low sodium soy sauce*
½ T **sage**
1 ½ tsp sugar
½ tsp **Thai peppers**
1 tsp canola oil
1 T **ginger**, minced
2 tsp **garlic**, minced
2 tsp sesame oil
2 **green onions**, sliced thin, diagonally
1 T canola oil
2 c brown rice, cooked

Step 1: Make sauce in small bowl. Mix soy sauce and next 4 ingredients. Sauté ginger and garlic in canola oil; stir well. Pour half of sauce over salmon.

Step 2: Grill fish until an internal temperature of 145 degrees is reached. Transfer salmon to a serving plate and cover with sauce. Sprinkle with onions and serve with brown rice.

*This food item either is not naturally gluten free or may contain gluten due to preparation and processing. Read food label to ensure that food product does not contain gluten.

Nutrients per serving:
Calories: 540
Carbohydrate: 75g
Protein: 25g
Total Fat: 15g
Saturated Fat: 2g
Omega-3 fatty acids: 1.94g
Dietary Fiber: 4g
Sodium: 240mg
Cholesterol: 80mg

Salmon Supreme and Penne Pasta

Serves 4

1 c penne pasta, cooked and drained**
2 T canola oil
½ c **mushrooms,** washed and sliced
15 ½ oz can Salmon, drained and flaked
⅓ c Parmesan cheese, shredded
½ tsp **nutmeg**
1 c light sour cream
Paprika, to taste

Step 1: Cook pasta and set aside.
Step 2: In medium size pan, add canola oil, mushrooms, Salmon, Parmesan cheese, and nutmeg. Cook over low heat until hot. Sprinkle with paprika and serve.

**This food item contains gluten. You may substitute a gluten-free product for this item to make this a gluten-free recipe.

Nutrients per serving:
Calories: 690
Carbohydrate: 85g
Protein: 48g
Total Fat: 17g
Saturated Fat: 3.5g
Omega-3 fatty acids: 2.01g
Dietary Fiber: 4g
Sodium: 580mg
Cholesterol: 80mg

White Fish Bake

Serves 6

½ c low-fat sour cream
4 T grated Parmesan Cheese
3 T Italian bread crumbs**
1 lb white fish
½ c **mushrooms**, diced
1 T canola oil
½ tsp **black pepper**
Pinch **parsley** and **paprika**, to taste

Step 1: Mix together sour cream, Parmesan and bread crumbs; set aside.

Step 2: Rinse fish and pat dry. Arrange fish in 9x13 greased pan. Sauté mushrooms and onion in canola oil until lightly brown. Spoon mixture over fish and sprinkle with pepper. Spoon sour cream and cheese on top. Cook uncovered at 350 degrees until internal temperature reaches 145 degrees (about 35 minutes). Sprinkle with parsley and paprika before serving.

Serve with your favorite salad or light pasta and vegetable dish.

**This food item contains gluten. You may substitute a gluten-free product for this item to make this a gluten-free recipe.

Nutrients per serving:
Calories: 180
Carbohydrate: 4g
Protein: 17g
Total Fat: 11g
Saturated Fat: 3.5g
Omega-3 fatty acids: 0.23g
Dietary Fiber: 0g
Sodium: 160mg
Cholesterol: 50mg

Fish Made Easy

Serves 4

1 c Italian bread crumbs**
2 T chopped mixed fresh **tarragon** and **dill**
Zest of 1 **lemon**
4 white fish fillets, skinned
2 T all-purpose flour**
2 T canola oil
1 **omega-3 egg**, beaten
Black pepper, to taste
Lemon wedges to serve

Step 1: Blend the bread crumbs, herbs and lemon zest in food processor until fine.
Step 2: Prepare each fillet as follows: sprinkle with salt and pepper, then coat with flour and shake off excess. Dip each piece of fish in the beaten egg, then coat with bread crumb mixture.
Step 3: Heat oil in a large nonstick skillet. Add fish and cook over medium heat for 3 minutes on each side until an internal temperature of 145 degrees is reached (fish should appear golden brown and crisp). Serve with lemon wedges for squeezing.

**This food item contains gluten. You may substitute a gluten-free product for this item to make this a gluten-free recipe.

Nutrients per serving:
Calories: 460
Protein: 43g
Carbohydrate: 22g
Dietary Fiber: 1g
Saturated Fat: 2.5g
Total Fat: 21g
Sodium: 890mg
Omega 3 fatty acids: 13.97g
Cholesterol: 175mg

Garlic Shrimp (gluten free)

Serves 4

16-20 raw jumbo shrimp, peeled and deveined
5 T canola oil
3 **garlic** cloves, minced
Black pepper, to taste
8 oz can crushed **tomatoes**
Juice of ½ **lemon**
1 tsp superfine sugar
3 T fresh **parsley,** coarsely chopped
Zest of 1 **lemon**

Step 1: Place shrimp in large bowl with canola oil, garlic, salt and pepper. Toss well to mix.
Step 2: Heat a large nonstick sauté pan over high heat for 2 minutes. Add the shrimp with the oil and garlic and stir for 2 minutes, or until pink.
Step 3: Reduce heat to medium and add crushed tomatoes, lemon juice, and sugar. Cook and stir for 3-4 minutes.
Step 4: Check seasoning then top with parsley and lemon zest.

Nutrients per serving:
Calories: 220
Protein: 8g
Carbohydrate: 7g
Dietary Fiber: 1g
Total Fat: 18g
Saturated Fat: 1.5g
Sodium: 130mg
Cholesterol: 55mg
Omega 3 fatty acids: 1.78g

Scallops and Shrimp (gluten free)

Serves 6

1 T canola oil
2 large **carrots**, washed, peeled, and sliced
¾ lb large shrimp, peeled and deveined
½ lb scallops
1 medium Vidalia **onion**, diced
1 c light **coconut milk***
1 tsp sugar
Fresh **cilantro**
*May substitute evaporated skim milk for the coconut milk to reduce total fat and saturated fat.

Spices
3 garlic cloves, peeled
1 inch piece of fresh ginger, peeled
2 tsp mild curry powder
2 Tbsp canola oil

Step 1: Spices: Place ingredients in food processor and blend until smooth.
Step 2: In wok heat oil over high heat until very hot (~2 minutes). Reduce heat to medium, add carrots, and stir fry for 1 minute.
Step 3: Add spice mix and stir-fry for 2 minutes.
Step 4: Add shrimp, scallops, and scallions. Stir-fry over high heat for about 3 minutes, until shrimp are pink.
Step 5: Add coconut milk and sugar. Stir and heat until bubbling. Garnish with cilantro.

Nutrients per serving:
Calories: 260
Carbohydrate: 9g
Protein: 19g
Total Fat: 17g
Saturated Fat: 8g
Omega-3 fatty acids: 1.00g
Dietary Fiber: 2g
Sodium: 170mg
Cholesterol: 100mg

Grilled Seafood Kebabs

Serves 8

½ lb white fish fillet
½ lb Salmon fillet, skinned
8 jumbo shrimp, peeled and deveined
1 **zucchini**, washed and cut into thick slices
1 **yellow squash**, washed and cut into thick slices
16 cherry **tomatoes**

Seafood Kebab Marinade

6 T canola oil
1 T balsamic vinegar*
3 T fresh **tarragon,** chopped
3 **garlic** cloves, minced
Pinch of salt and **black pepper**, to taste

Step 1: To make the Seafood Kebab Marinade place all ingredients in a large bowl and mix well.
Step 2: Cut white fish and Salmon into equal-size pieces. Place fish and shrimp in the marinade and mix. Cover and refrigerate for 2 hours.
Step 3: Remove fish and shrimp from the marinade. Thread 2 pieces of each type of fish, 1 shrimp, 4 pieces of zucchini and squash and 2 tomatoes onto each skewers.
Step 4: Grill fish until it is opaque in the center. Serve on skewers on a large platter.

*This food item either is not naturally gluten free or may contain gluten due to preparation and processing. Read food label to ensure that food product does not contain gluten.

Nutrients per serving:

Calories: 210
Carbohydrate: 4g
Protein: 14g
Total Fat: 15g
Saturated Fat: 2g
Omega-3 fatty acids: 2.01g
Dietary Fiber: 1g
Sodium: 45mg
Cholesterol: 40mg

Easy Baked Fish

Serves 6

½ c bread crumbs**
½ tsp salt
⅛ tsp **garlic** powder
⅛ tsp **paprika**
Black pepper, to taste
1 lb favorite fish fillets
2 T skim milk

Step 1: Combine bread crumbs, salt, garlic powder, paprika and pepper.
Step 2: Dip fish in milk and roll in bread crumb mixture.
Step 3: Preheat oven to 350 degrees. Place fish in nonstick baking pan and bake uncovered at 350 degrees until internal temperature reaches 145 degrees (about 25 minutes).

**This food item contains gluten. You may substitute a gluten-free product for this item to make this a gluten-free recipe.

Nutrients per serving:
Calories: 140
Carbohydrate: 7g
Protein: 16g
Total Fat: 5g
Saturated Fat: 0.5g
Omega-3 fatty acids: 1.09g
Dietary Fiber: 0g
Sodium: 310mg
Cholesterol: 45mg

Cajun Style Shrimp

Serves 6

36 large raw shrimp, peeled and deveined
12 10 inch skewers

Cajun Style Marinade

¼ c canola oil
¼ c dry red wine
¼ c low-sodium soy sauce*
¼ c fresh **lemon juice**
2 **garlic** cloves, minced
½ tsp **cayenne pepper**
1 T **parsley**
2 T low-sodium Worcestershire sauce*
2 T red wine vinegar*
1 T dry **mustard**
½ T **paprika**
¼ tsp ground **red pepper**

Step 1: Put marinade ingredients in large bowl and mix well. Add shrimp and marinate at least 10 minutes, but no longer than 30 minutes. Drain marinade into a medium-size saucepan. Bring to a boil, reduce heat and simmer. Thread 6 shrimp on 1 or 2 skewers.
Step 2: Grill until shrimp are pink and just barely opaque in the center.
Step 3: Serve with hot Cajun Style Marinade as dipping sauce.

*This food item either is not naturally gluten free or may contain gluten due to preparation and processing. Read food label to ensure that food product does not contain gluten.

Nutrients per serving:

Calories: 150
Carbohydrate: 3g
Protein: 9g
Total Fat: 10g
Saturated Fat: 1g
Omega-3 fatty acids: 1.07g
Dietary Fiber: 0g
Sodium: 330mg
Cholesterol: 65mg

Baked Spinach with Tuna

Serves 4

1 10 oz package frozen **spinach**, thawed
2 T chopped **onion**
1 6 oz can low sodium tuna, drained and rinsed
3 hard boiled **omega-3 eggs**, sliced
1 can cream of **mushroom** soup
½ c low fat sour cream
¼ c butter
1 c bread crumbs**

Step 1: Spread spinach in a 9x13 pan. Sprinkle with onion, tuna, and sliced omega-3 eggs.
Step 2: Combine the soup with the sour cream. Pour over omega-3 eggs.
Step 3: Mix melted butter and bread crumbs and pour over top. Bake until hot, about 30-35 minutes at 350 degrees.

**This food item contains gluten. You may substitute a gluten-free product for this item to make this a gluten-free recipe.

Nutrients per serving:
Calories: 330
Carbohydrate: 23g
Protein: 22g
Total Fat: 17g
Saturated Fat: 9g
Omega-3 fatty acids: 0.26g
Dietary Fiber: 3g
Sodium: 330mg
Cholesterol: 205mg

Salmon and Yogurt Sauce

Serves 4

10 oz package frozen chopped **spinach**, cooked and drained
6 oz can Salmon, drained and flaked
3 hard boiled **omega-3 eggs**
¼ c sliced ripe or stuffed **olives**
1 T chopped **parsley**
1 tsp **dill**

Yogurt Sauce

½ c low-fat mayonnaise
1 c plain Greek yogurt
1 T Dijon **mustard***

Step 1: Make yogurt sauce, stir well and set aside.
Step 2: In a large bowl, combine spinach, Salmon, omega-3 eggs, olives, parsley and dill; spread into baking dish.
Step 3: Bake at 350 degrees for 20 minutes. Serve with yogurt sauce.

*This food item either is not naturally gluten free or may contain gluten due to preparation and processing. Read food label to ensure that food product does not contain gluten.

Nutrients per serving:

Calories: 240
Carbohydrate: 8g
Protein: 18g
Total Fat: 16g
Saturated Fat: 3g
Omega-3 fatty acids: 0.06g
Dietary Fiber: 2g
Sodium: 670mg
Cholesterol: 200mg

Grilled Salmon with Roasted Peppers (gluten free)

Serves 4

4 4 oz Salmon fillets, grilled

Roasted Red Pepper Sauce
2 **red bell peppers**, roasted on grill, skin and seeds removed
2 red **onions**, 1 inch slices grilled
6-8 **garlic** cloves
6 oz can **tomato juice**
2 T **black pepper**
3 T sugar

Step 1: To make the Roasted Red Peppers, combine all ingredients and then blend until smooth.
Step 2: Grill Salmon until internal temperature reaches 145 degrees.
Step 3: Serve the Roasted Red Pepper Sauce over the grilled Salmon.

Nutrients per serving:
Calories: 230
Carbohydrate: 17g
Protein: 24g
Total Fat: 7g
Saturated Fat: 1g
Omega-3 fatty acids: 1.98g
Dietary Fiber: 3g
Sodium: 70mg
Cholesterol: 60mg

Grilled Bass with Roasted Garlic Relish

Serves 4

4 4 oz striped bass fillets
Grilled sliced vegetables-1 **zucchini**, 1 **squash**, 1 **red bell pepper**, 1 **yellow bell pepper**
1 medium Vidalia **onion,** sliced
1 bunch **asparagus**, washed and ends removed
1 medium **eggplant**, peeled and sliced length-wise
3 c brown rice, cooked

Roasted Garlic Relish

10-12 **garlic** cloves, roasted in olive oil at 400 degrees for 30 minutes, drained and pureed
½ c rice wine vinegar*
½ tsp sugar
1 T **chives**, chopped
2 T **parsley**, chopped
1 T **black pepper**

Step 1: To make the Roasted Garlic Relish, combine all ingredients; taste and season as desired.
Step 2: Grill veggies and Bass fillets until fish has an internal temperature of 145 degrees.
Step 3: Serve veggies and bass over brown rice, topped with the Roasted Garlic Relish.

*This food item either is not naturally gluten free or may contain gluten due to preparation and processing. Read food label to ensure that food product does not contain gluten.

Nutrients per serving:
Calories: 450
Carbohydrate: 59g
Protein: 38g
Total Fat: 7g
Saturated Fat: 2g
Omega-3 fatty acids: 1.06g
Dietary Fiber: 13g
Sodium: 320mg
Cholesterol: 100mg

Southwest Shrimp (gluten free)

Serves 4

60 shrimp, peeled and deveined

Shrimp Marinade
¼ c **lime juice**
¼ c **lemon juice**
¼ c **orange juice**
2 T olive oil
1 tsp **cumin**
1 tsp chili powder
1 **garlic** clove, minced
2 tsp **cilantro**

Southwest Salsa
1 c **corn** kernels
1 c **tomatoes**, diced
1 c **onions**, diced
½ c **cilantro**, chopped
1 roasted green Chile, diced with seeds
1 c black beans, rinsed and drained
1 T **cumin**

Step 1: Prepare Shrimp Marinade and add shrimp. Let sit in the refrigerator for 2 hours.
Step 2: Combine corn, tomatoes, onion, cilantro, chile, black beans and cumin. Mix well and set aside.
Step 3: Cook shrimp on grill until done and serve with Southwest Salsa.

May add shredded lettuce, any type you prefer (for garnish).
Can be served over brown rice as a main dish or with tortilla shells.

Nutrients per serving:
Calories: 200
Carbohydrate: 21g
Protein: 18g
Total Fat: 7g
Saturated Fat: 1g
Omega-3 fatty acids: 0.36g
Dietary Fiber: 5g
Sodium: 360mg
Cholesterol: 105mg

Crab Dip

Serves 8

16 oz cream cheese, soft
½ c light mayonnaise
¼ c light sour cream
2 c canned crab meat, rinsed
1 tsp **lemon juice**
¼ tsp **dill**
1 tsp **chives** (may add more if desired)
1 tsp hot sauce*
Black pepper, to taste

Step 1: In large bowl combine all ingredients.
Step 2: Mix well until smooth.
Step 3: Taste and add additional seasoning, if desired. Chill until ready to serve.

*This food item either is not naturally gluten free or may contain gluten due to preparation and processing. Read food label to ensure that food product does not contain gluten.

Nutrients per serving:
Calories: 120
Carbohydrate: 1g
Protein: 8g
Total Fat: 10g
Saturated Fat: 6g
Omega-3 fatty acids: 0.23g
Dietary Fiber: 0g
Sodium: 190mg
Cholesterol: 50mg

Shrimp Scampi

Serves 4

20 oz shrimp, shelled and deveined, grilled
12 oz angel hair pasta, cooked**

Shrimp Scampi Sauce
4 **shallots**, chopped
2 **garlic** cloves, minced
1 T olive oil
4 T **lemon** juice
1 T butter
1½ T **chives**
1 T **parsley**

Step 1: Cook pasta and set aside.
Step 2: In small skillet sauté shallots and garlic in olive oil over medium heat until transparent.
Step 3: Add lemon juice, butter, chives and parsley. Pour sauce over pasta, add grilled shrimp and mix well. Serve and enjoy!

**This food item contains gluten. You may substitute a gluten-free product for this item to make this a gluten-free recipe.

Nutrients per serving:
Calories: 660
Carbohydrate: 88g
Protein: 44g
Total Fat: 14.5g
Saturated Fat: 4.5g
Omega-3 fatty acids: 0.08g
Dietary Fiber: 4.5g
Sodium: 335mg
Cholesterol: 240mg

Grilled Mahi Mahi with Lemon Caper Marinade (gluten free)

Serves 4

4 Mahi Mahi fillets

Lemon Caper Marinade
½ tsp olive oil
1 **shallot**, diced
1 caper, diced
1 T heavy cream
1 T **lemon** juice
2 T water
1 T fresh **parsley**, chopped
1 tsp **black pepper**

Step 1: In small mixing bowl, add all ingredients for the Lemon Caper Marinade. Mix well.

Step 2: Place the Mahi Mahi in a shallow pan and brush on the Lemon Caper Marinade. Cover and place in the refrigerator for 2 hours prior to grilling.

Step 3: Grill Mahi Mahi until internal temperature reaches 145 degrees. Enjoy with your favorite pasta or rice side dish.

Nutrients per serving:
Calories: 140
Carbohydrate: 1g
Protein: 26g
Total Fat: 3g
Saturated Fat: 1g
Omega-3 fatty acids: 0.16g
Dietary Fiber: 0g
Sodium: 255mg
Cholesterol: 105mg

Grilled Shrimp Kebobs

Serves 4

½ lb shrimp, peeled and deveined

Spicy Shrimp Marinade
6 oz plain Greek yogurt
1 tsp **paprika**
1 tsp pureed **ginger**
1 tsp wasabi
1 T teriyaki sauce*
3 **garlic** cloves, minced
2 T chopped **chives**
1 ½ T **lime juice**

Cucumber Relish
2 **cucumbers**, peeled and diced
2 yellow **onions**, diced
1 **yellow bell pepper**, diced
1 **red bell pepper**, diced
1 T **sesame seeds**
1 ½ T low-sodium soy sauce*
1 T brown sugar
1 T Dijon **mustard***
½ T **black pepper**

Step 1: Make Spicy Shrimp Marinade and allow shrimp to soak in sauce for at least 1 hour.
Step 2: Place 2 oz of shrimp on each skewer and grill until tender.
Step 3: Serve with plain couscous and Cucumber Relish.

*This food item either is not naturally gluten free or may contain gluten due to preparation and processing. Read food label to ensure that food product does not contain gluten.

Nutrients per serving:
Calories: 110
Carbohydrate: 14g
Protein: 11g
Total Fat: 1.5g
Saturated Fat: 0g

Omega-3 fatty acids: 0.20g
Dietary Fiber: 3g
Sodium: 270mg
Cholesterol: 55mg

Baked Goods

Flour, sugar, and shortening can be combined in the commercial market place and at home with other ingredients to produce an unbelievable array of products, from donuts to Mom's homemade apple pie. Unfortunately, baked goods have a bad reputation because so many of these products use refined flours and sugars combined with unhealthy fats and artificial ingredients. Breads and baked goods can be a wonderful source of wholesome ingredients, as our recipes demonstrate.

Banana Muffins

12 Muffins, Serving Size: 1 Muffin

1 c all-purpose flour**
¼ c packed brown sugar
½ tsp baking soda
1 tsp baking powder
½ tsp ground **cinnamon**
1 c oatmeal**
1 egg white
1 **omega-3 egg**
2 T canola oil
1 c mashed ripe **bananas** (about 2 bananas)
½ c plain nonfat Greek yogurt
½ c dried **cranberries**

Step 1: Line a standard muffin tin with paper liners, spray lightly with cooking spray. Set aside.
Step 2: In a large mixing bowl sift flour, brown sugar, baking soda, baking powder, cinnamon, and nutmeg. Add oats to the dry ingredients.
Step 3: In another bowl, beat the egg white until foamy (~3 minutes) and increased in volume. Stir in the omega-3 egg, oil, mashed bananas, Greek yogurt, and dried cranberries. Fold wet ingredients into the flour mixture.
Step 4: Spoon batter into the muffin tin and bake at 400 degrees for 25 minutes. Cool for 5 minutes. Place on cooling rack until completely cool. Serve and enjoy!

**This food item contains gluten. You may substitute a gluten-free product for this item to make this a gluten-free recipe.

Nutrients per serving:
Calories: 140
Carbohydrate: 25g
Protein: 3g
Total Fat: 3g
Saturated Fat: 0g
Omega-3 fatty acids: 0.01g
Dietary Fiber: 1g
Sodium: 110mg
Cholesterol: 15mg

Cranberry and Applesauce Muffins

12 Muffins, Serving Size: 1 muffin

2 c all-purpose flour**
1 T baking powder
½ tsp salt
½ tsp ground **cinnamon**
1 **omega-3 egg**
1 egg white
½ c evaporated skimmed milk
2 T canola oil
⅓ c packed brown sugar
¾ c **applesauce**
½ c dried **cranberries**

Step 1: In a large mixing bowl sift together flour, baking powder, salt, cinnamon.

Step 2: In another bowl, lightly beat the omega-3 egg with the egg white. Stir in evaporated skimmed milk, oil, brown sugar, and applesauce. Fold the wet ingredients into the flour mixture. Gently fold in the dried cranberries.

Step 3: Line a standard muffin tin with paper liners and spray lightly with cooking spray. Spoon the batter into the muffin tin and bake at 400 degrees for 25 minutes. Cool in the tin for 5 minutes. Serve and enjoy!

**This food item contains gluten. You may substitute a gluten-free product for this item to make this a gluten-free recipe.

Nutrients per serving:
Calories: 150
Carbohydrate: 28g
Protein: 3g
Total Fat: 2.5g
Saturated Fat: 0g
Omega-3 fatty acids: 0.3g
Dietary Fiber: 1g
Sodium: 260mg
Cholesterol: 15mg

Soft Pretzels

Serves 16

3 c all-purpose flour**
2 T granulated sugar
1 tsp salt
1 package of active dry yeast
1 c water
1 T butter
¼ c **flaxseed**
1 **omega-3 egg yolk**
1 T water
Coarse salt (optional)

Step 1: In a large mixing bowl combine 1 cup flour, sugar, salt, flaxseed and yeast.

Step 2: In a saucepan over medium-high heat, heat water and butter to 130 degrees. Add warm liquid to flour/yeast mixture; stir until well combined. Add enough flour to make a soft dough.

Step 3: Turn out onto a lightly floured surface. Knead, adding more flour as necessary until dough is smooth and not sticky. Place dough in a greased bowl, and cover. Let rise in a warm place for 1 hour.

Step 4: Line baking sheet with aluminum foil, lightly grease; set aside. Punch down dough, knead several times. Divide dough into 16 equal portions and keep portions not being rolled covered. Roll each portion into a 12 inch string; shape into pretzel. Place on baking sheet, cover, and let rise 5 minutes. Beat together egg yolk and water. Lightly brush on pretzels. Sprinkle pretzels lightly with coarse salt. Bake 15 minutes at 375 degrees. Serve and enjoy!

**This food item contains gluten. You may substitute a gluten-free product for this item to make this a gluten-free recipe.

Nutrients per serving:

Calories: 100
Carbohydrate: 19g
Protein: 3g
Total Fat: 2g
Saturated Fat: 0.5g

Omega-3 fatty acids: 0.6g
Dietary Fiber: 1g
Sodium: 150mg
Cholesterol: 20mg

Flaxseed Bread

One 5"x10" Loaf, Serving Size: 1 slice

1 ¼ c lukewarm water
2 T active dry yeast
2 T honey
2 T canola oil
2 c all purpose flour**
1 c whole wheat flour**
1 tsp salt
¼ c milled **flaxseed**
2 T **sunflower seeds**
1 T **poppy seeds**

Step 1: Combine flour, salt, and milled flaxseed in a large mixing bowl and set aside sunflower seeds and poppy seeds.

Step 2: Combine lukewarm water and yeast.

Step 3: Add honey and canola oil to dried ingredients. Mix together.

Step 4: Add yeast water and mix until dough forms a ball. Add additional flour if dough is sticky to the touch.

Step 5: Place dough in well greased bowl and let rise for 1 hour. Punch down dough, kneed and place dough in well greased bread pan. Bake at 375 degrees for 1 hour, checking at 45 minutes for browning on top.

**This food item contains gluten. You may substitute a gluten-free product for this item to make this a gluten-free recipe.

Nutrients per serving:
Calories: 140
Carbohydrate: 20g
Protein: 5g
Total Fat: 5g
Saturated Fat: 0g
Omega-3 fatty acids: 2.64g
Dietary Fiber: 3g
Sodium: 135mg
Cholesterol: 0mg

Flaxseed Muffins

12 Muffins, Serving Size 1 Muffin

1 c oat bran**
1 c all-purpose flour**
½ c milled **flaxseed**
½ T baking powder
½ tsp salt
1 **orange** (peeled and seeded)
1 c brown sugar
1 c buttermilk
¼ c canola oil
2 **omega-3 eggs**
1 tsp baking soda
1 c **raisins**

Step 1: Preheat oven to 375 degrees. In a large bowl, combine oat bran, flour, flaxseed, baking powder, and salt. Set aside.

Step 2: Using a food processor, combine: orange, brown sugar, buttermilk, oil, eggs and baking soda - blend well.

Step 3: Combine orange mixture and dry ingredients. Mix until blended. Stir in raisins.

Step 4: Fill paper lined muffin tins almost to the top. Bake at 375 degrees oven for 18-20 minutes. Cool 5 minutes before removing to cooling rack.

Note: For chocolate lovers, substitute white chocolate chips for raisins.

**This food item contains gluten. You may substitute a gluten-free product for this item to make this a gluten-free recipe.

Nutrients per serving:
Calories: 260
Carbohydrate: 43g
Protein: 6g
Total Fat: 9g
Saturated Fat: 1g
Omega-3 fatty acids: 0.45mg
Dietary Fiber: 4g
Sodium: 310mg
Cholesterol: 30mg

Coffee Cake

One 9"x13" cake

¼ pound (½ cup) butter
Juice of 1 large **orange**
¾ c light brown sugar, packed
2 **omega-3 eggs**
½ tsp salt
1 tsp baking powder
1 tsp baking soda
2 c all purpose flour**
¾ c buttermilk
½ c dried **cherries**
½ c dried **cranberries**
½ c chopped **walnuts**

Step 1: Preheat oven to 350 degrees. Butter and flour baking pan.

Step 2: Cream butter and sugar until light and fluffy.

Step 3: Add eggs and beat until smooth. Stir in orange juice and salt, baking powder, and soda.

Step 4: Alternately add flour and buttermilk, in thirds, beating just until smooth, then fold in the dried fruits and walnuts.

Step 5: Pour mixture into baking pan and bake at 350 degrees until lightly browned, about 45 minutes.

**This food item contains gluten. You may substitute a gluten-free product for this item to make this a gluten-free recipe.

Nutrients per serving:
Calories: 260
Carbohydrate: 37g
Protein: 5g
Total Fat: 11g
Saturated Fat: 5g
Omega-3 fatty acids: 5.79g
Dietary Fiber: 2g
Sodium: 410mg
Cholesterol: 55mg

Cranberry Bread

One 6"x12" Loaf, Serving Size: 1 slice

1 ½ c dried **cranberries**
6 T butter
¾ c light brown sugar, packed
2 **omega-3 eggs**
1 c buttermilk
2 ½ c all-purpose flour**
pinch of ground **cloves**
1 tsp baking soda
1 ½ tsp baking powder
½ tsp salt
1 c **walnuts**, finely chopped

Step 1: Preheat oven to 375 degrees. Butter and flour bread pan.
Step 2: Cream butter and sugar in a mixing bowl until light and fluffy, add eggs and beat until smooth.
Step 3: Add buttermilk.
Step 4: Combine dry ingredients except the nuts and stir half into the batter.
Step 5: Add cranberries and the remaining flour, and fold in the nuts.
Step 6: Pour batter into pan and bake on center rack until brown on top. Turn out onto a cooling rack.

Cooking time: ~ 1 hour 10 minutes

**This food item contains gluten. You may substitute a gluten-free product for this item to make this a gluten-free recipe.

Nutrients per serving:
Calories: 310
Carbohydrate: 43 g
Protein: 6 g
Total Fat: 14 g
Saturated Fat: 4.5 g
Omega-3 fatty acids: 10.97g
Dietary Fiber: 3 g
Sodium: 210 mg
Cholesterol: 55 mg

Omega-3 Walnut Pie

Serves 8

4 **omega-3 eggs**
¾ c maple syrup
2 T **lemon juice**
½ tsp **cinnamon**
2 tsp **vanilla extract**
½ tsp salt
2 c chopped **walnuts**
1 unbaked 9 inch pie crust (or you can make your own from scratch)**

Step 1: Preheat oven to 375 degrees.
Step 2: Beat together eggs, maple syrup, lemon juice, cinnamon, vanilla extract and salt until light and frothy.
Step 3: Spread walnuts into the unbaked crust and cover with the batter. Bake for 30 minutes at 375 degrees. Remove from oven and cool.

**This food item contains gluten. You may substitute a gluten-free product for this item to make this a gluten-free recipe.

Nutrients per serving:
Calories: 410
Carbohydrate: 35g
Protein: 9g
Total Fat: 27g
Saturated Fat: 4g
Omega-3 fatty acids: 2.69g
Dietary Fiber: 2g
Sodium: 330mg
Cholesterol: 110mg

Homemade Granola Bars

24 Bars, Serving size: 1 Bar

¼ c butter
2 c miniature marshmallows
1 c rolled oats
½ c almond slivers
¼ c **flaxseed**
½ c **raisins**, chopped
¼ c raw **sunflower seeds**
¼ c dried **cranberries**

Step 1: In a large saucepan over low heat, melt butter. Add marshmallows and stir constantly until marshmallows are melted and mixture is smooth. Remove from heat.

Step 2: Stir in oats, almonds, flaxseed, raisins, and sunflower seeds until thoroughly coated. Press into a 9"x13" pan. Cool and cut them.

**This food item contains gluten. You may substitute a gluten-free product for this item to make this a gluten-free recipe.

Nutrients per serving:
Calories: 230
Carbohydrate: 33g
Protein: 6g
Total Fat: 9g
Saturated Fat: 1g
Omega-3 fatty acids:
Dietary Fiber: 4g
Sodium: 5mg
Cholesterol: 0mg

Dark Chocolate Chip Omega-3 Cookies

48 Cookies, Serving Size: 2 Cookies

1 c shortening
1 c brown sugar
½ c granulated sugar
1 tsp **vanilla**
2 **omega-3 eggs**, beaten
2 c all-purpose flour**
1 tsp baking soda
½ tsp salt
1 c **dark chocolate** chips
¼ c ground **flaxseed**

Step 1: In medium sized mixing bowl, cream shortening, brown sugar and granulated sugar. Add vanilla and eggs, mix well.

Step 2: In a separate medium sized mixing bowl combine flour, baking soda, salt, ground flaxseed and dark chocolate chips. Mix well and then add to shortening mixture.

Step 3: Spoon onto greased cookie sheets. Bake for 10 minutes at 350 degrees. Remove from baking sheet and allow cooling.

**This food item contains gluten. You may substitute a gluten-free product for this item to make this a gluten-free recipe.

Nutrients per serving:
Calories: 180
Carbohydrate: 21g
Protein: 2g
Total Fat: 10g
Saturated Fat: 2g
Omega-3 fatty acids: 0.01g
Dietary Fiber: 1g
Sodium: 240mg
Cholesterol: 20mg

Omega-3 Buns

12 Buns, Serving Size: 1 bun

1 T fast rising instant yeast
4 c all purpose flour**
⅓ c ground **flaxseed**
¼ c granulated sugar
1 **omega-3 egg**
½ tsp salt
1 ½ c lukewarm water

Step 1: In a small mixing bowl combine yeast, 2 cups flour and ground flaxseed.
Step 2: In a large mixing bowl combine sugar, egg, and salt. Add water and stir. Add flour mixture to the liquid and beat until well blended. Add remaining flour and knead.
Step 3: Let rise in a warm place for 15 minutes. Punch down and let rise again 15 minutes. Punch down and divide into 12 buns. Place on greased baking sheet with a 2 inch space between the buns. Let rise one hour.
Step 4: Bake 20 minutes at 350 degrees. Remove and cool on a rack.

**This food item contains gluten. You may substitute a gluten-free product for this item to make this a gluten-free recipe.

Nutrients per serving:
Calories: 107
Protein: 3.3g
Carbohydrate: 19.4g
Dietary Fiber: 1.7g
Saturated Fat: 0.1g
Sodium: 100mg
Cholesterol: 15mg
Omega-3: 0.5g

Flax Fruit Crisp

Serves 4 (½ cup serving)

4 plums, 4 apricots
⅓ c granulated sugar
2 T fresh **lemon juice**
2 tsp cornstarch*
1 c oatmeal**
¼ c ground **flaxseed**
2 T butter

Lemon Cream
1 c light sour cream
¼ c powdered sugar
3 T fresh **lemon juice**

Step 1: Preheat oven to 350 degrees.

Step 2: Lightly grease a 8"x8" baking dish. Quarter plums and apricots into the baking dish.

Step 3: In small bowl, mix granulated sugar, lemon juice and cornstarch. Pour mixture over fruit.

Step 4: In a medium bowl, mix oatmeal, ground flaxseed and melted butter. Sprinkle over fruit. Bake 25 minutes.

Step 5: In a medium bowl, mix sour cream, powdered sugar, and lemon juice. Chill and serve.

*This food item either is not naturally gluten free or may contain gluten due to preparation and processing. Read food label to ensure that food product does not contain gluten.

**This food item contains gluten. You may substitute a gluten-free product for this item to make this a gluten-free recipe.

Nutrients per serving:
Calories: 410
Carbohydrate: 80g
Protein: 6g
Total Fat: 11g
Saturated Fat: 4g
Omega-3 fatty acids: 0.15g
Dietary Fiber: 10g
Sodium: 0mg
Cholesterol: 15mg

Nutty Cookies

3 Dozen, Serving Size: 1 Cookie

¼ lb butter
¾ c light brown sugar, packed
1 **omega-3 egg**
1 ½ tsp **vanilla**
¼ tsp salt
1 ¼ c flour**
1 c **walnuts**, finely chopped
Powdered sugar

Step 1: Preheat oven to 375°F.
Step 2: Cream butter and sugar until smooth and light. Beat together egg, vanilla and salt and add to butter/sugar mixture. Stir in flour, and then the nuts.
Step 3: Drop dough onto cookie sheets. Bake until lightly browned on top, about 8 to 10 minutes.
Step 4: Cool on rack, and then dust with powdered sugar.

**This food item contains gluten. You may substitute a gluten-free product for this item to make this a gluten-free recipe.

Nutrients per serving:
Calories: 80
Carbohydrate: 8g
Protein: 1g
Total Fat: 5g
Saturated Fat: 2g
Omega-3 fatty acids: 0.31g
Dietary Fiber: 0g
Sodium: 75mg
Cholesterol: 15mg

Honey Cracked Wheat Bread

2 Loaves, Serving Size: 1 slice

¼ c warm water
1 ½ tsp sugar
2 ¼ tsp active dry yeast (one envelope)
1 ½ c hot water
1 ½ c buttermilk
¼ c honey
3 T canola oil
1 tsp salt
1 c cracked wheat**
2 c whole-wheat flour**
2 ½ c all-purpose flour**

Step 1: Combine ¼ cup warm water with the sugar and yeast in a small bowl and set aside, about 10 minutes. Grease two 8"x4" bread pans for the dough.

Step 2: In a mixing bowl, combine 1 ½ cup hot water and milk. Stir in molasses, oil, and salt. Add yeast and begin mixing in the flour. Turn onto a lightly floured surface and knead until smooth, adding flour a little at a time. Place dough in a canola oiled bowl, turn once to coat the top, then cover with a clean cloth and set aside to rise until doubled in bulk, about 1 ¼ hours.

Step 3: Push the dough down and turn it out, dividing it in two halves. Shape into two loaves and place in cooking sprayed 8x4 bread pans. Cover again and let rise until the dough has risen to the top of the pan, about 40 minutes. Preheat the oven to 375 degrees. Bake for 45 minutes or until well browned.

**This food item contains gluten. You may substitute a gluten-free product for this item to make this a gluten-free recipe.

Nutrients per serving:
Calories: 170
Carbohydrate: 31g
Protein: 5g
Total Fat: 3g
Saturated Fat: 0g
Omega-3 fatty acids: 4.11g
Dietary Fiber: 3g
Sodium: 160mg
Cholesterol: 0mg

Granola with Cranberries

Serves 8, Serving Size: ½ cup

5 c oatmeal**
1 c **almonds**, chopped
½ c wheat germ**
1 tsp **nutmeg**
1 T ground **cinnamon** (more if desired)
½ c **raisins** or ½ c dried **cranberries**
¼ c canola oil
¾ c honey

Step 1: Preheat oven to 300 degrees.

Step 2: Mix together the dry ingredients, excluding the raisins. Add oil and honey and toss again.

Step 3: Spread mixture on two sheet pans and bake until golden, turning every 10 minutes so that it browns evenly. After 30 minutes add raisins and let cool.

Step 4: As the granola cools, it will become crunchy. Store in a tightly covered jar.

**This food item contains gluten. You may substitute a gluten-free product for this item to make this a gluten-free recipe.

Nutrients per serving:
Calories: 254
Protein: 5.7g
Carbohydrates: 34g
Dietary Fiber: 3.3g
Saturated Fat: 1.2g
Sodium: 139mg
Cholesterol: 0mg
Omega 3: 0.7g

Cinnamon Muffins

12 muffins, Serving Size: 1 Muffin

1 c all purpose flour**
½ tsp baking soda
1 tsp baking powder
1 tsp salt
1 tsp ground **ginger**
½ tsp ground **allspice**
½ tsp ground **cinnamon**
1 c cornmeal
1 **omega-3 egg**
1 egg white
¾ c **prune** puree (1 cup prunes blended with ¼ cup water)
½ c plain yogurt
¼ c skim milk
¼ c honey
2 T canola oil

Step 1: In a large bowl, sift together flour, baking soda, baking powder, salt, ginger, allspice and cinnamon. Stir in the cornmeal.

Step 2: In another bowl, lightly beat the whole egg with the egg white. Stir in prune puree, yogurt, skim milk, maple syrup, and oil. Fold the wet ingredients into the dry ingredients.

Step 3: Spoon batter into greased muffin tins and bake for 25 at 400 degrees. Cool for 5 minutes and run a knife around the edge of each muffin before tipping it out of the tin. Place on cooling rack until completely cool. Serve and enjoy!

**This food item contains gluten. You may substitute a gluten-free product for this item to make this a gluten-free recipe.

Nutrients per serving:
Calories: 160
Carbohydrate: 31g
Protein: 3g
Total Fat: 3g
Saturated Fat: 0g
Omega-3 fatty acids: 0.3g
Dietary Fiber: 2g
Sodium: 210mg
Cholesterol: 15mg

Omega-3 Crackers

24 Crackers, Serving Size: 1 Cracker

¼ c whole **flaxseeds**
¼ c milled **flaxseeds**
1 ½ c all purpose flour*
½ tsp baking powder
1 tsp salt
4 tsp butter, softened
½ c skim milk

Step 1: In mixing bowl add whole flaxseeds, milled flaxseeds, flour, baking powder, salt and butter. Blend until the mixture is course in texture.

Step 2: Stir in milk and mix until soft dough is formed. Cover dough and chill 10 minutes.

Step 3: Divide dough into quarters. Turn out onto a lightly floured board. Roll out very thin and cut into 2 ½ inch squares. Place on an ungreased baking sheet. Bake 20 minutes at 325 degrees, until crisp and golden.

**This food item contains gluten. You may substitute a gluten-free product for this item to make this a gluten-free recipe.

Nutrients per serving:
Calories: 45
Carbohydrate: 7g
Protein: 2g
Total Fat: 1.5g
Saturated Fat: 0g
Omega-3 fatty acids:
Dietary Fiber: 0.5g
Sodium: 115mg
Cholesterol: 0mg

Part III
Identifying Personal Problem Foods

The recipes in the previous section are desinged for healthy people who can eat whatever they choose without adverse consequences. This next section is for those who do not enjoy excellent health.

For some people, eating a wholesome nutritious food can have devastating consequences due to an allergy or food intolerance. Food allergies are discussed later in this section. Food intolerances can arise for a host of reasons that are different from allergy. In addition to common and well understood food intolerances, there are one-of-a-kind, highly individualized food intolerances that can be uncovered by attention to what one eats.

An example of a well-studied food intolerance is celiac disease caused by intolerance to gluten that is found in wheat, barley, and rye. For people with celiac disease, gluten is highly toxic to the lining of their small intestine, leading to digestive problems and a loss of the ability to absorb essential nutrients. The good news is that these individuals can be "cured" of celiac disease by avoiding gluten, though this is not easy in a society where prepared and packaged foods can have 10, 20, or even 30 ingredients with gluten hiding among them. Gluten intolerance goes way beyond celiac disease. Some but not all autistic children benefit from a gluten free diet. A woman with the autoimmune disease polymyositis achieved wellness when wheat was eliminated from her diet. There are epidemiological studies showing a low incidence of schizophrenia in populations that do not eat cereal grains, though the exact relationship is uncertain and may relate to infestations of grain with fungus producing toxins that are known to cause psychosis.

Some people with rheumatoid arthritis have had remarkable improvement after eliminating one or more foods from their diet. A woman who had sudden onset of severe rheumatoid arthritis was told by her rheumatologist that she would be in a wheel chair in a few years. Her husband was a scientist who went to the local medical school library and found the book, *Food Allergy and Intolerances, 2nd Edition,* edited by Dr. Jonathan Brostoff and Dr. Stephen J. Challacombe. After reading the chapter on rheumatoid arthritis, he suggested that his wife try avoiding milk and other dairy products. After a few days with no milk or milk products, her joint pain and swelling improved and then went away. Twenty years later she was still free of any signs of arthritis. Occasionally she will go to a wine and cheese party, try to get away with eating a few cubes of cheese, and have achy joints for a few days. Unfortunately, every patient with rheumatoid arthritis will not have a remission by avoiding milk. Food intolerances are highly individualized. What it does mean is that some people with rheumatoid arthritis may find foods that modulate their disease and may benefit from systematically eliminating foods from their diet.

Another illness that can be ameliorated by food eliminations in some individuals is bipolar disorder. This disease is characterized by extreme ups and downs. Irrational periods of hyperactivity, known as manic phases, alternate with depression. In controlled clinical situations with simplified diets, it has been observed that some bipolar patients become manic after eating certain foods. After the manic phase resolved, a period of depression followed.

241

Irritable bowel syndrome is just as it sounds. Victims have an irritable gut that over reacts to stimuli, producing crampy abdominal pains and diarrhea alternating with constipation. Elimination diets can sometimes identify foods that are best not put into an irritable gut. Dr. Myers had a patient who developed irritable bowel syndrome. She had been suffering with this condition for several months. When her diet was examined, it was noted that around the time of her illness, she had starting chewing cinnamon gum, using cinnamon flavored mints, and eating granola that contained cinnamon. After eliminating cinnamon from her diet for a week, the woman's irritable bowel syndrome improved and slowly went away.

A woman in our community developed an unusual illness where she would have attacks of swelling of her body with low blood pressure, called capillary leak syndrome. In this disease, capillaries periodically open up so that fluids in the bloodstream leak into tissues and cause swelling. Every time an attack occurred, she would have to go to the hospital emergency department and get infusions of saline and albumin to support her circulation. After each attack, the swelling would persist for days. She was tortured by this ailment until she figured out that attacks followed eating pork. Medical science has not caught up with her discovery. The point is that all sorts of illnesses can be triggered by intolerances to constituents in foods. Discovering food intolerances can give some people their lives back, eliminating suffering and the need for expensive medical care.

There are one-of-a-kind food intolerances that are not described in the medical literature. A physician learned this in a dramatic way when he was eating in a hospital cafeteria one day and suddenly developed a severe pain in the center of his chest. He sipped some water that came back up. He was astute enough to diagnose that his esophagus—the tube that connects the throat to the stomach—had gone into a spasm. He leaped from the table and ran to the men's room where he each time he tried to drink water, it came back up. After fifteen minutes or so, the spasm was relieved and he returned to work.

Over the next ten years, he had attacks about once a year but only when eating in a restaurant. After eating a restaurant dish covered with coarse flakes of black pepper. he had the most severe esophageal spasm ever. Could black pepper be triggering the awful attacks of esophageal spasm? He did not care for black pepper and never used it at home. Painful experimentation verified that indeed, black pepper produced the spasms. A little was tolerated, but eating coarse black pepper flakes was devastating. A chemical in black pepper is known to bind to receptors on nerve cells. A reflex arc had developed in this individual. Black pepper excited nerve cells, causing a spasm of the muscles of his esophagus.

It is important to note that these food-illness correlations are highly individualized. Just because one rheumatoid arthritis victim found relief by eliminating dairy products, or one sufferer of irritable bowel syndrome found cinnamon provoked her symptoms, does not mean that dairy products cause rheumatoid arthritis or cinnamon is the cause of irritable bowel syndrome. Medical scientists have sometimes mistakenly tried to study a single food-disease connection with dismal results and concluded that dietary factors do not play a role in disease exacerbations. A proper study would use a broad elimination program that is individualized for each subject.

Organ systems that can be affected by food intolerances, with some of the diseases that can be exacerbated by them, are listed in Table III-1. These are based on the discussions presented in Brostoff and Challacombe's book. A wonderful reference to this topic is their paperback book for the public, *Food Allergies and Food Intolerance: The Complete Guide to Their Identification and Treatment,* published by Healing Arts Press in 2000. A welcomed aspect of food intolerances is that individuals can sort them out at home, without resorting to expensive medical testing.

Table III-I

Diseases that are reportedly caused or exacerbated by food intolerances in some individuals.

Organ System	
Oral	Recurrent mouth ulcers, swelling of mouth and tongue, itching and burning of the mouth, lichen plantus & lichemoid reactions, cheilitis
Respiratory	Rhinitis, secretory otitis media, sinusitis, asthma, alveolitis
Gastrointestinal	Irritable bowel syndrome, Crohn's disease, ulcerative colitis, Celiac disease
Skin	Atopic dermatitis, eczema, urticaria, angio-edema, urticarial vasculitis, contact dermatitis, dermatitis herpetiformis
Central nervous system	Panic disorder, depression, narcolepsy, hyperactivity, migraine headaches, fatigue, neuropathic pain, antisocial and criminal behavior
Musculoskeletal system	Joint pain and inflammation, muscle pain and inflammation

Ref: *Food Allergy and Intolerances, 2nd Edition,* edited by Dr. Jonathan Brostoff and Dr. Stephen J. Challacombe. Saunders Ltd.; 2 edition (August 9, 2002).

The reader may be surprised to find antisocial and criminal behavior in the table of food intolerances. A number of studies in prisons have verified that diet can modulate criminal behavior.

A distinction is made between food allergies and food intolerances. Food intolerances are more general and often highly specialized, while food allergies are a specific type of reaction to foods in which a person makes antibodies of the IgE class to proteins in foods. Food allergies can be devastating. They are a particular kind of immune reaction to substances in foods. Proteins in the food bind to antibodies on the surface of two types of cells—mast cells and basophils—that are loaded with powerful substances including histamine that produce inflammation. Symptoms of a food allergy vary in different people. In some, there is abdominal bloating, crampy abdominal pain, nausea, vomiting, diarrhea, and swelling. Some people get itchy whelps called hives after eating a food they are allergic to. Runny noses, wheezing, and even shock can occur in severe cases.

There are skin tests for food allergy. A drop of fluid containing the food is injected into the skin. A screening test is usually done for more sensitive individuals; a drop of the fluid is placed onto the skin and a prick is made in the center of the drop. An itchy bump surrounded by an area of redness at the site of the injection indicates an allergy to the food. There are also blood tests to detect the antibodies to the food, though these are not as good as the skin tests because the antibody levels in the blood are very low. Most of the antibody is on the surface of the mast cells and basophils. Food allergies are increasing dramatically in the United States, particularly among young children, but at the time of this writing, no one knows why.

Sample Page for Food Diary

Date	Time	Foods ingested and/or symptoms

A woman with severe asthma who was spending several hundred dollars a month on medications saw Dr. Meggs for allergy testing. Tests for the most likely allergens to cause asthma—pollens, molds, dust mites, cat and other animal proteins—were all negative. The only positive food test was eggs. She was advised to stop eating eggs and come back in a month. A month later she returned and said, "I didn't have to keep this appointment but I wanted to come and tell you in person. My asthma is a thing of the past. Every morning I would get up, eat eggs for breakfast, start wheezing, and wheeze all day. Since you told me to stop eating eggs, I have not used a single inhaler."

This woman could have used another approach to find triggers of her asthma. She could have started keeping a diary of everything that she ate and everywhere that she went. The onset of every asthma attack could also be recorded. She would have recognized that attacks started after breakfast. Her breakfast foods—eggs, toast, coffee, orange juice, and milk—would come under suspicion. She could have systematically eliminated each food, or gone for broke and stopped them all. Using a trial and error approach of systemically eliminating foods, she could have discovered the connection between eating eggs and asthma attacks.

Physicians in the United States have been criticized for ignoring dietary and environmental causes of illness and reaching for the prescription pad. Asthma, the quintessential environmental illness, is treated by many physicians as a deficiency of the drugs albuterol and steroids such as prednisone. Most people who have environmental triggers of illness sort them out for themselves, using techniques such as those described here as a guide, with the exception of allergies to things like pollens, for which allergy testing is very useful. We recommend allergy skin testing for all people with asthma and rhinitis.

Eliminating foods from one's diet is a chore that requires a period of attention to everything one eats, but for some people the payoff is great. People who suffer from a chronic disease, no matter the nature, can undertake a period of observation and dietary manipulations to see if their chronic illness improves. One can use a symptom approach and a disease approach. Some of the diseases that have been reported to improve with eliminating offending foods are given in Table III-1. These are the diseases discussed in Dr. Jonathan Brostoff's books.

The symptoms that can be related to foods (and also chemicals, as described in part IV) in some individuals are given in Table III-2. These are based on clinical experience as described in the writings of Dr. Theron Randolph, a twentieth century Chicago allergist who over a lifetime of medical practice—Dr. Randolph continued to treat patients well into his eighties—treated tens of thousands of patients using elimination routines. Dr. Randolph described *Stimulation Symptoms* and *Withdrawal Symptoms*. Stimulation symptoms occur after eating the food, while withdrawal symptoms occur in a period of time after the food is eliminated from the diet. The onset and duration of stimulation and withdrawal is variable. Generally, stimulation symptoms start minutes to hours after eating the food. Withdrawal symptoms usually begin a few hours to a day or so after not eating the food and can last up to five days, and sometimes even a week.

Table III-2. Randolph's Intermittent Stimulatory and Withdrawal Symptoms Associated with Maladaption to Foods and Chemicals.

	Stimulatory symptoms	Withdrawal Symptoms
Devastating	Mania: agitation, excitement, blackouts, seizures in extreme cases	Depression: confabulation, hallucinosis, obsessions, delusions, transient amnesia
Severe	Hypomania: hyper-responsiveness, anxiety, panic attacks, mental lapses	Brain-fag (a term used to describe fatigue, mood changes, irritability, impairment of: cognition, concentration, poor reading comphrension, memory)
Moderate	Hyperactivity: restless legs, insominia, agressive forceful behavior	Systemic physical symptoms: fatigue, headache, myalgia, arthralgia, arthritis, edema, fast heart beat, arrhythmias
Mild	Stimulation: active, self-centered, suppression of symptoms	Localized physical symptoms: rhnintis, bronchitis, asthma, dermatitis, gastrointestinal and genitourinary symptoms

Based on Chapter 2 in *An Alternative Approach To Allergies* by Theron G. Randolph, MD, and Ralph W. Moss, PhD.

For those who want to investigate whether or not a food intolerance is causing an illness, the steps given below can be followed. Many will find answers after Step One, but those who do not can progress to Step Two and higher as needed.

Step One.

Begin by keeping a foods and symptoms diary.

Write down everything eaten, giving the date and time.

Remember that most commercially prepared foods contain numerous ingredients.

Herbs and spices added to foods should also be recorded, even salt and pepper.

For meats, record the animal it came from, not the cut. For example, for bacon and pork chops, put down pork. If a hot dog is eaten, read the label to determine if it contains beef, pork, or both, and record hot dog (beef and/or pork).

For cow's milk products, including yogurt, cheese, whipped cream, etc., record both the food, source, and other ingredients. For example, yogurt (cow's milk, cane sugar, raspberry, etc.).

Note should be made of artificial sweeteners consumed, such as aspartame and sucralose, as some individuals have been described who have adverse reactions to these substances.

Write down symptoms that one has, such has headache, achy joints, skin rash, feeling blue, diarrhea, nausea, and so forth.

Lucky individuals will be able to scan their food diaries and identify problem foods. For example, eating oranges three times each week and having a headache or upset stomach each time. If problems persist, continue to Step Two.

Step Two.

Continue to keep the foods and symptoms diary.

For a chronic condition, make a list of the foods that are eaten daily. For most of us, this list will include wheat, milk, and sugar. Some will have coffee, tea, eggs, beef, pork, and cola beverages.

Eliminate all foods that are eaten daily for a one week period. This may mean no coffee, no eggs for breakfast, and no bread or shredded wheat for a week. If symptoms improve, foods may be added back to the diet one-by-one to determine which ones were damaging.

Many people who eat a monotonous diet are dismayed at the thought of eliminating foods eaten every day and don't know what to eat. Our grocery stores are filled with a wide variety of foods from all over the world. Goat milk or soymilk can be substituted for cow's milk, duck for chicken, salmon for tuna, etc.

For no or partial success, proceed to step three.

Step Three.

Continue to keep a foods and symptoms diary.

Simplify the diet, eating only simple foods, such as a meal of baked cod, boiled sweet potato, and green peas.

Eat a wide variety of foods so that no foods are eaten regularly.

Pay close attention to symptoms. For stimulatory symptoms, look at the foods minutes to hours before the symptom began. For withdrawal symptoms, look at the foods eaten hours to a day before symptom onset. One man who suffered severe classic migraine headaches, with headaches on one side of his head of disabling severity culminating in nausea and vomiting, found that the headaches occurred around 4 pm on the day after oranges were eaten. He quit eating oranges and never had another migraine headache.

If problems still persist, the determined reader can proceed to step four.

Step Four. The Rotation Diet

Those who have not found the answers they are seeking and are determined can go to the most dramatic elimination routine, the rotation diet. Eat a rotation diet, eating one single food at each meal, and only repeating any food every five days. An example of a rotation diet would be to eat a serving of fruit for breakfast, rotating through a list of five or more fruits. Eat a vegetable or starch for lunch, paying careful attention to food groups (discussed below). Eat a protein food source for dinner, rotating through a list that could contain beans, beef, pork, goat, chicken, turkey, duck, and seafood. Mammals such as beef, pork, and goat would be considered different foods in the rotation. Fowl such as chicken, turkey, and duck would be considered different foods in the rotation. Sea foods are separate species and could be put in the rotation. For example, one could eat shrimp one day, salmon the next day, and cod the third day and still be eating no food more than every five days.

It is important to note that foods in the same biological family can contain the same or similar chemicals and toxins. A person with a disease related to one food in the family can also react to other foods in the family. The rotation diet approach must consider foods in the same class as the same food. For example, the cruciferous vegetables—cabbage, broccoli, cauliflower, bok choy—contain chemicals common to the family. Vegetables that contain solanine, such as potatoes, can be a problem if a person has intolerance to solanine. A list of food families can be found online at http:www/aaia/ca/en/food-groups.htm. When trying the rotation diet approach, one should treat the members of a food family as one food.

As part of his residency, Dr. Meggs received remarkable training at the Environmental Control Unit at Henroiten Hospital in Chicago. The unit was conceived of and run by the late Dr. Theron Randolph, an allergist in private practice in Chicago. Patients were admitted with a wide variety of severe chronic diseases, ranging from traditional allergic diseases like chronic urticaria, eczema, and asthma to inflammatory diseases like rheumatoid arthritis, chronic colitis, and multiple sclerosis. There were even patients with psychiatric diseases such as bipolar disorder and schizophrenia. These individuals—many of whom were chronically ill physicians who had not been helped at the most respected medical centers in the country—were there to see if Dr. Randolph could help them uncover environmental factors such as problem foods and inhalants that were driving their diseases.

Patients admitted to the Environmental Control Unit spent their first five or so days fasting on spring water. To prevent dehydration and problems with electrolytes and acidosis—people on a fast burn body fat for energy which produces acids—they added a salt mixture of two parts sodium bicarbonate and one part potassium bicarbonate to their water. The air in the environmental control unit was as pure as possible, with no synthetic materials that outgas volatile organic chemicals, no products of combustion, no perfumes nor fragrances, no harsh cleaning products, and a heavy duty air filtration system.

The fast was continued until their withdrawal symptoms improved. This generally took five to seven days. They then ate three meals a day with each meal consisting of a single pure food. Reactions to the foods were recorded. Foods that they had eaten every day before coming to the Environmental Control Unit were not put into the rotation until they had established a good safe diet of foods they tolerated. After a safe diet had been established—this generally took two to three weeks—they were exposed to chemical inhalants such as fumes from gas appliances and volatile organic chemicals out-gassing from synthetic materials. Some patients arrived with samples of materials from their homes, such as synthetic carpets, to be tested.

An amazing phenomenon was observed. Patients who had suffered from chronic daily symptoms had relief from their chronic illnesses. Instead, they developed acute reactions to a food or chemical that was causing the chronic illness. It was a trade off. Chronic illness with daily exposure converted to acute illness with episodic exposure. For example, prior to coming to the Environmental Control Unit, an arthritis patient might drink milk all the time and not have any reaction to drinking milk, but their joints hurt all the time. After the withdrawal period, their joints no longer hurt. When they drank milk, symptoms could include severe joint pains but might also include flushing, a racing heart, or other symptoms that never happened in association with milk exposures prior to a period without drinking milk.

The phenomenon was actually discovered in animal experiments in the 1930's and was called the *Adaptation Syndrome*. Dr. Hans Selye, a medical researcher in Montreal, was trying to purify a hormone by injecting rodents with an extract of body tissues. When exposed to the tissue, the strain of rat he was working with developed stomach ulcers, joint inflammation, shrinkage of the thymus gland, and enlargement of the adrenal glands. Dr. Selye was using a medical research technique sometimes referred to as *grind and find*. The body tissue such as a gland would be ground up, make into a solution, and injected. The fluid would then be separated into two components by some property, such as a component that dissolves in alcohol or by size of the molecule. Each component would be tested to see which one contained the active ingredient.

To his dismay, Selye found that every component had the property he was trying to isolate. One day while pondering the problem, he noticed a bottle of formalin—a deadly mixture of formaldehyde and methyl alcohol used to fix tissues—on the shelf of his lab. He injected the animals with sub-lethal doses of formalin and found it also produced the illness. As he continued his work, he exposed the animals to a variety of stresses, including emotional stress and surgical stress. No matter how he stressed his animals, the same illness resulted.

Selye continued his work by studying the reactions resulting from chronic exposure to small doses of toxins that were not sufficient to kill the animal. He found that mammals have an amazing ability to adapt to toxic exposures, but their adaptation breaks down and they become chronically ill. If they are removed from the exposure and then re-challenged, they can have a shock reaction and become extremely ill. He called his discovery the *Generalized Adaptation Syndrome.*

A group of allergists in the American mid-west—including Drs. Randolph, Rinkel, and Zeller—were using elimination diets to study food allergy in their patients. They were surprised when their patients reported an improvement in a variety of complaints when they eliminated a specific food from their diets. Joint pains, muscle aches, depression, fatigue, and what they termed brain fag (a term used to describe neuropsychological consequences including difficulties with memory, concentration, and cognition) improved. The allergists recognized immediately that the phenomenon they were observing was different from allergic reactions to food.

Randolph heard of Selye's work and proposed that individuals could become maladapted to one or more chemicals in commonly eaten foods. He noticed in some patients that elimination of a single food from the diet that was eaten daily could improve a medical condition. After a period of avoidance of five to seven days, eating the food could produce a shock reaction, which could range from a severe attack of the chronic condition to a new set of symptoms, such as flushing or racing heart. Randolph called this observation the *Specific Adaptation Syndrome.* One conclusion of this work is that eating a monotonous diet can lead to chronic illness. Certainly most of us eat a monotonous diet, consuming products such as coffee, wheat, sugar, eggs, and so forth, every day. Prepared and packed foods often contain a large number of ingredients which overlap, no matter the product. Soy, corn, wheat, and sugar are ubiquitous and heavily subsidized by the US government. It is amazing the diversity of products that can be produced with the first three ingredients being flour, sugar, shortening.

Many versions of the adaptation syndrome have been described. The way that we like to look at it has been termed the Chemical Stress Syndrome. In the breakdown of one's adaptation to the environment, including chemicals in foods, there are four stages.

Stages 0-3:

Stage 0 is normal health in which there are not chemical intolerances.

Stage 1 (-algia stage) is sensory hyper-reactivity, with symptoms related to exposures such as joint pain, headaches, burning of nasal passages, and so forth. It is termed the –algia stage because the suffix –algia in medical terminology refers to pain. For example, arthralgia means joint pain.

Stage 2 (-itis stage) is when the substances induce inflammation. It is termed the –itis stage because the suffix –itis in medical terminology refers to inflammation. For example, arthritis means joint inflammation.

Stage 3 (-osis stage) is when the inflammation produces tissue damage, such as joint destruction. It is the –osis stage because the suffix –osis in medicine refers to destruction. Fibrosis is the replacement of a normal tissue by scar tissue, which can be the endstage of an inflammatory process. Necrosis is the extreme of dead tissue. The end stage of arthritis is when the joints are destroyed and deformities occur.

Table III-3 gives the stages of the Chemical Stress Syndrome and shows how it manifests in various organ systems. By finding environmental factors that drive the inflammation, an afflicted individual can achieve wellness as long as the end stage 3 (-osis stage) has not been reached. At the present time, we have no way to reverse destruction of a tissue. Stem cell research offers promise as a way to reverse destroyed tissue, but unfortunately is periodically restricted in the United States for political rather than scientific reasons. Even if we achieve techniques to reverse scarring and tissue destruction, the rejuvenated tissue may be at risk if environmental factors driving the inflammation are not identified and eliminated.

Table III-3

	General	Musculoskeletal	Respiratory	Gastrointestinal
Stage 0. Normalcy	Tolerance of chemical exposures, wellness without symptoms	No symptoms	No symptoms	No symptoms
Stage 1. –algia	Sensory Hyper-reactivity. Subjective symptoms associate with chemical exposures. (arthralgias, myalgias, etc.)	Joint pains, muscle aches, pains, and spasms	Itching and or burning of nasal passages, sinus headaches, wheezing	Nausea, vomiting, diarrhea, abdominal cramps, irritable bowel syndrome
Stage 2. –itis	Inflammatory reactions to chemicals (arthritis, myositis, etc.)	Arthritis, myositis	Asthma, rhinitis	Inflammatory bowel disease, colitis
Stage 3. –osis	Fibrosis. Tissue destruction (arthritic deformities, muscle atrophy and necrosis,etc.)	Deformed joints, muscle scarring	COPD (chronic obstructive pulmonary disease), emphysema, pulmonary fibrosis	Bowel scarring, obstruction

An amazing obesity epidemic, perhaps one of the greatest public health disasters ever, has hit the United States and other developed nations. The number of overweight and obese people has increased dramatically over the last twenty years. This epidemic is dramatically depicted at the

Centers for Diseases Control web site, with color-coded maps showing the percentage of obese people in each state over the past decade or so (http://www.cdc.gov/obesity/data/index.html). One of the things reported by Dr. Randolph and his collaborators was that eliminating a single food from the diet could sometimes result in dramatic weight loss. This may relate to effects of obesogens or hypersensitivity to endocrine disruptions in foods, though our knowledge of these biological processes has not been developed. Obesogens are chemicals that induce obesity. The scientific investigation of obesogens is in its infancy at this writing.

Part IV

Beyond What We Eat – Where We Live and Work, Clean Air, Healthy Lifestyles, Good Mind States, Exercise, Supplements, The Chemical Environment, What Medicine Can Do

Where We Live and Work

Clean Air

When Dr. Meggs was a resident working in a cardiac unit in Rochester, New York, a fierce unseasonable cold front moved through in mid June. As temperatures fell below freezing and leaky old furnaces fired up all over town, the cardiac unit filled up with heart attack victims. At that time, little was known about the relationship between air pollution and heart attacks, other than the dangers of both primary and second hand tobacco smoke. A literature search uncovered articles relating surges of heart attacks with cold fronts moving through, but there was no understanding of why. Some were related to shoveling snow, but most were not.

Since that time, a rich body of scientific evidence has accumulated relating the products of fossil fuel combustion to heart attacks. The air of cities is filled with tiny particles from burning fossil fuels in furnaces and internal combustion engines. These particles are on the order of a millionth of a meter in size—about the size of a bacteria—and pass from the lungs into our blood vessels. White blood cells called neutrophils line the walls of our blood vessels waiting for something to fight. The neutrophils ingest the tiny particles. This triggers inflammation along the walls of blood vessels including those of the heart. The inflammation produces changes in the blood vessel walls that lead to heart attacks. The same process takes place from exposures to cigarette smoke.

Data from London has established that when concentrations of tiny particles in the air increase, heart attack rates increase. In the United States, the high heart attack rates in New York City and Houston are attributed to the large concentrations of tiny particles in the air. It is now known that exposure to traffic fumes is a risk factor for heart attacks. In addition, non-smokers in cities have higher rates of lung cancer than non-smokers living in the country, which is again attributed to air pollution. The major carcinogen in cigarette smoke can also be found in car exhaust.

Forced air furnaces are problematic. Over time, the constant heating and cooling of the metal between the combustion chamber and the air ducts leads to metal fatigue and leaks, so that products of combustion leak into the house. Thermostats turn furnaces on and off many times a day. When the furnace is off, cold air flows down the chimney and into the house. When the furnace turns on, furnace fumes flow into the living space until the air column in the chimney becomes hot enough for the fumes to flow up the chimney. When the thermostat turns the furnace off, cold air again flows down the chimney bringing with it any remaining fumes in the firebox and chimney.

Many people living in cold climates with long heating seasons complain of winter malaise, with headaches, dry skin, fatigue, nasal congestion, and so on. Those with such problems should inspect their heating systems. An inspection should demonstrate that there is no evidence of furnace fumes being released into the house, such as soot in the heat ducts. The air intake of the furnace should be vented to the outside air. Furnaces located in basements can be enclosed in a room with a window open to the outside, to allow the air intake to receive air from the outside instead of the breathing air of occupants in the house. Some health conscious people install ducts to bring outside air to the air intakes of the furnace so when flows reverse, pollution will not be swept into the breathing air of the house. Ideally, there should be no combustion taking place in the breathing spaces of our home.

Wood stoves and wood burning fireplaces can be sources of indoor air pollution. Small children are particularly vulnerable. A number of studies have shown that respiratory infections including pneumonia are more common in children living in homes heated with wood rather than cleaner fuels. Kerosene heaters are a serious source of indoor air pollution and should be avoided.

Gas appliances pollute the indoor air. Gas cook stoves are generally not exhausted to the outdoors. The flames are commonly burned in the open air so that the fumes go directly into the breathing air of occupants rather than being vented to the outdoors. A study found that homes with gas cook stoves had levels of sulfur dioxide and oxides of nitrogen above the levels allowed in factories. The gas industry developed a catalytic converter for gas cook stoves when there were fears that indoor air pollution would be regulated. Since the United States has no indoor air regulations, the product was shelved. The outlook for public health measures to protect us from indoor air pollution is very dismal in the United States where commercial interests trump public health, so it becomes our individual responsibilities to protect ourselves.

Those with chronic or recurrent conditions who have gas cook stoves can do a simple test to see if the fumes are exacerbating to their problems. Have the gas turned off for a week and cook with electric appliances, such as electric frying pans, toasters, and hot plates. Leave the gas off for 5 to 7 days, then have the gas turned back on. Such an experiment can be very enlightening and has led to amazing improvements in health in some individuals.

Studies by the US Environmental Protection Agency found that air inside our homes contains organic solvents such as toluene and benzene. Insecticides—even insecticides that are now banned because they are too toxic to use—were found in the indoor air of our homes. Bringing home clothes from the dry cleaners raises levels of dry cleaning solvents in the air for up to a week. Many materials contain toxic volatile organic compounds that evaporate into the air. Unhealthy concentrations of these toxins develop in tightly sealed buildings with poor fresh air exchange. For example, pressboard and some insulation materials can emit formaldehyde into the air, which is a respiratory irritant and causes cancer.

Synthetic carpets can also emit fumes into the air, particularly immediately after installation. A major epidemic occurred at the Environmental Protection Agency's facility in Washington, D.C., when new carpets were installed. A number of individuals became ill with respiratory, neurological, and other complaints. Exposed workers fell into three groups: a group that tolerated the exposure without difficulty, a group that became acutely ill but recovered after remediation, and a group that became chronically ill and had a generalized intolerance to fumes. In the air of the newly carpeted building, EPA chemist Dr. William Herzy identified an extremely irritating compound in the air. We now know how even one single exposure to irritating chemicals can produce lifelong disability. The irritation inflames the lining of our airways and produces changes called remodeling. The remodeled airway has a lower threshold for irritants to induce inflammation, so that respiratory irritants like tobacco smoke, diesel exhaust, perfumes, fragrances, and air fresheners at levels that were previously tolerated can produce symptoms. A vicious positive feedback loop is set up so that ongoing low level exposures keeps the airway inflamed, remodeled, and sensitive to irritants.

Healthy Lifestyles

Good Mind States

In his memoir, *Anatomy of an Illness,* American intellectual Norman Cousins described his mysterious inflammatory illness that had stumped the best medical advice he could find. He had just returned from Russia where he had stayed in a hotel near a construction site, with diesel trucks plying outside the open windows of his second floor room. It was 1964, a time before medical science had fully appreciated the toxic, inflammatory, and carcinogenic properties of diesel exhaust. It was not until 2012 that the International Agency for Cancer Research upgraded diesel exhaust from probable to known human carcinogen.

Cousins invented a program of positive attitude, love, faith, hope, and laughter as a vehicle to regain his health. In this pre-VCR era, he arranged to have viewings of Marx Brothers movies from his sick bed. He outlived the predictions of medical experts and survived for an additional 26 years. Since Cousins' time, much research has verified the beneficial effects of positive mental states on modulating negative inflammatory states on the body. Conversely, negative states such as anger can accelerate destructive effects of inflammation. The brain modulates the inflammatory response and can send signals to all parts of the body. Emotional states such as anxiety and anger put the immune system on alert that there is danger present, and any nidus of inflammation in the body will be enhanced. We now know that depression is connected with a host of other inflammatory conditions, from asthma to obesity and coronary artery disease, through the inflammation connection. Current thinking is that behavioral conditions such as depression can result from inflammation in the brain.

A number of scientific studies have unequivocally proved the benefits of meditation and related practices. Benefits of meditation include reduced blood pressure, reduced anxiety, relief from stress, improved sleep and mood, increases in ability to concentrate, and sharpening of memory. Meditation can benefit a number of pathological conditions, including fibromyagia and other chronic pain syndromes, generalized anxiety disorder, depression, substance abuse, and post traumatic stress disorder. The table on pages 170-171 of *The Inflammation Cure* outlines some of the techniques that can be used.

Dr. Bretta Holzel and her colleagues at Harvard Medical School have studied the effects of an integrated practice called Mindful Based Stress Reduction on generalized anxiety disorder and chronic pain syndromes. Mindful Based Stress Reduction was developed by Dr. Jon Kabat-Zinn at the University of Massachusetts Medical Center Stress Reduction Clinic. It combines gentle yoga with mindfulness meditation. Changes in the brains of study subjects after an 8 week program of Mindful Based Stress Reduction were detected by Dr. Holzel's group using functional and structural magnetic resonance imagining. The men and women in the study demonstrated changes in the areas of their brains related to things like memory and mood.

The best way to undertake a program of meditation is with instruction. There are over 200 centers around the country giving instruction in Mindful Based Stress Reduction. Zen Buddhism is based on a form of meditation called zazen which is undertaken—not for health improvement—but as a religious practice to achieve religious enlightenment. Nonetheless, its health benefits have been proven in scientific studies. Zen Centers around the country give workshops on their highly developed meditation practice. One should be cautioned that many Zen Centers are sometimes heavily saturated with incense smoke which, like all products of combustion, carries health risks. There are numerous other groups and gurus offering instruction in meditation.

The Chemical Environment

Planet Earth is a poisoned planet. It always has been and always will be. The thin sliver of air and ocean we call the biosphere is so toxic that life only survives by adapting to the poisons. The toxicity of the planet is ever changing. Humans have created tens of thousands of new chemicals that never existed on the planet before the human age. In addition to our own mucking around, natural processes on the planet also change the concentrations and composition of the biosphere's poisons. Those who make the distinction between natural and synthetic as being non-toxic versus toxic are off the mark. The synthetic chemist cannot rival the natural toxins on earth. The most toxic substance known, botulinum toxin, is made by a bacteria. Great extinctions have been related to increased levels of hydrogen sulfide in the atmosphere millennia ago.

The Centers for Disease Control has a well-equipped laboratory in Atlanta that monitors levels of toxins in the blood and urine of Americans. Periodically, reports are released; the latest report released in 2009, is available at http://www.cdc.gov/exposurereport/pdf/FourthReport.pdf. It was found that we have measurable levels of a host of chemicals in our bodies at levels below those that produce acute toxic effects. These include organic solvents, neurotoxic insecticides, toxic metals, chemicals from plastics, and a host of others. The effects of these chemicals on human health are a subject of great debates. Some believe that the levels are too low to be a threat. Others believe that a number of illnesses that are becoming more common, such as depression, obesity, asthma, allergies, attention deficit disorder, hyperactivity, autism, diabetes, Parkinson's disease, and a host more, are due to either the toxic effects of chemicals, or a combination of chemicals combined with genetic susceptibility.

There is a difference in philosophy between western Europeans and North Americans. Europeans have adopted what is called the *Precautionary Principle*, that it is prudent to reduce one's exposures to chemicals which are not known to be safe. In the United States, chemicals are assumed innocent until proven to be hazardous. The science is difficult because to show an effect at low levels is extremely expensive. Dr. Meggs' identical twin brother developed the most deadly form of leukemia known. This form of leukemia can be caused by benzene, a component of gasoline. Could the small inhalational exposures we all get to benzene while pumping gasoline have caused the leukemia? The probability has to be very low if not zero, but when a billion or more people on planet Earth are exposed to such low levels, could there be some cases of leukemia from pumping gas?

A way to sort out the role of toxins in causing specific illnesses was developed by Dr. Theron Randolph when he introduced the Environmental Control Units, as discussed in Section III. Sick individuals would be housed in a specially designed hospital wing where they would breathe clean air while eating organic foods on a rotation diet. Several Environmental Control Units were constructed throughout the country, for clinical but not for research use. In the early 1990's, government panels of experts were formed to examine the problem of chemical exposures and their role in diseases. They recommended the construction of a research environmental control unit to study the hypothesis that the chemical environment could cause or exacerbate diseases like hyperactivity in children. The recommendations have not been implemented.

The importance of research into the effects of environmental chemicals cannot be over emphasized because we are sick people on a poisoned planet. Our children suffer in ever increasing numbers from asthma, autism, cancer, hyperactivity, dyslexia, and other illnesses. The number of women with breast cancer continues to rise; the prevalence has doubled since the middle of the last century. Brain cancer among children has increased. Depression is ever more common, particularly among the young. Obesity among both children and adults is increasing at an alarming rate. Diabetes and kidney failure go hand-in-hand with obesity and are also increasing. Pulmonary fibrosis, in which scar tissue takes over the lungs and one suffocates, increases. More people are reporting allergies to common pollens, molds, and dust. Sleep disorders are reaching epidemic proportions. In order to describe environmental diseases, a host of new syndromes have been described—Gulf War Illness, Sick Building Syndrome, solvent neurotoxicity, Chronic Fatigue Syndrome, Spanish Toxic Oil syndrome, World Trade Center syndrome, and the Multiple Chemical Sensitivity Syndrome—to name a few.

Until scientific investigations catch up with the disease epidemics, we favor the European precautionary principle and recommend limiting one's exposure to environmental chemicals. Commercial interests that believe their profits are threatened by environmental medicine have used the same techniques to discredit environmental medicine that the tobacco manufacturers used to discredit the science linking cigarette smoking to cancer, or that fossil fuel industries have used to discredit the science relating burning fossil fuels to climate change.

Healthy Lifestyles

Exercise

Use it or lose it sums up the importance of exercise. Both aerobic exercise and strength training are beneficial. Even the extremely frail elderly can benefit from exercise, even if limited to walking and curling or bench pressing a soup can. Aerobic exercise increases cardiopulmonary reserve. Exercise benefits weight control beyond the obvious benefit of burning calories. A number of studies have shown that exercise reduces markers of inflammation in the blood, including interleukin-6, a signaling molecule that revs up inflammation in the body. The benefits of exercise in moderating specific disease states related to inflammation, from coronary artery disease to asthma, have been demonstrated. Exercise can modulate depression and chronic pain. The current recommendation for exercise is 60 minutes every day. We suggest that you find activities you enjoy (that way you are more likely to stick with it) and recruit some friends to join you. Dr. Myers walks or swims at least 60 minutes every day. Dr. Meggs walks, swims, bikes, or gardens at least 60 minutes every day. There is one caveat to reduce harm from exercise—excessive repetitive motions can stress a body part and lead to inflammation, pain, and damage. When Dr. Meggs swims, he alternates through different strokes, changing his stroke with every lap. He once ignored the admonition of an orthopedist that he needed to cross train. The result was damage to his knees from excessive running. Just as we recommend a variety in diet, we recommend a variety of exercises over excessively pursuing one exercise.

Avoiding tobacco products

When *The Inflammation Cure* was published, Dr. Meggs had numerous interviews with media. On journalist requested, "Dr. Meggs, please list the top ten things in order of importance that one should do to reduce the risk of diseases related to inflammation and to slow the aging process." This was a difficult request after the first few, but number one was easy.

"A person who uses tobacco products should quit," was the number one recommendation. Tobacco products significantly increase the risk of coronary artery disease, heart attack, strokes, asthma, and cancer. The respiratory system is permanently damaged. Aging is accelerated. The skin of long time smokers is easily recognized, with the leathery texture and deep fine wrinkles. The accelerated aging of the skin is a visible manifestation of accelerated aging throughout the body.

Complaints are made about smokers driving up health insurance premiums for non-smokers. Many insurance companies increase premiums for smokers and restrict access to the higher coverage categories to non-smokers. Studies have shown that even though non-smokers subsidize healthcare coverage for smokers, smokers subsidize retirement for non-smokers. One study found that a 30 year old smoker in the United States has a life expectancy to age 66, while a non-smoker's life expectancy is into the eighties. When the numbers are crunched, non-smokers actually come out ahead.

So why do people smoke? The answer is simply that cigarettes are a drug delivery system. Nicotine may be the most addicting chemical on the planet. Dr. Meggs treated a patient whose lungs had been so damaged by smoking that he had to be on continuous oxygen. Even so, he was unable to quit smoking. He lit a cigarette while breathing pure oxygen. The cigarette became a blow torch that scorched his face. Another smoker only quit after repeatedly passing out every time he took a drag on a cigarette because his brain was not getting enough oxygen.

At the peak of the smoking epidemic, over half of adults living in the United States smoked. That number has fallen to less than 20% in 2010. Many people have managed to quit, and anyone can quit. Some smokers quit cold turkey after years of smoking, while others need aids such as nicotine gum and patches to quit. Smoking withdrawal can be horrific in some. One man became homicidal every time he tried to quit. The drug varenicline (brand name Chantrix®) binds to nicotine receptors in the brain and can be helpful in severe cases of nicotine addiction. It must be used under close supervision though, because adverse reactions include changes in behavior including anxiety, aggression, and suicidal thoughts.

Second hand smoke is also dangerous. Dr. Meggs took care of an older woman with severe emphysema. She had the deep clusters of wrinkles that characterize older smoker's faces. She had never smoked, but had lived with a three pack per day smoker for four decades before he passed away. Her inheritance was a miserable life struggling to breathe.

One of the greatest public health initiatives in recent years is the banning of smoking in public places. California led the way. Public health scientists took the opportunity to study respiratory problems of non-smoking bartenders before and after the ban occurred. Before the ban, 70% of bar tenders had chronic respiratory problems. That number that fell to 25% after the ban went into effect. When the ban spread to New York, restaurateurs and bar owners yelled and screamed that their businesses would be adversely affected. After the ban, business increased. People who had avoided their establishments due to poor air quality from tobacco smoke flocked back, while smokers were happy to step out onto the sidewalk in order to satisfy their addiction to nicotine.

The good news for smokers is that if they quit, their risk of diseases related to smoking goes away with time. The added risk of heart disease from smoking go away in as little as two years. Reduction of cancer risk takes longer, but after a decade or so it is greatly reduced. Even after the onset of emphysema, lung function can stabilize and in some cases even improve if a smoker can quit.

Weight Control

Obesity is part of the infamous *inflammation connection*. Obese individuals have elevated levels of inflammatory markers in their blood and are more likely to suffer from a host of diseases related to inflammation—asthma, heart disease, arthritis, gum disease, depression, and so forth. Losing weight is rewarded with a decline in markers of inflammation measured in blood. In animal studies, caloric restriction has extended life expectancy more than any other intervention.

The obesity epidemic is perhaps the greatest health calamity of the modern age. Beginning in the 1970's or so, there has been a rapid increase in obesity among adults and children, even infants, in the United States. Obesity increased from about 5% in the 1970's or so to over 30% in some states. Over the last decade, the number of obese people has increased at about 1% a year and is projected to reach 42% by 2030. Another projection has this rate rising to 51%. When Dr. Meggs was in elementary school, the one or two fat children in each class were regarded as somehow very different from the norm. Now, in many schools, half the class or more will be overweight and a third will be obese. Twelve year old children weighting 200 pounds or more are not rare, while in prior generations they would be candidates for the freak show at the circus.

The standard explanation for obesity, sedentary life styles and junk food diets, is only part of the problem. Are we to believe that an additional 1% of the population—3 million people each year—decide to start eating junk food and quit exercising each year? Dr. Meggs and his long time scientific collaborator, Dr. Kori Brewer, have studied neuropsychological effects on rats exposed to low doses of a common insecticide found in the blood of many Americans (for information on the chemicals in our bodies, see http://www.cdc.gov/exposurereport/pdf/FourthReport.pdf). It comes from eating foods from sprayed fields. This neurotoxic chemical (chlorpyrifos) was widely used in homes, schools and offices until the Environmental Protection Agency restricted that use in 2001 due to concerns about effects on the developing brains of children. One day Dr. Brewer—whose hands are smaller than her collaborator's—observed that some of the rats were getting so big that she had trouble holding them in her hand. The rats exposed to the insecticide were getting fat. A literature search turned up data showing that the insecticide interferes with an enzyme involved in appetite regulation. This was one of the first examples of an obesogen, a newly coined word referring to chemicals that induce obesity. The relationship between insecticides at low doses and the human obesity epidemic is unknown at this time.

Another chemical that has received attention is bisphenol A (BPA), which is found in soft plastics and other products. Two reviews of the scientific literature found that BPA may be a contributor to the obesity epidemic, particularly in children. Canada and the European Union have banned BPA in plastic baby bottles. We recommend avoiding products that are contaminated with BPA, which includes foods delivered in soft plastic bottles.

The Inflammation Cure food choices can be an effective treatment for obesity. To summarize, obese people should avoid fast food, junk food, caloric beverages, and all products that contain simple sugars including corn syrup. Eat lots of fruits, vegetables, and whole grains while eating a variety of foods and avoiding a monotonous diet. Some may want to go on a rotation diet to see if there are specific foods that are *personal problem foods.* One physician who suffered from obesity and an arthritic condition called anklosing spondylitis went on a rotation diet and found that potatoes were one of his personal problem foods. After eliminating potatoes from his diet, his weight normalized and the progression of his arthritic condition ceased. If there are foods that one does not want to give up because eating them gives great pleasure, put them on the No-No list. They may be personal problem foods. Exercise is a vital part of a weight reduction program that has benefits that go beyond burning calories.

Good Dental Hygiene

A study estimated that flossing one's teeth once a day adds two to four years to life expectancy. While this fact may seem crazy, it makes great sense in the context of *the inflammation connection.* The mouth is loaded with bacteria that can form biofilms and plaque on the teeth, producing an inflammatory response. Inflammation in one area of the body revs up inflammation in other areas. In particular, inflammation in the mouth is connected to inflammation of the lining of the arteries. This accelerates atherosclerosis—hardening of the arteries that can lead to heart attacks and strokes. A daily program of good dental hygiene is highly recommended. Dental floss is known to remove plaque and should be used at least once a day to floss the teeth. A number of web sites demonstrate proper technique.

Teeth should be brushed at least twice a day, again using proper technique. One can under brush but also over brush. Vigorous brushing can actually lead to retraction of gums which can be a problem. A number of web sites which demonstrate proper technique can be found by searching *brushing teeth proper technique.*

Adequate Rest

People with hectic lifestyles often get too little rest. Sleep is essential. Our brains require sleep to regenerate and process information. Sleep disorders are rampant in our society. They have risen along with obesity, asthma, and a host of other conditions related to the inflammation connection. For those with sleeping difficulties, following the general prescriptions of this book, with a good diet, clean air, exercise, reduced stress, and so forth can promote healthy sleep along with general wellness. Avoidance of stimulants can be important for those with difficulty sleeping. The half life of caffeine is eight hours, so limiting consumption of caffeine can be helpful in many cases. There is a correlation with sleep disturbances and rhinitis—inflammation of the upper airway—so identification of allergies and irritants that cause rhinitis can help with sleep. Consultation with a competent allergist or environmental physician can help sort these out. Individual food intolerances, as discussed in section III, can induce sleep disturbances. Dr. Myers has learned that if she drinks even a relatively small amount of red wine at night, she wakes at 2 or 3 am and has difficulty falling back to sleep. Dr. Meggs has learned not to drink caffeinated beverages after lunch because they can interfere with his sleep. At the same time, he has had patients who must drink a strong cup of coffee at bedtime or suffer sleep deprivation, which points to the highly individualized nature of reactivity to foods and chemicals. As Socrates said, *Know Thyself!* We are each unique individuals and *One person's meat is another person's poison.*

What Medicine Can Do

The section on medications and their role in disease prevention in *The Inflammation Cure* can be consulted for further information on this topic. A number of medications have been shown to reduce one's risk of diseases related to inflammation. Cholesterol lowering drugs are recommended for those who cannot control their cholesterol with diet and exercise. For some individuals, difficulty with cholesterol levels is related to genetic control of cholesterol. There are well studied genetic profiles of cholesterol and fat metabolism that carry an increased risk of heart disease, even in childhood. One's pediatrician, internist, or family physician can screen for this with blood tests. If blood pressure cannot be controlled with diet, exercise, and weight loss, blood pressure medications may be necessary, particularly in aging individuals. The majority of elder folks have blood pressure problems, which may be related to the planned obsolescence to do us in as we pass reproductive years. Some can benefit from an aspirin a day, while this may be harmful for others. Medication regimens are highly individualistic and should be undertaken with the help of one's physician.

Supplements

Americans spend billions of dollars a year on nutritional supplements. It can be reasonably argued that a person eating an ideal diet will never need supplements. Few of us, however, devote the care and attention to eating that a perfect diet demands. Nutritional supplements are a topic of great controversy. There are strong political forces that want to increase government regulation of supplement use. Others demand individual freedom to choose both the type and dose of supplements to take. In the national congress, there is a stalemate between senators and representatives who want to extend federal regulations over supplements and those from districts where supplement manufacturing takes place.

There is even controversy over what constitutes a supplement. Current law in the United States gives the Food and Drug Administration (FDA) the right to regulate drugs. Pharmaceutical companies must spend millions of dollars establishing both the safety and effectiveness of a drug before bringing it to market. To regulate a supplement, the FDA must prove that the supplement is harmful. A company can claim that its product is a nutritional supplement and market it without approval. This has led to some weird products being marketed as supplements. The drug ephedrine, a powerful amphetamine, was marketed for decades in the United States as a nutritional supplement. It achieved that status by being in a Chinese herbal medicine that has been used for centuries to treat asthma, low blood pressure, and nasal congestion. It was marketed in this country as a stimulant and widely sold at truck stops and convenience stores. Like all amphetamines, ephedrine does keep one awake. Adverse events including deaths did occur. To ban ephedrine, the FDA had to collect data to support the ban. The manufacturers then sued the FDA to keep their supplement on the market, but the FDA prevailed in the courts.

Another example of a drug that was marketed as a supplement is GHB (gamma hydroxybutyrate), which was readily available in health food stores. This naturally occurring substance in the brain is metabolized to the neurotransmitter GABA. It causes an intoxication similar to alcohol. Unfortunately, taking just a little too much can lead to coma and death, particularly if alcohol is taken at the same time. When GHB became a popular drug of abuse on college campuses in the 1990's, a number of deaths occurred. It is no longer legally available as a supplement.

Scientific support for supplement claims is often lacking, but there are some studies which show some supplements can be of benefit. Studies have established that others can even be harmful, particularly if taken in large doses. We do recommend some supplements in special cases, but again feel that a healthy person eating an ideal diet will have little need for supplements. Healthy choices in food with a proper balance of different foods will supply just about everything that we need.

Fish Oil Supplements.

Fish oil supplements have become the most commonly consumed supplement in the United States due to widespread publicity about their benefits in persons with coronary artery disease. For a healthy person with no risk factors for coronary artery disease who consumes two to four servings of fish per week, the recommendation is that supplements are not necessary. Fish oil contains two omega-3 fatty acids, EPA (eicosapentaenoic acid), and DHA (docosahexaenoic acid). Our bodies use these compounds to manufacture signaling molecules that dampen inflammation. Omega-6 fatty acids are used to manufacture signaling molecules that enhance inflammation. The theory is that by consuming more omega-3 fatty acids than omega-6 fatty acids, inflammation will be dampened because our bodies will make more of the signals to dampen inflammation. Since inflammation plays a role in atherosclerosis, a natural process that damages our arteries as we age and leads to heart attacks and strokes, many believe that taking daily fish oil supplements will reduce the risk of heart attacks and strokes. Scientific studies supporting an association are conflicting. Theoretically, optimum health requires a proper balance of omega-3 and omega-6 fatty acids for an individual. An excess of either can be harmful. For some individuals, producing an imbalance may be beneficial, but such a recommendation is highly individualized. People with certain genetic profiles may be harmed by taking omega-3 supplements. *Nutrigenomics* is the science of personalizing dietary recommendations based on a person's genome. Several companies are developing or have marketed commercial tests to analyze a person's genome from a cheek swab. One such company is Nutrigenomix (http://nutrigenomix.com/).

Because inflammation plays an important role in producing blockages in and hardening of arteries, many cardiologists recommend fish oil supplements. Hardening of the arteries is a natural part of the aging process that is the programmed obsolescence built into the human genome. Inflammation plays such an important role in the degenerative processes of aging that the term *Inflam-aging* has been coined to describe this process. The typical American diet is high in vegetable oils that contain large amounts of omega-6 fatty acids that enhance inflammation.

An important study demonstrated that taking omega-3 fatty acid supplements can reduce the risk of sudden cardiac death. A recent meta-analysis, which attempts to combine the data from other studies, did not find that taking fish oil supplements preventing heart attacks and strokes but had limitations. Eating fish was found to be of benefit, suggesting that the benefits of eating fish go beyond the omega-3 fatty acids in fish. Perhaps people who eat fish eat less red meat, or there are other beneficial substances in fish such as selenium.

The downside of fish oil supplements is that too much fish oil can have negative effects on blood clotting, leading to an increased risk of hemorrhagic strokes—bleeding into the brain. Consumption of total omega-3 fatty acids should be limited to less than 3 grams a day.

The American Heart Association recommendation (http://www.heart.org/HEARTORG/GettingHealthy/NutritionCenter/Fish-101_UCM_305986_Article.jsp) is that individuals without coronary artery disease consume two servings of fish each week and oils and foods that contain significant amounts of alpha-linoleic acid (oils of soy, flaxseed and canola, flaxseed, and walnuts). Persons with known coronary artery disease should take supplements with one gram of EPA & DHA a day. Like many supplements and hormones, at high doses fish oil becomes a pharmaceutical.

There is a legitimate indication for prescribing 2 to 4 grams of EPA & DHA each day as therapy for people who have dangerously high levels of triglycerides in their blood. In Dr. Meggs' experience, some people with super high levels of triglycerides in their blood have had normal levels within a week of eating a vegetarian diet. Rather than begin high levels of omega-3 fatty acids, we first recommend that anyone with elevated triglycerides try a vegetarian diet, eating lots of fruits and vegetables, with a variety of nuts, beans, and whole grains for protein. The triglyceride levels should be measured one to two weeks after the trial to see if this is a viable solution for that individual. Under medical surveillance with frequent blood tests to monitor triglyceride levels, portions of lean chicken, turkey, and fish can then be introduced into the diet, while greatly limiting consumption of red meats and high fat dairy products (fat free and low fat dairy products are a good source of calcium and vitamin D).

An Aspirin a Day

As people age, their risk of coronary artery disease, heart attacks, and strokes increases. There is a wonderful web site hosted by the National Institute of Heart, Lung, and Blood Diseases that allows one to calculate their risk of having a heart attack or stroke in the next ten years (http://hp2010.nhlbihin.net/atpiii/calculator.asp?usertype=pub). If the risk exceeds 10%, taking daily low doses of aspirin (81 milligram a day, which is one baby aspirin a day) is recommended. Low dose aspirin is not without its risks. Dr. Meggs reached an age where he decided that low dose aspirin might be of benefit. A month or so after he started taking a baby aspirin each day, he went downhill skiing and had a fall onto his hip. A hematoma (blood collection under the skin) the size of a grapefruit developed at the site of the impact. He was grateful that he fell onto his hip and not his head. It is important that all recommendations be individualized. What is harmful to one may benefit others. A study of physicians who were randomized to take aspirin or a sugar pill each day showed that an aspirin a day reduced to risk of heart attacks but increased the risk of bleeding, including fatal cerebral hemorrhages. Of note, in this study the same number of people died in each group. Statistically, what taking an aspirin a day changed is not whether people died, but the cause of death. The importance of individualizing preventive therapies cannot be overemphasized. A sedentary person with multiple risk factors for heart attacks is more likely to benefit from and not be harmed by taking an aspirin a day than a person who participates in contact sports and dangerous activities.

Vitamin Supplements

Inadequate intake of vitamins can lead to specific vitamin deficiency diseases (see table). These diseases are rare in developed countries. A healthy person eating a balanced diet with five or more servings a day of a variety of fruits and vegetables may not need vitamin supplements. Notable exceptions include pregnant women, for whom prenatal vitamins are recommended to ensure the nutritional needs of the developing fetus are met. In particular, folic acid is an essential nutrient in pregnancy because inadequate levels are associated with the birth defect spinal bifida in the developing fetus. Vegetarians need vitamin B12 supplements because this vitamin is produced by yeasts and fungi but not vegetables and is found in animal products. The primary antioxidants protecting the lens of our eyes from cataracts are vitamin C and glutathione. Those with heavy sunlight exposures are advised to take vitamin C supplements and wear UV protective sunglasses to reduce the risk of cataracts. A study of oyster harvesters who are doubly exposed to ultraviolet radiation—direct plus reflections from the water—demonstrated a benefit to vitamin C supplements in reducing risk of cataracts. Alcoholics can develop vitamin deficiencies, particularly of thiamine. Individuals who are not exposed to the sun or use sun screen may need vitamin D supplements.

There is a belief among some that taking high doses of vitamins can offer protection against diseases such as cancer. Unfortunately, a number of scientific studies have been conducted to determine whether or not vitamins protect against specific diseases. None of these studies have been successful in proving benefits from high doses of vitamins, and some have found harm. A study of multivitamin pills found that men taking more than one multivitamin pill a day in the mistaken belief that if a little is good, a lot is better, were found to have an increased risk of prostate cancer. What has been demonstrated over and over again is that eating a diet high in fruits and vegetables is beneficial. Every semester Dr. Myers challenges her Introduction to Nutrition class for 1 week to try to consume their recommended intake of fruits and vegetables each day. The recommendation for **women** for fruits and vegetables combined is **5-7 servings per day**. The recommendation for **men** for fruits and vegetables combined is **7 – 9 servings per day** (men get more because typically men are bigger/taller/larger than women). At the end of the week they share how they did (actual servings of fruits and veggies each day), what they learned, and strategies they can use to continue to increase the number of fruits and vegetables in their diet. Her students are always surprised at how this experiment made them feel more energetic and clear headed. This exercise in many cases changed their typical eating patterns. Students reported feeling less sluggish and more focused in their school work. By making this one simple change in their diets, these students are able to see almost instant results.

Table IV-1 lists the symptoms of deficiency and toxicity of fat soluble and water soluble, while the same data is given for water soluble vitamins in Table IV-2.

Table IV-1

Fat Soluble Vitamins	Deficiency	Toxicity
Vitamin A	Leading cause of non-accidental blindness worldwide, night blindness, skin thickening, follicular hyperkeratosis (bumpy skin), abnormal corneal dryness	Yellow-orange harmless color to skin from over consumption of beta-carotene Reduced bone-density, liver malabsorption, birth defects
Vitamin D	In children: Rickets, bone deformities. In adults: Osteomalacia or osteoporosis, soft bones due to loss of calcium	Elevated blood calcium and calcium deposits in heart, kidney, and other soft tissues
Vitamin E	Anemia, peripheral neuropathy, insufficient bile production	Influences anticoagulation drugs
Vitamin K	Hemorrhage, poor skeletal mineralization	Not likely, interactions with anticoagulation drugs

Table IV-2

Water Soluble Vitamins	Deficiency	Toxicity
Thiamin	Beriberi (ranging from nerve damage to heart failure), peripheral neuropathy	None reported
Riboflavin	Ariboflavinosis (cracked skin around mouth), throat disorder	None reported
Niacin	4 D's of Pellagra: diarrhea, dermatitis, dementia, & death; skin rash when exposed to light, decreased appetite and weight	Hives and skin rash, nausea, vomiting, liver damage, impaired glucose tolerance
Pantothenic Acid	Rare, nausea, vomiting, stomach cramps, insomnia, muscle cramps, burning foot syndrome	None reported
Vitamin B6	Anemia, dermatitis, convulsions, depression, confusion, decreased immune response, peripheral nerve damage	Nerve damage, depression, skin lesions, fatigue, irritability
Biotin	Depression, lethargy, hallucinations, hair loss	None reported
Folic acid/Folate	Anemia, neural tube defects, depression, elevated homocysteine, mental confusion	Masks vitamin B12 symptoms, epilepsy, skin and respiratory disorders
Vitamin B12	Anemia, tingling and numbness, fatigue, memory loss, disorientation, nerve degeneration	None reported
Vitamin C	Scurvy, anemia, pinpoint hemorrhages, poor wound healing, muscle degeneration and associated pain	Kidney stones, nausea, abdominal pain, diarrhea, hot flashes, rashes, may interfere with medical tests, rebound scurvy

Trace Metals (Minerals)

Supplements of the trace minerals such as copper, manganese, zinc, chromium, molybdenum, and iodine, and even the essential nutrient iron, have to be taken with caution because these metals become toxic in higher doses. It is a paradox of human biology that while a little is essential, a little more can be harmful. Except for iron, only tiny amounts are needed. High doses of manganese can cause nerve damage that results in a movement disorder that is similar to Parkinson's disease. Copper is toxic to nerve cells. Zinc compounds can be very irritating to the digestive system. Chromium, while there are many forms, becomes toxic to the liver and is known to cause cancer when inhaled in occupational settings.

What's a person to do? In an ideal world, we would have our levels of these essential nutrients monitored and adjusted as needed. The good news is that our bodies have a complex set of mechanisms to adjust the absorption of nutrients, their transport in the blood to cells, and their elimination from our bodies. The bad news is that these mechanisms can be overwhelmed when one consumes excessive amounts of these essential nutrients.

Conclusion

Overall this book has provided you with the key ingredients to a sound diet that can aid in the treatment and prevention of inflammatory processes and diseases. Over seventy-five percent of all diseases and conditions can be treated and prevented by what we eat. With almost 200 recipes, we have demonstrated ways to incorporate good sources of vitamins, minerals, carbohydrates, proteins, healthy fats, fiber and phytochemicals into the fundamentals of your daily cooking. A well balanced diet that focuses on whole ingredients is one key element in the prevention and treatment of inflammation related diseases. There are steps you can take to decrease your risk, and your family's risk, of developing devastating health conditions. Clean living is essential to basic health. Being active and incorporating physical activities into your daily routine that you enjoy can provide multiple health benefits to you and your loved ones. Limiting exposures to toxic fumes and chemicals that are found everywhere is another important step. It is up to the individual to be pro-active in their health care, including day-to-day living. By being active, eating healthy, avoiding unhealthy chemicals and being aware of your environment, you have the potential to decrease your risk of diseases related to aging, and to increase and sustain your quality of life.

Further Reading

The Inflammation Cure. William J. Meggs and Carol Svec. McGrawHill. 2003.

An Alternative Approach to Allergies, by Theron G. Randolph. Harper Perennial. 1990.

Food Allergy and Intolerances, 2ⁿᵈ Edition, edited by Dr. Jonathan Brostoff and Dr. Stephen J. Challacombe. Saunders Ltd.; 2 edition (August 9, 2002).

Food Allergies and Food Intolerance: The Complete Guide to Their Identification and Treatment, Jonathan Brostoff M.D., Linda Gamlin and Jonathan Brostoff. Healing Arts Press, 2000.

Reversibility of Chronic Degenerative Disease and Hypersensitivity (4 volume set). William J. Rea and Kalpana Patel. CRC Press. 2012.

Optimum Environments For Optimum Health and Creativity: Designing and Building a Healthy Home or Office. William J. Rea. American Environmental HeatlhFoundation. 2002.

Prescriptions for a Healthy House, 3rd Edition: A Practical Guide for Architects, Builders & Homeowners. 3ʳᵈ edition. Paula Baker-Laporte, Erica Elliott, John Banta. New Society Publishers. 2002.

Chemical Exposures: Low levels and high stakes. 2ⁿᵈ Edition. By Nicholas A. Ashford and Claudia s. Miller. Wiley Interscience. 1998.

Tyler's Honest Herbal: A sensible Guide to the Use of Herbs and Related Remedies. 4ᵗʰ edition, Varro.E. Tyler; 1999.

The Gluten-free Bible, by Jax Peters Lowell. St. Martin Press. 2005.

About the Authors

Dr. Kimberly B. Myers is an Associate Professor in the Department of Nutrition Science, and is Adjunct Faculty in the Department of Kinesiology at East Carolina University in Greenville, North Carolina. Dr. Myers earned both of her BS degrees and Masters in Health Science from Western Carolina University in Cullowhee, North Carolina. She completed her internship for eligibility to become a Registered Dietitian Nutritionist (RDN) also through Western Carolina University and has been a RDN since 2002. She earned her PhD in Human Nutrition from the University of Nebraska at Lincoln in 2003. Dr. Myers is a licensed Dietitian Nutritionist within the state of North Carolina. She is engaged in the university community and serves on numerous departmental and university committees. Dr. Myers has served as the faculty senator representative for the Nutrition Science Department for six years and has served on the Eat Smart, Move More, Weigh Less Committee at East Carolina University. She is an active member of the Academy of Nutrition and Dietetics and the American Society for Nutrition. She consults with corporations in the DC area. She has contributed to nutrition position papers for the Academy of Nutrition and Dietetics and continues to conduct on-going research in the area of omega-3 fatty acids and obesity. She has authored numerous peer reviewed articles on a variety of nutrition related topics that were published in journals including the *Journal of the American Dietetic Association, Journal of American College Health,* the *Sport journal,* and *Advances in Medical Sciences.* Dr. Myers has presented numerous presentations at the prestigious Federation of American Societies for Experimental Biology and is an active member of the United States Department of Agriculture NC-1199 research group, which contributes to the scientific body of work regarding omega-3 fatty acids.

William J. Meggs, MD, PhD, FACMT, FACEP, is a physician with a strong interest in environmental toxicology and the environmental aspects of health and disease. Dr. Meggs currently practices in Greenville, NC, where he is a professor of Emergency Medicine and Director of the Division of Toxicology at the Brody School of Medicine at East Carolina University.

Dr. Meggs is Author of *The Inflammation Cure,* a widely acclaimed book on the role of inflammation in chronic diseases. The book addresses environmental and nutritional modifiers of the inflammatory response and how individuals can reduce their risk of a host of diseases related to inflammation, from cardiovascular disease and asthma to Alzheimer's disease. It was favorably reviewed by the *New York Times,* the *Library Journal,* and other national publications. Dr. Meggs is very active in medical research and has authored numerous publications. Current research interests include acute and chronic poisonings, irritant sensitivities, and the physics of living systems. He formulated the biological homing theory of life and the neurogenic switching theory of inflammation.

Dr. Meggs has served on numerous advisory boards, including the Research Advisory Committee on Gulf War Illness and the National Academy of Sciences subcommittee on immunotoxicology.

Born in Newberry, South Carolina, Dr. Meggs received his undergraduate degree from Clemson University. He received a PhD in physics from Syracuse University and an MD degree from the University of Miami. Post graduate training was a residency in internal medicine at the University of Rochester, Medical Staff Fellow at the National Institute of Allergy and Infectious Diseases, and a fellow in Medical Toxicology at New York University. Dr. Meggs is Board certified in Medical Toxicology, Allergy and Immunology, Internal Medicine, and Emergency Medicine.

Made in the USA
Lexington, KY
29 June 2014